Mike Anderson is a senior employee of one of the world's oldest private banks. He considers himself fortunate to have stumbled across this extraordinary true story and has been relentless in his pursuit of the tale of Britain's only war crimes prosecution and the parallel lives of Ben-Zion Blustein and Andrei Sawoniuk.

Neil Hanson is the author of a dozen acclaimed works of narrative non-fiction, including *The Unknown Soldier*, *The Confident Hope of a Miracle*, *The Custom of the Sea* and *The Dreadful Judgement*. They have been hailed by critics around the world as 'astonishing', 'brilliant', 'haunting', 'extraordinary', 'a triumph' and 'a masterpiece', and compared by one to 'Siegfried Sassoon, Robert Graves and a dozen other immortals'.

Praise for *The Ticket Collector from Belarus*

'In this brilliantly gripping mix of true crime and narrative history, Mike Anderson and Neil Hanson tell the story of the first and only war crimes trial to be held on British soil . . . To their great credit, Anderson and Hanson avoid piling on the horror, letting the court transcripts speak for themselves.'
Kathryn Hughes, *Sunday Times*

'Here we meet the gulf whose existence is so well illustrated in this book – that between court truth and historical truth. One of the great values of Anderson and Hanson's excellent work is to demonstrate that there are several distinct kinds of justice.'
David Aaronovitch, *The Times*

'A riveting and haunting book that raises important questions about how far justice should reach when confronted with the worst of crimes.' **Roger Alton,** *Daily Mail*

'Sawoniuk ignored the advice of his own lawyers and took the stand. The old man's angry testimony is the high point of the book ... The authors have interviewed most of the key players in this heart-rending tale and the result is a sensitive and well-balanced account of an extraordinary moment in British legal history.' **Saul David,** *Sunday Telegraph*

'An extraordinary tale, not least because of the light it throws on the persistence and thoroughness of the British legal system ... The account of how he was finally identified and tracked down makes lively reading.' **Caroline Moorehead,** *Spectator*

'Engrossing. The book ... arrive[s] in gift-wrapped form for any smart TV or film producer – with characters who don't so much as jump but leap off the page and into your imagination. Forgive the hyperbole but this is the story with everything ... A terrific achievement.' **Adrian Hennigan,** *Haaretz*

THE TICKET COLLECTOR FROM BELARUS

An Extraordinary True Story of the Holocaust and Britain's Only War Crimes Trial

MIKE ANDERSON and NEIL HANSON

SIMON &
SCHUSTER

London · New York · Sydney · Toronto · New Delhi

First published in Great Britain by Simon & Schuster UK Ltd, 2022

This edition published in Great Britain by Simon & Schuster UK Ltd, 2023

1 3 5 7 9 10 8 6 4 2

Simon & Schuster UK Ltd
1st Floor
222 Gray's Inn Road
London WC1X 8HB

www.simonandschuster.co.uk
www.simonandschuster.com.au
www.simonandschuster.co.in

Simon & Schuster Australia, Sydney
Simon & Schuster India, New Delhi

A CIP catalogue record for this book is available from the British Library

Paperback ISBN: 978-1-3985-0329-8
eBook ISBN: 978-1-3985-0328-1

Typeset in Perpetua by M Rules
Printed and Bound in the UK using 100% Renewable
Electricity at CPI Group (UK) Ltd

*To Ben-Zion, the Blustein family and
to all who resist Fascism*

'What haunts are not the dead, but the gaps left within us by the secrets of others'

Nicolas Abraham and Maria Torok,
The Shell and the Kernel

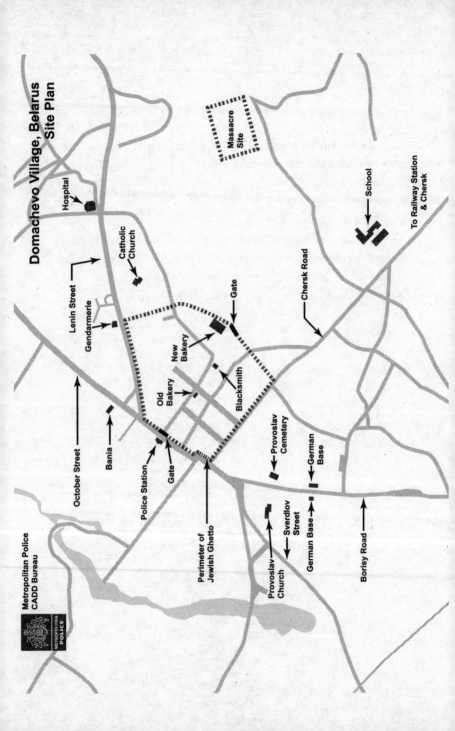

Domachevo Village, Belarus
Site Plan

Metropolitan Police
CADD Bureau

Hospital

Catholic Church

Lenin Street

Gendarmerie

October Street

Bania

Police Station

Gate

Old Bakery

New Bakery

Blacksmith

Gate

Perimeter of Jewish Ghetto

Provoslav Church

Sverdlov Street

German Base

German Base

Provoslav Cemetery

Chersk Road

Borisy Road

Massacre Site

School

To Railway Station & Chersk

In the course of its modern history, the country that is now Belarus has been known by several other names: White Russia, Byelorussia, Belorussia and the Byelorussian Soviet Socialist Republic, and was also part of Poland between the wars. To avoid confusion, its modern name has been used throughout.

PROLOGUE —
16 FEBRUARY 1999

Early one slate-grey, late-winter morning, three rusting, single-decker buses left Warsaw. Relics of the Soviet era, they trailed black smoke and stinking diesel fumes behind them as they headed east. A distinguished British High Court Judge, two eminent QCs and their junior counsel led the convoy, along with court stenographers and several officials of London's Central Criminal Court of England and Wales, better known as the Old Bailey. The next vehicle held the jury – eight men and four women – with six court officials and two Metropolitan Police Jury Protection Unit officers, there to ensure the jurors were kept well clear of the British press pack in the third bus. They were travelling to a country none of them knew but they were also journeying into the past, visiting the scenes of crimes that had been committed 57 years before. The alleged perpetrator, who for over 50 years had lived in Britain, unsuspected and unrecognised, had been left behind in London, with his trial put on hold for this unprecedented visit by a British jury to a foreign land.

The snow-covered landscape through which they passed was flat and marshy, broken only by birch woods and small, impoverished villages. The 100-mile journey took four hours, often slowed to a crawl by sudden snowstorms whipped up by the bitter east wind. As they approached the frontier with Belarus, where sullen border guards routinely took hours or even days just to check visitors' documents, they found a queue snaking back several kilometres. An enterprising vendor had set up a roadside stall selling hot soup to the delayed drivers and a few equally enterprising prostitutes, wearing mini-skirts and low-cut tops despite the bitter cold, could be seen climbing into the cabs of some of the trucks. They were said to have bribed the border guards to keep the delays long enough to make the drivers more receptive to their approaches.

However, with the local police chief acting as a 'fixer', the convoy of buses swept past the queue and cut in right at its head. He distributed packs of Western cigarettes to the guards and customs officials, but increasingly dog-eared forms still had to be inspected and stamped at every stage of the process. By the time they cleared the final hurdle, the forms carried a dozen stamps, but after a mere 65-minute delay, the buses were waved through. Even so, as one of the reporters cynically remarked, it had taken them longer to cross the frontier than the German Army in 1941.

The previous night the British party had stayed in the relative luxury of a four-star hotel in Warsaw, but on their first night in Belarus they had to settle for the rather less salubrious Intourist Hotel in Brest-Litovsk, 'a hostelry,' said *The Times*, 'exuding all the charm of a tax office'. It was rumoured to have undergone an urgent refurbishment before their arrival, but there was little sign of it in the drab, spartan and frigid interior. Some of the bedroom windows were broken, there were no plugs in the sinks or the bathroom down the hall, and if guests ran out of toilet paper, they had to take the empty cardboard tube to the reception desk before being issued with another roll.

Detectives from Scotland Yard's War Crimes Unit had already made several trips to Belarus to interview potential witnesses, and had learned to take food, heaters and even gaffer tape with them to cover the cracks in the windows, but the jurors and court officials had not been forewarned and had no option but to endure the cold and the other hardships.

As in Soviet times, an old woman presided over every floor of the establishment, sitting on a chair opposite the clanking lift and noting the comings and goings of the guests, while the telephones in the rooms emitted strange buzzing and crackling noises, suggesting they were being tapped. Prostitutes patrolled the hotel corridors, knocked on the bedroom doors and propositioned guests in the bar, which the UK press quickly drank dry. The menu in the hotel restaurant promised a range of gourmet delights, but every attempt to order a dish was greeted with '*Nyet! Nyet! Nyet!*' It turned out that everything was off except the boiled chicken.

The first of the British party bowed to the inevitable.

'And I'll have the same,' his companion said.

'*Nyet!*' The waiter pointed to the first man. 'He's had the chicken.'

Fortunately, there was a curry house not far away. When the owner was asked how he came to be in this unlikely place, he told them that he had bought it unseen before leaving India, thinking it was in Brest in France. He'd only discovered his mistake when the papers confirming the sale arrived in the post. Unable to get his money back, he came to Brest-Litovsk anyway, and had been running one of the very few Indian restaurants in Belarus ever since.

The food was good and the prices so low that it was impossible to spend more than £2 or £3 on dinner, much to the disgust of one senior journalist. When they were presented with their bills, he said, 'No, no, no! These are no good at all.' He then borrowed the owner's receipt pad and treated himself and his colleagues to a much more satisfactory addition to their expenses claims.

At ten the next morning, after the almost inedible complimentary breakfast – served with a cup of coffee only on payment of a surcharge – the convoy set off on the last rough and potholed leg of their journey. A police escort of rusty, dark-blue Ladas led the way, lights flashing and sirens blaring, while other traffic was halted by more policemen who saluted the convoy as it passed. An hour later, the buses descended through pine forests and rumbled across the ramshackle bridge over the frozen River Bug, where old men with fishing rods crouched over the holes they had cut in the thick ice. The townspeople also cut blocks of ice from the frozen river and stored them under layers of sawdust in their cellars for summer use. In the spring, when the ice and snowfields of the mountains began to melt, soldiers had to blast apart the huge ice floes on the river with explosives to prevent them destroying the bridge.

Just beyond the river lay Domachevo. The buses halted on a broad expanse of waste ground at its centre. There was no main square lined with flower beds and benches, just this empty space where the heart had been torn out of what was now little more than a village over half a century before, when the Jewish ghetto was obliterated. Nothing had been built there since. It had remained bare and derelict, as if even weeds could get no purchase on that poisoned soil.

The temperature had fallen to -25 Celsius the previous night and the pale winter sun had done little to raise the daytime reading before grey clouds brought a fresh fall of snow and a strengthening wind that sent it plummeting again. The shivering passengers clambered down from the buses and formed up in a strange procession. His Honour Sir Humphrey Potts led the way, dressed in a bright-red, pointed felt hat with ear-flaps that one observer likened to 'an arctic-grade judicial wig', and even the august correspondent of *The Times* was unable to resist describing it as 'a Noddy hat'. The judge was accompanied by his court clerk, not much more than half his size, who was wearing a pointed green hat like a leprechaun's.

Puffing on his pipe, the prosecuting counsel, Johnny

Nutting, QC, resembling a patrician KGB officer in his full-length coat and fur hat, 'strode about in the manner of a grand Shakespearean actor-manager'. The much shorter and rounder defence counsel, Bill Clegg, QC, was clad in a brightly patterned Austrian ski jacket with a hood which he pulled over his head when the freezing Siberian wind whistled through. Underneath his jacket he had so many layers of woolly jumpers that one of the pressmen said he 'looked like an escapee from a local asylum'. When a little old lady came shuffling along and stopped to ask their interpreter something, he laughed and shook his head. She had wanted to know if Clegg was the defendant.

One of the journalists, blowing on his frozen fingers to try to warm them, cast a baleful glance around Domachevo and said, 'What the fuck are we doing here?' Only then did he realise the judge was within earshot but, as he braced himself for a stern judicial reprimand, he heard Sir Humphrey say, 'That's the most sensible thing I've heard today.'

As a retinue of mangy stray dogs trailed after them, Potts led the jurors through the streets like a guide showing a group of tourists the sights, while they tried to picture the crime scenes. From time to time, the Foreman of the Jury raised his umbrella, signalling that one of them had a question.

The reporters had been forbidden to speak to the jurors, or get closer than 40 paces from them, and marshalling officers in bright-yellow bibs kept them at bay. Belarusian police also escorted the party, while militiamen in camouflage uniforms, their heavy boots ringing like iron as they stamped on the icy ground, barked orders through megaphones, keeping the townsfolk at a distance. Two Belarusian KGB men, straight out of central casting, kept a wary eye on proceedings from the confines of a small red Lada.

Many of the inhabitants, old men in fur hats and overcoats with astrakhan collars, and women wearing drab-coloured coats and headscarves, had formed small, silent knots at street corners. Inured to the savage cold, their exhaled breath froze in mid-air and fell in tiny, sparkling ice crystals around their feet, with the faint sound that Russians call the 'whispering of the stars'. They stared, baffled, at this column of invaders. There had probably not been as many strangers passing through Domachevo since the Red Army liberated it in 1944.

Life had always been a struggle here. In the course of their lives, the oldest inhabitants had endured successive rule by Tsarist Russia, Imperial Germany, Poland, Nazi Germany, Soviet Russia, Nazi Germany again, Soviet Russia again, and finally by yet another authoritarian regime as part of an independent Belarus. There was a stolidity about the people but also a pervasive sense of weariness. Life must have held few surprises in this rural backwater, and their expressions suggested that fewer still had been pleasant ones.

Fleet Street photographers, unable to speak the language, tried their usual cajolery in English: 'Ladies, can I take a picture of you? All right, ladies, look this way and smile.' While the flash-guns popped, the ladies stared back, uncomprehending and unsmiling.

In the 1920s and 1930s, Domachevo had been a slow, sleepy town for most of the year but summer saw it undergo a metamorphosis into a bustling spa resort, with visitors flocking to the small hotels and boarding-houses in the fringes of the forest. They came on doctors' recommendations – the fresh air, sandy soil and dry climate were thought to be good for TB and asthma sufferers – or just for a holiday. Famous rabbis from other towns and cities had summer homes where they and their disciples stayed, and Jewish welfare organisations also built holiday homes for orphans and deprived children.

Shaded by the pine trees from the fierce heat, the visitors could walk in the forest or around the lake, swim in the broad reaches of the River Bug, or stroll down the broad main street, planted with aspen, cherry, maple and rowan trees, and dance to an orchestra in the evening.

As well as two synagogues, there were three churches then: the onion-domed, blue-painted Russian Orthodox church, the Lutheran church for the Protestants, and the Catholic church where most of the Poles worshipped. It had been a polyglot community, mainly Jewish, but with Russian, Polish, German and Ukrainian minorities, who had all found ways to coexist until the Nazi invasion in 1941 brought that world to a brutal conclusion.

The village council building, flying the red and green flag of Belarus – the one flash of bright colour in the otherwise drab and monochrome scene – had been the police station during the Nazi occupation, a commandeered Jewish house facing one of the two entrances to the ghetto. A building alongside it had been used to house prisoners.

As the east wind drove stinging flurries of dry, gritty snow into their faces, the jurors were ushered along the dirt road that led from there to the forest. Officially named Pushkin Street, to its inhabitants it was still known as the 'Road of Death'. As the jurors plodded through the snow, the ghosts of thousands of Nazi victims walked with them.

One Sunday morning in September 1942, the eve of the Day of Atonement – Yom Kippur, the holiest date in the Jewish calendar, when Jews fast and pray to God for forgiveness for their sins – Nazi *Einsatzgruppen,* SS death squads with skull insignia on their caps, ordered the Catholic congregation out into the street. They forced them to watch as the inhabitants of the ghetto were stripped naked and then kicked, punched and rifle-butted towards the sand-hills just outside the town where, in the space of a few hours, 2,900 of them – men, women and children – were machine-gunned to death in the huge burial pits they had already been forced to dig.

The lack of any attempt to conceal what the SS were doing

suggested they were either attempting to intimidate the non-Jewish population – inducing terror in subject populations was a standard tactic – or trying to make them complicit in what was happening. Although much less pronounced than in other Eastern European countries, there was an undercurrent of anti-Semitism in Belarus, and as well as instilling fear, the public show of force was perhaps intended to demonstrate that violence against Jews would not only be condoned but actively encouraged.

The naked victims were first thoroughly searched for any remaining items of value that they might have secreted on their persons, with 'particularly close attention paid to the women'. After this final humiliation, they were forced at gunpoint onto planks laid across the pits, so that when they were shot, they would tumble straight into their graves. Like butchers in a slaughterhouse, the machine-gunners standing at the edge of the pit wore rubber aprons. Erwin Cerecke, a local policeman who witnessed the slaughter, having helped to herd the Jews to the killing ground, was later so tormented by his memories that he made a voluntary confession to his part in the massacre. He said that the Jews had been 'very calm. Many of them prayed and I think that some even sang. All the Jews were shot: men, women and children. For us it was a terrible sight.'

The only pause in the executions was when the barrels of the machine-guns became so hot that they had to be changed to allow them to cool. Wearing asbestos gloves to protect their hands, assistant gunners removed the barrels and replaced them, but it was a routine task and so well practised that less than ten seconds would elapse before the firing resumed.

Reporting to his superiors, as if describing the policing of a football match, the commander of the German *Ordnungpolizei* [Order Police] merely noted that 'On September 19–20, 1942, an anti-Jewish *Aktion* was carried out in Domachevo by a special commando of the SD [*Sicherheitsdienst* – Security Service], together with the cavalry squadron of the Order Police and the *Schutzmannschaft* [the auxiliary police recruited from the local, non-Jewish population] and in total some 2,900 Jews were shot. The *Aktion* took place without any disturbance.'

When the killing was at last over, the auxiliaries shovelled the sandy soil back into the pit to cover the mounds of victims; there were now not enough Jews left alive to do the work. For days after the slaughter, as the bodies began to decompose and rats burrowed into the mound, the surface of the mass grave continued to move as if the victims buried beneath it were still struggling to escape.

The Road of Death still led to those sand-hills at the edge of the forest, where a huge concrete slab covered the mass grave of those who were slaughtered there. The concrete obelisk standing over it, a Soviet memorial topped with a red star, carried the inscription: 'To the victims of the German fascist terror 1941–45'. Like other Soviet memorials to the war dead, there was no reference to the fact that most of the victims of that fascist terror were Jews.

The burial plots in the town's graveyard were almost all marked by Christian symbols, many of them Russian Orthodox crosses with a diagonal bar below the horizontal crosspiece. There were no Stars of David visible anywhere in Domachevo, other than the graffiti that someone had drawn on the Soviet memorial in red chalk. Nor was there now a single Jewish resident – another grim reminder of the Nazi genocide.

The SS had soon moved on to fresh slaughters elsewhere, leaving the task of hunting down and eliminating those Jews who had somehow escaped to the *Schutzmannschaft* police auxiliaries. Some Jews had gone to ground in cellars and hiding places inside the ghetto; others had fled to the forest or joined the partisans fighting the invaders. Perhaps a couple of hundred had survived.

The jurors were now to be shown the places where many of those, too, had been exterminated. At the age of 75, dressed in his Sunday best clothes and an imitation leather coat, with a fur hat on his shock of white hair, Fedor Zan stood ramrod straight while the interpreter passed on the judge's instructions to him, and then led the way along a track through the forest, reliving the events of many years before, when he was just a boy of 18. In a suffocating silence, broken only by the desolate cawing of crows, the jurors trudged in single file after him. He stopped three times on the one-mile walk, not out of frailty, but to point out a particular location.

Zan worked as a 'river leveller', opening and closing a network of sluices and dams to ensure that the River Bug through Domachevo remained at a consistent depth. He lived in a shack without electricity or running water and had to wash in the river or, once a year, use the *bania* – the decrepit public bathhouse – in the town. When he was flown to London to give evidence, he had to be shown how to use the shower and toilet in his hotel room and, with limitless hot water at his disposal, as one of the lawyers involved in the trial remarked, 'If he wasn't in court, he was in the bath; he took about six baths a day.' When the junior prosecution counsel, John Kelsey-Fry, offered Zan a Marlboro cigarette instead of his usual Russian black tobacco, hand-rolled in a scrap of newspaper, Zan's eyes widened and he took it with reverence. 'You'd have thought I was giving him the keys to Fort Knox,' Kelsey-Fry said, 'he was so thrilled.'

Late one winter afternoon in 1942, Zan had called on his sister – her remote and modest wooden cottage, its corrugated iron roof festooned with yard-long icicles, still stood in the tiny hamlet of Kobelka – and then walked home through the forest. Fifty-seven years later, he paused and raised his hand to indicate the point where he had first heard screams.

He walked on for another 400 yards, as he had done that day, then left the path, demonstrating how he had crept through a thicket of bushes and hidden behind a tree trunk to witness what was happening in the clearing beyond it. Pine and birch trees had grown dense and tall on this site in the intervening years but Zan did not hesitate. Pushing his way through a tangle of dead bracken crusted with hoar-frost, he peered through the branches of a pine and then stood motionless, raising his arm above his head. When the interpreter asked if he was on the exact spot where he had been standing that day, he said, 'Da. Da. Da.' A translation was scarcely needed.

On the far side of that clearing Zan had seen a member of the *Schutzmannschaft*, a man he had known since he was a child: Andrei Sawoniuk, known to everyone in Domachevo by the diminutive Andrusha – 'Little Andy'. Armed with a sub-machine gun, he had lined up 15 terrified women in front of him. Zan could see the yellow patches on their clothes that the Nazis compelled Jews to wear. He watched, powerless, as Sawoniuk forced them to strip naked, then shot them in the back and pushed and kicked their bodies into a freshly dug pit. Almost 60 years had passed since then, but Zan still had to wipe away the tears forming in his eyes.

One at a time, floundering in the softer snow under the trees, the judge and the jurors pushed their way through the branches. They then watched as Zan walked on to the execution site 100 metres away, once more raising his arm to indicate when he was standing on the spot. His work done, he gave a small bow to the judge and then walked away through the forest, alone with his memories.

Back in Domachevo, the jurors were shown several other landmarks that would be constant reference points in the trial, including a blacksmith's forge – now in ruins – from where Ivan Stepaniuk had seen Sawoniuk force-marching Shlemko, a 50-year-old Jew, towards the forest, repeatedly striking him with a spade. Shlemko kept collapsing but, each time, Sawoniuk forced him back to his feet and drove him on. They passed out of Stepaniuk's sight, but soon afterwards he heard a single shot and Sawoniuk then returned alone, still carrying his spade.

The jurors were also taken to the place where 12-year-old Alexandre Baglay and his friend were arrested by Sawoniuk as they scavenged for clothes in the deserted ghetto. 'Crying, thinking we would be shot as well,' the boys were marched down the Road of Death to a clearing a quarter of a mile away. There they saw two more auxiliaries guarding two dishevelled and emaciated middle-aged Jewish men and a young woman, who had all been found hiding in a cellar.

Sawoniuk ordered them to strip naked. The men did so, but the young woman was too embarrassed to remove her underwear until Sawoniuk shouted and threatened her with a club and she finally complied. He then made them turn away from him to face a newly dug grave, pulled out a pistol and shot each of them in the back of the head. He pushed them into the hole with his knees and then handed spades to the two terrified boys and ordered them to fill it in. He searched the Jews' clothes for hidden valuables and, not finding any, told the boys they could have them when they'd finished but, fearing a trick to catch them out, they left them there.

More than half a century later, defence solicitors had put up posters around the town asking for information from anyone who recalled Sawoniuk. They were looking for 'eyewitnesses who might be able to give an account of events that cast suspicion on someone else', or failing that, who could at least cast doubts on the prosecution witnesses' statements. They were not successful, and nor did they find any potential witnesses to Sawoniuk's good character. No one who came forward had a good word to say about him. Instead, according to an observer, there were 'huddles of old people in their eighties, volunteering information about more murders and pointing to sites where people had been killed'.

As they described a series of terrible crimes, Lee's heart sank. Sawoniuk, they claimed, had given one young Jewish girl a savage beating when he caught her trying to smuggle a few potatoes into the ghetto. There had been more murders in nearby Chersk, where he was said to have led a mopping-up operation, picking off fleeing survivors as a Nazi execution squad wiped out 54 children in an orphanage on the edge of the town. One of the village elders also witnessed him shooting 'a young Jewish girl of twenty-five years. He shot her in daylight on the street near the church.' He also shot all the members of the Yankel and Khalalyuk families in the sand-hills outside Domachevo, and killed the baby of yet another family. One 60-year-old local, Ivan Tribunko, had a plain message. 'My mother's family were killed and Andrusha was responsible. He was an animal. If they brought him back here, he wouldn't leave alive.' Any thoughts the defence might have had about attempting to establish Sawoniuk as a man of good character were not pursued further.

The jurors next paused outside Number 6 Sverdlov Street, a blue-painted, wooden dwelling with green shutters and a corrugated iron roof. Owned by a Jewish family, it had once stood inside the ghetto, but after the massacre, Sawoniuk had instructed a carpenter to dismantle the building timber by timber and rebuild it outside. When the man asked for payment, Andrusha brandished his rifle and told him, 'If you come here again, the first bullet will be yours.'

While the jurors, reporters and photographers were studying the facade, as if it could offer some clue to Sawoniuk's guilt or innocence, one of the yellowing lace curtains was pushed aside. Nose pressed against the window, a young boy peered out at the horde of people staring back.

The jurors were led on around the perimeter of the ghetto,

all traces of which had long since been erased. The fences and the coils of barbed wire that surrounded it were removed after the massacre and the homes of its occupants burned or demolished. The town had never recovered and remained a place of desperate, almost medieval poverty. Ploughing was still done by oxen, not tractors, and horse-drawn carts were as common as cars on the roads and tracks, most of which were unsurfaced. Every vehicle that did pass seemed to be a rattling, clanking rust-trap with a blown exhaust.

There was no reliable electricity supply and the inhabitants – mainly subsistence farmers – still drew their water from wells. A few of the wealthier ones had diesel-powered pumps, but most still hauled up buckets by hand. Cast-iron stoves were their only source of heat and almost all had to make do with the light from oil lamps and candles, like their ancestors a century before. They lived in shabby wooden houses with outside toilets and ramshackle sheds. When the dairy had made a batch of butter, any remaining hot water from the process was carried to the *bania*, and those who were quick enough could briefly enjoy the relative luxury of a warm bath.

There were only two shops in Domachevo and their shelves were mostly bare. In the bakery, an abacus was used to calculate the price of bread in a country where, on the black market, whatever the official rate might be, runaway inflation meant that even 250,000 Belarusian roubles might not be enough to buy one US dollar. The counter in the state-owned food store was presided over by eight women in white coats – far outnumbering the customers. A cool cabinet for fish, cooked meats and dairy products ran the entire length of the shop, but there was one small lump of cheese in its 30 yards of shelf space and absolutely nothing else. The Soviet era might have ended but shortages of basic goods evidently still continued, and most of the townsfolk bartered with each other for basic necessities.

If anything, the economic situation had got worse, not

better, in the years since the fall of the Berlin Wall. In exchange for their new freedoms – and in Belarus, they were of dubious value anyway – people had lost whatever small sums they might have had in the collapsed Bank of Savings, and with guaranteed employment at an end, thousands had fallen into even deeper poverty. The only obvious signs of capitalist freedom were the pathetic handwritten signs held up by people trying to sell whatever personal belongings they had left, and the only growth industries appeared to be crime, smuggling and prostitution.

The sky was darkening when Judge Potts finally brought the tour to an end. Once more escorted by Belarusian police, and belching out fresh clouds of oily, black smoke, the three buses made the return journey to Brest-Litovsk where, to the audible relief of the journalists, the Intourist Hotel bar had been restocked. The dining room remained as devoid of food as the Domachevo store and, to the owner's delight, Belarus's only Indian restaurant was soon packed once more. The press and the legal teams could relax and mingle freely there and in the hotel bar, since they were operating under the 'Chatham House Rule' that everything was off the record – the rule having originated in the 1920s at the London headquarters of the Royal Institute of International Affairs.

As a thank-you to the local police chief for his role as fixer during the visit, the prosecution and defence teams took him out for dinner at the curry house that night and ordered a couple of bottles of wine. 'He was obviously suspicious of this liquid,' Bill Clegg said, 'so I asked him if he'd prefer a vodka and he brightened up no end. So I ordered a vodka and, instead of a glass, they brought a bottle. He drank the lot and then drove us back to the hotel.'

The next morning, the jurors were given some time off before flying home and, still escorted by bailiffs, were allowed to go shopping for souvenirs in the GUM department store. It was so badly lit that it was almost impossible to see anything, but there was precious little to choose from anyway. The home appliances department contained nothing but a solitary antique electric toaster and a small TV on which the assistant was watching a football match and studiously avoiding catching the eye of any potential customers.

Even in Britain, judges were sometimes anxious about protecting jurors from unwanted influences, but taking them abroad with a press pack in tow had made it an even more fraught process, and Potts and the court officials exhibited an almost palpable sense of relief once their charges had been ushered back onto their bus for the flight home.

Several of them had been visibly moved by the memorial to the dead in Domachevo, and seeing the other murder sites had brought the crimes to life with a vividness that, no matter how eloquent the prosecuting counsel, could never have been achieved in a dusty courtroom. It would inevitably colour their perspective through the remainder of the trial, making the task of defending Sawoniuk even more challenging. Yet it was the defence, not the prosecution, who had prompted the visit, after being caught in a trap of their own making.

During the pre-trial hearings, on 5 November 1998, defence counsel Bill Clegg had applied to the judge, Sir Humphrey Potts, to have the proceedings 'stayed' as an abuse of process and the charges thrown out. He argued that there was no forensic or other physical evidence to link his client to the crimes, while the decades that had elapsed made it impossible to rely on the accuracy of any eyewitness testimony.

The prosecution counsel, Johnny Nutting, countered that the lack of physical evidence was 'likely to be of greater disadvantage to the Crown than the defence, bearing in mind the burden of proof, since in a criminal trial, the defendant does not have to prove anything'.

Clegg then added that, had the crimes taken place in Epping Forest, the jury could have been taken there and shown the scene of the crime and the places where the murderer, his victims and the witnesses had been standing, so that they could decide whether the evidence was plausible. 'If this issue were raised in a trial concerning a crime committed in England,' Clegg said, 'then no judge would refuse a defence request for a view of the scene by the jury. Indeed, no fair resolution of the issue could take place without such a view. We're denied that in this case, because the crime scene is in Belarus and we can't go there.'

A doyen of the Criminal Bar, Clegg would not have dreamed of saying such a thing had he thought there was even the slightest chance of it happening, and must have believed he was on safe ground, since no British jury had ever visited a foreign crime scene. However, the 1991 War Crimes Act, allowing charges to be brought for crimes committed by foreigners, against foreigners, on foreign soil, had changed the rules of the game. The judge simply said, 'Well, why can't we?'

The delighted Johnny Nutting was only too happy to agree, and to Clegg's horror – he later described it as 'one of the biggest own goals of my career; I was hoist with my own petard!' – the visit to Domachevo went ahead.

That was undoubtedly helpful to a prosecution hampered by a lack of physical evidence and credible witnesses. Many had been killed during the war; others had died of natural causes in the intervening decades; the memories of yet more had faded over the years and others simply did not wish to testify. The stories of still others had been so embellished in the retelling, that neither they nor their audience could any longer have sworn to what was truth and what was fiction.

Some of the few remaining potential witnesses were ruled out as too old and infirm to travel to London. Filmed interviews were recorded with some of them and Bill Clegg still recalls 'the surreal experience, walking through knee-high snow to a cottage in the pitch darkness, hammering on the door and then taking evidence from an old woman, who was sitting in front of the fire with a cat on her lap, about things that had happened nearly sixty years before'.

'Everybody knew what Sawoniuk had done,' was a frequent comment from the townspeople, but that was not admissible as evidence in a court of law. Nor was the fact that someone else had seen the crime and then told a witness about it. So each of the four specimen charges of murder he faced would rely on the evidence of a single witness. Fedor Zan, Alexandre Baglay and Ivan Stepaniuk still lived in Domachevo. The fourth, Ben-Zion Blustein, the only Jew, had emigrated to Israel after the war. Like the others, he would give his testimony at the Old Bailey when the trial resumed.

Sawoniuk had not been forgotten by any of the older inhabitants of the town, and most of those interviewed by journalists – interviews that could not be published until after the proceedings had been concluded – expressed satisfaction that he was finally being brought to trial. 'It's a pity he couldn't go on trial in our country,' 60-year-old Vera Eskin said. 'I wish he could look into the eyes of Domachevo's people.' But not everyone agreed. 'This is fifty years too late,' 70-year-old Olga Yashmuk told the *Guardian*. 'The trial is meaningless now. There is no point in punishing him now. I don't know whether he killed all those people . . . If he killed the Jews, he will be cursed by God.'

An editorial in the *Independent* also warned that the visit might prejudice the proceedings. 'The jury will find visiting mass graves distressing. They will feel disgusted. They may seek means to provide the dead with justice. Conveniently, there is at hand an object for their righteous anger: Mr Sawoniuk. This is the way miscarriages of justice happen.'

James Heartfield echoed that warning in *The Times*:

It is not possible to put evil on trial, only men. A Court of Law cannot re-run historical events, it can only punish people for what they did. And in the case of these trials the real danger exists that people will be punished to satisfy an emotional need, whether they are guilty or not . . . The original Nuremberg hearings had gravitas, with the Nazi elite such as Goering and Hess in the dock. Today we have the sorry spectacle of pensioners on trial. History repeats itself – the first time as tragedy, the second time as farce.

Whether it would ultimately prove to be tragedy or farce, the trial of Andrei 'Andrusha' Sawoniuk would resume at the Old Bailey the following week, when a succession of witnesses from Domachevo would be called to testify about his alleged crimes.

CHAPTER I

The story of Great Britain's first and only successful war crimes trial is also the tale of the intertwined lives of two men. Childhood friends in Domachevo, they were on opposite sides after the German invasion, with one fighting against the Nazi atrocities that the other was helping to inflict. For over half a century after the war, they lived thousands of miles apart, each unaware that the other had even survived, but fate was to bring them together again, in Court 12 of the Old Bailey in London, in February 1999, where one would face possible retribution, while the other sought some vindication at last for the suffering and loss he had endured.

Ben-Zion Blustein was born in Domachevo, then part of Poland, in 1924. His father died from TB when Ben-Zion was just ten months old, and with his older sister and, later, a sister and little brother seven and eight years younger than him, he was raised by his mother, Shaindel, who ran a grocer's shop, and his stepfather, Noah, a furrier. One of his first memories was of his mother wrapping him in a thick wool blanket, putting him on a sledge and pulling him through the snow to the schoolhouse so that the rabbi could begin teaching him Hebrew. She asked him first to teach Ben-Zion to say *Kaddish* – the prayer of remembrance for the dead – so that he could recite it over his father's grave on the fourth anniversary of his death.

Belarus had been part of the Russian Empire until the

October Revolution in 1917, and under the old Tsarist laws, Russian Jews had been forbidden to live in cities or agricultural communities, or own land. That forced them to move to villages and small towns like Domachevo where, since they were not allowed to farm, many became merchants, artisans and shopkeepers. They remained there after the Tsars were overthrown and Domachevo became part of the independent Poland, which existed briefly between the First and Second World Wars, and many grew to be relatively prosperous.

There was no ghetto then, no walls or barbed wire separating the communities, but the Jews, who formed the majority of the town's population, lived separately from the Gentiles, in wooden houses with steeply pitched roofs to shed the winter snow, wide verandas at the front and neat gardens at the rear. On Friday and Saturday evenings, every family dressed in their best clothes and, in a Jewish equivalent of the Spanish *paseo*, promenaded along the main street to see and be seen, exchanging greetings with friends and neighbours, while their teenage sons and daughters swapped furtive glances.

There were two synagogues: the Great, in the marketplace where the wealthy businessmen and merchants prayed, and the Small, in a side street for workers and tradesmen. The two rabbis matched their congregations. Reb Yankel, who presided over the smaller synagogue, had the powerful build of his tradesman father. The other, Leizer Wolf, was a tall, thin, ascetic man who earned his living as a rabbinical judge and studied day and night until he was claimed by TB. His wife, a much smaller, stooped woman, took care of their more fundamental needs, having secured the monopoly of selling yeast for the *challah*, the traditional egg bread baked for the Sabbath.

On Sundays the inhabitants of all the neighbouring villages came to Domachevo to pray at the Catholic, Russian Orthodox or Lutheran churches. They wore their Sunday best clothes, but to save their shoes, they hung them around their necks and walked through the fields barefoot, only putting them on when they reached the town. After church, they sat on the edge of the verandas on the main street, cracking sunflower seeds, chatting and watching the passers-by, before returning to their home villages. When a wedding took place, a procession of horse-drawn farm wagons decorated with flowers and ribbons would make its way past, accompanied by accordion players, drummers and trumpeters, whose music and singing echoed through the streets.

Once a fortnight, there was a market in town, with farmers on wagons laden with vegetables, eggs, butter and cheese, and firewood gathered from the forest. They also set up pens of pigs, cattle and horses, jostling for space with the stalls of Jewish merchants selling oil, salt, sugar, paraffin, clothes, shoes, pots and pans, and sweets for the children.

There was no industry in Domachevo, but it was a beautiful town and a thriving resort. Straddling the main railway line linking Warsaw with Minsk and Moscow, it drew sufficient visitors from Brest-Litovsk, Bialystok and as far as Warsaw and Wolyn, 300 kilometres away, to ensure many of the permanent inhabitants made enough money to see them through the rest of the year.

The town was ringed by *dachas* built in the fringes of the forest, overlooking the lake and the river. There were several guest- and boarding-houses where people suffering from TB and other chest complaints came for the benefit of their health, but where many others – families, teachers, writers, intelligentsia, political party members and trade unionists – also came to enjoy a vacation. Domachevo was the summer home of the Grand Rabbi of Lebartov, and hundreds of his followers would come to him on the Hasidic High Holy Days. There were two holiday homes for Jewish orphans, children with various psychological and physical disabilities, and those who had been abandoned in the streets as babies so their mothers could avoid the shame of illegitimacy. They were given Yiddish names after the days upon which they were found: *Sabadski* for Saturdays, *Nigelski* for Sundays, and so on.

It was a far from wealthy region, but Domachevo was a relatively affluent place. There was a bank and a loans fund, two libraries, a small cinema, a literary club that held cultural evenings and discussions, and regular visits by touring Jewish theatre groups. A number of political parties – including Communists, Socialists, Zionists, the Zionist youth movement Gordonia, and the Socialist labour organisation known as 'the Bund' – jostled for position in a much more progressive and liberal environment than other, fiercely traditional Jewish towns in Poland and Belarus.

Although there was some anti-Semitism, notably in the school where Polish teachers openly discriminated against Jewish children, relations between the different ethnic groups were generally cordial, and the Jews employed many Belarusians, Poles and Ukrainians for menial labour. One of those was Andrei ('Andrusha') Sawoniuk. Born in 1921, he never knew who his father was. His mother, Pelagia, never revealed his identity, but local gossip, and indeed Andrusha's half-brother, Nikolai, were less constrained. 'People in the village said that my brother was the son of the schoolmaster. I think the same.' Pelagia had worked as a cleaner at the school and for the headmaster, Josef Jakubiak, who left Domachevo soon after the birth.

Whoever the father was, he never acknowledged the child, nor his responsibilities to Pelagia, and Andrusha took the surname of his mother's deceased first husband. Andrusha's favourite hobby earned him the nickname 'pigeon boy', but he was more widely known as 'Andrusha the bastard'. Illegitimacy was a considerable stigma, and he was relentlessly taunted by older boys.

Even by Belarusian standards, the family was desperately

poor. They owned no land on which they could grow food and lived near the Provoslav Russian Orthodox church in a one-room house that was little more than a shack, with log walls, a thatched roof and an earth floor. Pelagia took in washing and Andrusha and Nikolai, nicknamed Kola, worked as *Shabbat goys*, chopping wood, lighting fires and ovens, fetching water from the well, feeding the horses and doing other chores forbidden to Orthodox Jews on the Sabbath.

Scorned and shunned by his peers, Andrusha's only friends were younger boys, like Ben-Zion, who was three years his junior and probably flattered by the friendship of the older boy. Despite the age difference, they shared a school desk and became close friends. Andrusha had never had a father and Ben-Zion had never known his, and that must have strengthened the bond between them.

In summer Ben-Zion liked to take his morning wash in the stream that ran alongside Andrusha's house, so they saw each other every day. Andrusha encouraged him to help with the pigeons he reared, showing him how to handle them and the squabs he reared from their eggs. They played in the fields and forest together, climbing trees and building dams on the stream. In spring they collected frogspawn from forest ponds and they swam in the river on hot summer days, inching out along a thick branch of a huge tree growing from the riverbank near the bridge, and then launching themselves outwards, making a huge splash as they hit the water several metres below. In the autumn they would go foraging for berries and nuts in the forest, until the first snowfall signalled the onset of the cruel Belarusian winter, when all the inhabitants retreated indoors.

The friendship began to fade as they grew older. Ben-Zion's best friend was now Meir Bronstein, a boy of his own age, and he rarely saw Andrusha, who had left school at the age of 14. He was virtually illiterate, having only completed 'six classes of general school', which gave his peers another reason to scorn and denigrate him, but even those who pitied him tended to patronise him. When his mother died of cancer before the war, he was left even more friendless and alone. Even Nikolai had little to do with him. 'He had his own life,' Andrei Sawoniuk later said, 'and he did not seem to care much about me.' They had very different personalities. A female contemporary said, 'Kola was very calm, as opposed to Andrei who was very pushy.'

He had grown into a powerful young man and began picking on those – both boys and girls – who were smaller and weaker than him. He gained a bad reputation around the town and, rightly or wrongly, the blame for any petty theft or vandalism tended to be laid at his door. When Ben-Zion's mother warned him not to associate with Andrusha, the last traces of their friendship were at an end.

The rise of the Nazis in Germany during the 1930s had been viewed with considerable alarm by the Jews of Domachevo, where older inhabitants were still haunted by the destruction of the town in the First World War. As the German armies advanced, the entire population had fled east, deeper into Russia, leaving almost all of their possessions behind. When they returned at the end of the conflict, their property had been looted and their houses burned to the ground; they had to completely rebuild their lives.

On 1 September 1939, the radio carried the news of the invasion of Poland, and within days German troops were in Domachevo. Most of the Jewish population fled to the surrounding villages but, after a few days, thinking that children would be safe, Ben-Zion and his friend Meir were sent back into the town to find out what was happening. They saw German soldiers in the streets and the local Poles and Ukrainians stripping the Jewish shops and houses, but the looting stopped for fear of Soviet reprisals when the Wehrmacht rapidly withdrew again under the terms of the Molotov–Ribbentrop Pact, which divided Poland between Germany and the Soviet Union.

The River Bug was now the frontier, with Domachevo just inside the Russian zone. The Soviet Union was thought to be all-powerful, yet when their troops arrived, Ben-Zion saw 'soldiers in torn uniforms on horses which hardly moved, with old weapons. We could not believe our eyes; this was the famous Red Army?'

The Soviet system was at once introduced. The Radziwills, Polish aristocrats who had previously owned all the land, were dispossessed. Larger farms were collectivised, factories nationalised, capitalist occupations like merchant prohibited and tradesmen ordered to form co-operatives. Apprentices in trades such as tailoring were sent to work on the land 'to cleanse them of bourgeois values'. Food became scarce and the daily bread-line grew longer. The schools reopened, but now teaching in Russian rather than Polish although, unlike their predecessors, the Russians did not discriminate against the Jews.

The Soviet occupation lasted almost two years, during which Jews fleeing across the river from the German zone told terrifying stories of violence and massacre. At the beginning of June 1941, Ben-Zion's family received a postcard from Jewish friends in the German zone. It read, 'Be prepared! The slaughterer is on his way.'

On midsummer's night, 21 June, Ben-Zion and his friend, Meir Bronstein, went to the cinema. They noticed a number of strangers in the audience but it was the first week of the holidays and summer visitors were nothing new, so they thought little more about it, even when one of the newcomers turned to look at them and said, 'Isn't this a great movie? Tomorrow you will see an even better one.'

The film, *The Life of Bogdan Chmielnicki* – 'Chmiel the Wicked' in Jewish folklore – was the story of the seventeenth-century leader of a Cossack and peasant uprising in the Ukraine, who slaughtered tens of thousands of Jews in a series of terrible pogroms. It was a strange, unsettling choice for a town with such a large Jewish population.

When the two boys went outside, they found themselves in darkness. The street lights had all been vandalised and the telephone wires cut, isolating Domachevo from the outside world. Soviet border guards were patrolling the streets with tracker dogs and, fearful without exactly knowing why, the two boys ran for their homes. Only later did Ben-Zion realise that the strangers they had seen were fifth columnists and German saboteurs, who had disguised themselves as teachers at a conference and were using the cinema as their rendezvous point after wrecking the town's infrastructure. They had evidently switched the film reels as a final cruel joke.

In the early hours of the following morning, Sunday 22 June 1941, 'Operation Barbarossa' – the invasion of the Soviet Union – was launched. The largest invasion force in history: 3 million men with 600,000 motor vehicles including tanks, armoured vehicles, troop-carriers and artillery pieces, crossed the border on a battlefront that stretched almost 3,000 kilometres from north to south.

The sky over Domachevo was filled with wave after wave of aircraft flying east, as the ground erupted, pounded by bombs, artillery, tank shells and mortars. When Ben-Zion went outside, looking for Soviet soldiers who could tell him what was happening, he saw German ones emerging from the darkness. He ran home to tell his family that their worst fears had been realised.

Less than an hour after Operation Barbarossa had begun, the German 487th Infantry and 22nd Cavalry had swept aside the Soviet defenders – there had only been 40 guarding the bridge over the Bug River and they put up no more than token resistance – and occupied Domachevo. Constant explosions, machine-gun and rifle fire, shouts and screams provided the soundtrack to the elimination of the last shreds of resistance. Huddled together in their house, Ben-Zion's family felt as much as heard the bass rumble of heavy armour as a succession of smoke-belching tanks ground relentlessly onward, their tracks shattering the neat paving of the main street. A lurid red glow lit up the sky as the wooden buildings went up in flames, destroying half the town.

Jews rendered homeless by the destruction were given shelter by family or friends. 'We began to bury the dead and waited for what would happen next.' Over the next few days, the sound of fighting diminished and then ceased altogether as the battlefront moved rapidly east. Every day Ben-Zion and his friends hid in the surrounding wheat fields to watch the columns of tanks, armoured cars, troop-carriers, motorcycles and lorries dragging artillery pieces behind them, as they rumbled across the bridge and roared through the town.

The initial occupiers of Domachevo were regular army and most did not appear to share the Nazi ideology. When Jewish families asked the medics in the German field hospital for help treating civilians wounded during the invasion, they performed a series of life-saving operations – but told them to beware the SS who would arrive in their wake.

In August 1941, Heinrich Himmler had declared that the attack on the Soviet Union would result in the extermination of 30 million Slavs, but the scope of the *Generalplan Ost* – the Nazi blueprint for the transformation of the whole of Eastern Europe and Russia – was even more ambitious; it foresaw the elimination of 50 million people. Three-quarters of the population of Belarus were destined for deportation, and the future of the Jews living there was to be even more bleak.

On the third day after the invasion, the first SS-*Einsatzgruppe* (operational group) appeared in Domachevo, 'Angels of Destruction' with skull symbols on their caps. According to

Hitler, their commander, SS-*Obergruppenführer* Erich von dem Bach-Zelewski, was a man who could 'wade through a sea of blood', and his men were no less ruthless. They were tasked with eliminating potential resistance leaders such as politicians, intellectuals, priests and rabbis, but also with targeting Jews, Bolsheviks, gypsies and the mentally ill.

Einsatzgruppe B – one of the four *Einsatzgruppen* sweeping through conquered Eastern Europe – had been given responsibility for Belarus and at once they began snatching and killing Jews in Domachevo, instilling terror in the rest. The first to be murdered was one Mendel Rubenstein, and Leibel Detkis followed on the same day, along with five others who were buried with him in the courtyard of his house.

The next victims were a barber, Herschke Greenstein, and his three sons, Baruch, Michael and Wolf. They were marched at gunpoint into the centre of the town and made to dig a grave for themselves. The SS shot the three boys and then forced their father to bury them. As he began to do so, blinded by his tears, Wolf, wounded but not yet dead, stirred and said, 'Father, what are you doing? I'm alive.' Greenstein pleaded with them but they forced him to carry on filling in the grave, burying the boy alive alongside the bodies of his brothers. When he had finished, as a final inhuman cruelty they did not kill Greenstein himself, condemning him to live with the terrible knowledge of what he had been forced to do.

The slaughter was not confined to Domachevo. Between 22 June and 14 November, *Einsatzgruppe B* killed 45,000 Jews across Belarus, but terror of the SS kept everyone off the streets, so no one knew exactly how many others were being annihilated. Some Jews managed to convince themselves that the killings were just the work of a few rotten individuals rather than a systematic slaughter, until *Einsatzgruppe* soldiers broke into the Rabbi of Lubartov's compound. They marched him and 40 of his followers to the watermill on the edge of the town and forced them to load sacks of flour onto a wagon. Some were then harnessed to it like horses, while the others were made to push and manhandle it down to the river. The unpaved roads were full of potholes and the fierce summer heat made the ordeal even worse, but anyone who collapsed was kicked and whipped back to his feet. When they at last reached their destination, the exhausted men were forced to dig a pit and line up in front of it, whereupon they were all shot. When they heard about the massacre, the Jews of the town bribed some Ukrainians to show them the site and help them exhume the bodies in the dead of night for reburial in the Jewish cemetery.

On one of the last warm days before autumn closed in, Ben-Zion and six other Jews were rounded up at gunpoint by two Germans, marched to the woods outside the town and told to get into one of the old Soviet defensive trenches. When one of the older Jews made a run for it, he was shot in the head. The rest did as they were told and bowed their heads, certain of their fate, but one of their captors suddenly said, 'Do you want to live?' He then told them they would be released if they brought him three suit lengths and three leather hides to make boots. Touching Ben-Zion's shoulder with his rifle, he motioned to him to get out and fetch the ransom.

His mother had seen him taken by the soldiers and had followed them to the woods, picking up small branches to make it look as if she was collecting firewood, but she had given her son up for lost until she saw him climb out of the trench. They hurried back into the town together and told the relatives of the other hostages what the Germans wanted. The leather and cloth were quickly produced and, for once, the Germans kept their word and released them.

In occupied territories, the Nazis operated a hierarchy. At the apex were the feared security police, including the Gestapo. Beneath them and very few in number – there were only three in Domachevo – were the *Ordnungpolizei* (Order Police) whose green uniforms led to them being known as the *Grüne Polizei,* though they were also confusingly known as *Gendarmerie.* Too old to be drafted into the army, the Order Police were nonetheless conscripted for wartime service and given four weeks' training before being posted.

Lower still in the pecking order were the men of the *Schutzmannschaft* (guarding troops) – the auxiliaries recruited from the local population to maintain order in the expanding German Empire. By the summer of 1941, Heinrich Himmler was already complaining that, 'The tasks of the police in the occupied Eastern territories cannot be implemented by the units of the police and SS currently and soon to be deployed there.'

The Nazis regarded 'Eastern people' – Belarusians, Poles, Ukrainians and Russians – as backward peasants, only slightly less racially inferior than the *Untermenschen* (sub-human) Jews. However, there were not enough native *Volksdeutsche* (the name given to Poles of German origin) or 'Germanic' or 'Baltic' people (Dutchmen, Norwegians, Danes, Latvians and Lithuanians, who the Nazis regarded as more racially pure than Russians and Eastern Europeans) to fill the ranks of the *Schutzmannschaft.* As a result, Belarusians, Poles and Ukrainians were recruited, albeit at only one-third of the wages paid to Germanic auxiliaries. In the cities and large towns of Belarus, posters advertised jobs in the local constabulary for young, single, able-bodied men of 'suitable' political and racial background. In the smaller towns and villages, volunteers applied to the mayor or village elders, or were approached by them. Most of the recruits had been unemployed, but fear of deportation to Germany for forced labour was another powerful incentive.

The *Schutzmannschaft* was a scratch force, badly fed, sometimes lacking uniform and boots, and often unpaid. They were also poorly armed, at least partly because of German fears that the auxiliaries might one day turn their weapons on their overlords. At first, most of them were equipped only with rubber coshes or wooden batons, with only the most trusted given rifles or pistols. Their designated tasks were to combat local crime, provide protection against partisan attacks and 'lend effect to the occupation policy of the German state' – a policy that included the extermination of the Jews.

Ben-Zion's childhood friend Andrusha Sawoniuk had been one of the first to volunteer, swearing the oath 'to be true, brave and obedient and to carry out their duties conscientiously in the struggle against murderous Bolshevism'. His half-brother Nikolai signed up with him, but resigned again as soon as he realised that their work would actually involve killing Jews. Andrusha had no such compunction; for him, the German invasion represented a career opportunity. He had been the lowest of the low in the town's hierarchy, but when he put on the blue police uniform with its sleeve badge reading *Vertrauen, Gehorsam und Mut* – Trust, Obedience and Courage – for the first time in his life he became a man of authority, with the power of life and death over the townsfolk who had previously jeered at him. They may still not have respected him, but they soon learned to fear him. He was, as his QC, Bill Clegg, later said: 'A classic example of someone who has been bullied all his life, making the most of an unexpected chance to get his own back.'

Having carried out the first wave of killings, the SS moved on, leaving the German *Ordnungpolizei* and their *Schutzmannschaft* auxiliaries in charge. On the tenth day of the occupation, orders were published imposing humiliating restrictions on the Jews. Everyone over the age of 12 had to wear a yellow circle on their chest and another on their back. They had to remove their hats in the presence of Germans and were forbidden to walk on the pavement, although only the main street in Domachevo was paved anyway. 'When you met a German, you had to bow down to him,' Ben-Zion Blustein later said. If the Jews did not, they would be beaten for lack of respect, but if they did, they might also be beaten because *Untermensch* Jews were not fit to salute the *Herrenvolk* – the master race. Schools were closed, all forms of social gathering were banned, and a dusk-to-dawn curfew was imposed. Wireless sets were impounded and no contact with the non-Jewish population was permitted. All deliveries of food from the neighbouring villages were stopped.

A short time later, the Jews were herded into the ruins that had been blitzed during the invasion, forming a crowded ghetto surrounded by fences and barbed wire, where no one could enter or leave without a permit. Posters were put up in the surrounding streets warning Gentiles that they would be shot if they had any contact with them. Meanwhile many Jews, young and old, were shot on the least pretext and buried in graves they were forced to dig themselves.

Fit young Jewish men and women were taken away and used as slave labourers, and treated with equal brutality. Some were forced to build a new iron bridge over the River Bug, replacing the narrow wooden one. Many more were forced to dig peat for fuel and others were transported to Aleksandrova, 25 kilometres from Domachevo, where they worked on a new autobahn – *Hitler Strasse*. They were made to uproot trees using only axes and spades, and those who were unable to do so were savagely beaten. For no reason other than their own entertainment, the German supervisors also stripped them naked and forced them to beat each other. Jewish labourers were also forced to climb up into trees, and remain there while they were felled, causing them to plummet to their deaths.

The living saw their money stolen and their property looted, and all were slowly starved, forced to exist on a bread ration of 150 to 200 grams per person. Smuggling food was punishable by death – Ben-Zion saw the body of Buche, a 12-year-old orphan boy with two younger sisters, hanging from the barbed wire, shot in the back after being caught trying to sneak out of the ghetto to buy food. Despite the risks, some farmers still swapped potatoes and other vegetables for money and valuables. Prices rose daily, but the Jews were in no position to argue.

The auxiliary police also went from house to house in Domachevo searching for prohibited items. 'They found a bit of soap belonging to a Jew, Shaya Partzever, and they led him away,' a witness said, 'along with two other Jews who tried to bribe those bastards in an attempt to rescue him.' All three were taken to the forest, where another Jew was ordered to dig their graves. The auxiliaries shot the three men dead, but then claimed the fourth 'didn't do a good enough job digging the graves, so they shot him too. Then they brought two other Jews, who were ordered to dig his grave. When they were done, they wanted to shoot them too, but the mayor got involved, because he wanted to ensure he had a labour force, and so at this point the executions halted.' The remaining inhabitants of the ghetto, like Ben-Zion and his family, could only watch and await their own fate.

CHAPTER 2

The winter brought fresh misery to the surviving inhabitants of Domachevo, for it was one of the harshest of the century, with temperatures falling below -30 Celsius. There was so little fuel that 'people broke their last items of furniture in order to heat the houses for their children'. The one slight benefit of the terrible cold was that, although the killings never completely ceased, the frosts penetrated so deep into the ground that digging burial pits became impossible.

A few Jews had escaped the ghetto and fled to the forest, where some joined partisan groups, but the religious beliefs of Orthodox Jews required them to turn the other cheek and leave resistance and retribution in God's hands. There was also a fear of terrible reprisals if they did resist, for stories circulated that at first 20, and then 100 Jews were being slaughtered in Warsaw for every German killed. The vast majority remained in the ghetto, passively accepting their fate, and hoping only that the tide of war would eventually turn and save them.

A few were allowed out to carry out work for the Nazis. When leaving the ghetto, they were given a jacket to identify them as approved workers: white for skilled men and blue for menial labourers; without them, they were likely to be shot on sight. Ben-Zion, now 17, had worked at the hospital as a cleaner and water-carrier – there was no running water and the well was some distance away – but then he and seven other young men were chosen to install and repair telephone wires. For six months they left the ghetto every Monday morning and worked outside until the Saturday, doing work the Nazis regarded as critical to the war effort, although none of them were paid.

During that terrible winter, morale in the ghetto had sunk so low that, as one inhabitant said, 'if somebody died, people were jealous of him.' Yet, despite the misery they were enduring, the Jews had some grounds for optimism, because as they worked on the telephone lines, Ben-Zion and his comrades would often see long trains bringing back wounded and frostbitten troops from the Eastern Front. 'The temperatures were thirty, thirty-two below zero,' Ben-Zion later said. 'But however cold it was, we were happy because we knew the Germans on the front were suffering from this cold as well.'

Following the failure of 'Operation Typhoon' – the German assault on Moscow that had begun in October 1941 – Russia's 'General Winter' was now taking its toll. The sight of those trains raised hopes among the Jews that they might be able to survive until Germany was defeated. 'We will live on after them' became a mantra that helped them to endure their privations and suffering.

When the weather relented, the pressure on the ghetto's inhabitants increased again. One cold, wet evening, all of them were ordered to assemble on a nearby field, ready to move elsewhere. Each person was told only to take with them a ten-kilogram bundle of food and clothes. Anyone defying the order would be killed. Distraught and terrified, they went to the field where armed auxiliary police took their cash and valuables and handed them over to the watching Germans.

Men, women and children were then forced to stand for hours, cold and soaked to the skin by downpours, before eventually being told, without explanation, to return to the ghetto. When they did so, they found their homes had been torn apart, windows broken, doors hanging from their hinges, and the few possessions that had not been stolen, smashed to pieces.

Andrusha had shown few overt signs of anti-Semitism before the war, but he had now adopted his Nazi paymasters' creed with enthusiasm. Ben-Zion never understood how Andrusha and the other auxiliaries could switch so easily from friends to brutal foes. 'These policemen, who knew us well, who had studied with us at school, whose families had made a living trading with us, were now the worst of our enemies. The minute they put on the uniforms, they rivalled the Germans in their cruelty. Like angels of destruction, they roamed around the ghetto, looking for any pretext to beat up or kill Jews. Andrusha had been a bad sort, even before the German Occupation, but during the ghetto period, he was infamous for his cruelty. He wanted to sleep with one of the Jewish girls and killed her when she refused.'

The Jews were not the only Nazi victims; two million Soviet PoWs were killed within nine months of the launch of Operation Barbarossa, but that horrific number was soon dwarfed by the wholesale slaughter of Jews under *Endlösung der Judenfrage* – the 'Final Solution of the Jewish Question'.

In August and September 1942, the Germans recaptured hundreds of Red Army soldiers who had escaped from prisoner-of-war camps and were trying to cross the River Bug to get back to the Soviet Union. Groups of them, so heavily manacled that they could barely walk, were force-marched through Domachevo while the Germans beat them and set their ferocious dogs on any who collapsed or marched too slowly. When they reached the forest outside the town, they were shot dead and buried in huge pits excavated by Jews from the ghetto.

In neighbouring areas, the Germans had forced Jews to dig ditches, beating them with their rifle butts while they did so, and when they finished, made them fill them in, over and over again. The Domachevo pits were always used to bury the dead, and the horrors they witnessed spread even greater terror in the ghetto.

On Friday 19 and Saturday 20 September 1942, 20 men were rounded up once more and forced to dig huge new craters in the sand-hills at the edge of the forest. Unusually, the Germans offered an explanation: they were going to execute thousands more Russians who had rebelled at a PoW camp. However, on the Saturday evening, hundreds of German SD *Sonderkommandos* – the SD was notionally the intelligence service of the SS but frequently performed the same functions – and *Schutzmannschaft* auxiliaries surrounded the ghetto. The terrified inhabitants spent the night in the streets, unable to sleep for fear of what the morning would bring.

Early the next day, the eve of Yom Kippur, everyone was ordered to assemble at a nearby field. In February of that year, a census of the ghetto's inhabitants totalled 3,316. A number had not survived the following months, but the *Judenrat* (the elders appointed by the Germans as the Jews' representatives) were ordered to warn them all that if anyone was missing from the roll-call, it would lead to the immediate death of their entire family.

On the previous occasion when they had all been ordered out, they had eventually been allowed to return, but this time, Ben-Zion's mother, Shaindel, told her family: 'I do not believe the Germans only want to check numbers. I am sure this is the end. We will not leave.'

As rumours had filtered in from other towns and cities in Belarus about extermination *Aktionen* that had already taken place, many of Domachevo's Jews had tried to create hiding places. Ben-Zion's stepfather, Noah, had constructed a concealed bunker under the floor of the storeroom in their yard. Ben-Zion's older sister, Nechama, was now living with her husband in a village to the east of Domachevo, beyond their help, but the rest of the family took refuge there. It was tiny, just two metres long, a little over a metre wide and one metre high, so they had to sit squashed together in a row, knees drawn up to their chins, as the world around them fell silent.

During anti-Jewish *Aktionen*, *Schutzmannschaft* auxiliaries forced Jews out of their homes and took them to an assembly point where a head count could be made and they could be stripped of clothing and valuables. They then force-marched them to the killing ground, and cordoned off the area, more to prevent escapes than to bar witnesses, since instilling terror remained part of the process. The naked victims were either forced to lie face down in rows in the burial pits – which some of their tormentors dubbed 'the sardines method' – or lined up at the edge of the pit or on planks laid across it, and then shot in the back of the head. Groups of up to 20 soldiers carried out the killings but were relieved at intervals 'for psychological reasons'.

Initially the auxiliaries watched, often reportedly drunk while doing so, but in tune with the Nazi policy of involving local non-Jewish populations in the genocide, they increasingly took over the task as some German soldiers, particularly those with families, became traumatised by shooting women and children. Himmler's deputy, Reynard Heydrich, issued orders to the *Einsatzgruppen* following the Wehrmacht troops into the newly occupied territories that, 'No obstacles should be put in the way of strivings for *Selbstbereinigungsbestrebungen* [self-cleansing]' by local anti-Communist or anti-Semitic groups. 'On the contrary,' he wrote, 'they are to be instigated (of course imperceptibly), intensified, and directed into the right course.'

In some parts of Poland and Lithuania where anti-Semitism had always been particularly virulent, some of the non-Jewish population appeared to treat the wholesale slaughter as entertainment. On 30 August 1941, the head of the Gestapo,

Heinrich Müller, had to order the *Einsatzgruppen* to prevent 'the crowding of spectators during the mass executions', and in Lithuania in particular, Nazi propaganda roused the local inhabitants to carry out their own pogroms. This was not the case in Belarus, but it still became a killing ground not only for local Jews, but for those transported there from Germany, Austria, Czechoslovakia and the Nazi-occupied countries of Western Europe. Fearing that massacres there might cause unrest or be reported and used as propaganda against them, the Nazis chose to carry them out far from those prying eyes, first by mass shootings in Belarus and later, in the gas chambers of the extermination camps in Eastern Poland.

In their own propaganda, the Nazis made every effort to reinforce the crude stereotype of rich and avaricious Jews, and once the effects of *Aktionen* were understood, whenever one was rumoured to be imminent in any town or city, locals with wheelbarrows and empty sacks would crowd around the entrance to the ghetto, ready to begin looting and pillaging the deserted houses even as their owners were being led away to their deaths.

Einsatzgruppe soldiers, perhaps aggrieved that their own share of the booty was being pilfered, complained that there were not enough police to prevent 'the local population's thirst for robbery'. That was echoed by the *Gebietskommissar* (local commissioner) for Brest-Litovsk, who protested to his superiors that, since he had not been informed that an *Aktion* was about to take place 'my local administrator could only take over a part of the Jewish assets while the majority . . . have been ransacked unilaterally'.

Although *Einsatzgruppe* commanders sent reports of village elders travelling 40 or 50 kilometres to ask for their communities to be 'cleansed of Bolshevist and Jewish elements', and the *Anzeigestellen* [information posts] where people could denounce Jews or Communists and reveal their whereabouts were well used, *Einsatzgruppe B* complained that 'a pronounced anti-Semitism' was lacking in Belarus.

However, if the general population did not participate in this persecution as wholeheartedly as some did elsewhere, the police auxiliaries were soon 'wading through blood' with as much enthusiasm as their SS masters. Whatever their initial reservations – and in Sawoniuk's case, any he might have felt seem to have been easily overcome – brutality, theft, rape and murder soon became routine. Not only did such crimes go unpunished, they were the route to approval by their masters, promotion and material benefits, including the chance to take a share of the loot.

Einsatzgruppe B had only 650 soldiers to cover the whole of Belarus, and since the proportion of order police to *Schutzmänner* (members of the *Schutzmannschaft*) was only between one to ten and one to twenty, the mass killings could not have occurred so swiftly, nor on such a scale, without the willing participation of auxiliaries. Himmler saw their use as an efficient means of achieving the destruction of the Jews, and the majority in Domachevo were indeed killed not by Germans, but by *Schutzmänner*, who were often given the *Schmutzarbeit* (dirty work) of shooting the children, which even hard-bitten Nazi killers sometimes balked at.

During that long, never-to-be-forgotten day, Ben-Zion had crept out of the bunker where they were hiding several times to find out was happening. The house and the ghetto were silent, with no voices or movement, but in the distance he could hear 'shooting that went on for hours and the sounds of screaming which made my blood freeze'.

Surrounded by armed troops and auxiliary police with ferocious dogs, the Domachevo Jews had all been stripped naked. Anyone trying to escape or disobeying orders was shot dead at once. The remainder, whipped and beaten into line, were marched in groups to the huge burial pits, where they were machine-gunned. 'They would barely wait for one group to fall into the graves before they brought another.'

The German MG-42s had such a high rate of fire that individual shots were no longer distinguishable. Some likened it to the sound of tearing cloth, others a buzz-saw. The nickname given to it by German troops – *Knochensäge* (bone-saw) – described the effect as well as the cacophony.

When no one returned that evening, Ben-Zion's family came to the only possible conclusion. A report by the Nazi police commander for the area confirmed that 2,900 Jews had been shot. He claimed that only 300 were now still alive in Domachevo and the rest of the rural area surrounding Brest-Litovsk: 200 working on road construction and 100 digging peat for fuel. He added that the soap factory in Domachevo had had to be closed down because every one of its workers had been killed.

The next morning, police and soldiers raided the ghetto looking for any missing Jews. Ben-Zion's family remained in the bunker, sitting 'like statues for hours, clutching each other's hands as soldiers walked to and fro above our heads, breaking windows and furniture and spraying shots in every direction. We heard steps approaching the entrance to the bunker and held our breath for what felt like an eternity until we were sure every last soldier had left.' They heard more screams and shots as other Jews were found and killed.

The main German force then moved on to the next ghetto to be liquidated, leaving the auxiliary police, with Andrusha playing a leading role, to hunt down and murder any remaining Jews. The ghetto was searched every day and, trapped in the bunker, the family's food and water rapidly dwindled and ran out. Their position seemed hopeless. If they managed to escape, they knew of no safe refuge; they were in the heart of enemy territory that now stretched for thousands of miles, from the Mediterranean to the Arctic Circle, and the Atlantic coast to the gates of Moscow. Even if they could somehow reach the forest and hide there, Noah also knew that, with winter approaching, the youngest children would not survive.

He briefly harboured thoughts of escaping with Ben-Zion and leaving Shaindel with the other children, but abandoned the idea almost at once, telling them that even if he survived the war and lived to see the Germans defeated, 'How could I live with myself? The thought that I saved myself and abandoned my wife and children would never let me rest. I could not live like that.'

On their seventh night in the bunker, weak from hunger and thirst, Noah made the terrible decision that it was better for them all to commit suicide than be captured and killed by the Nazis. At first his wife refused, arguing that they could use a can of fuel they still had to set fire to their own and the neighbouring wooden houses and use the confusion as the ghetto was wreathed in smoke and flames to try to escape. However, when they emerged from the bunker in the dead of night, they heard low voices and movement from other houses and realised that some of their neighbours were also still in hiding.

Noah had a small bottle of morphine, taken from the clinic where he had worked as a medic, and some concentrated saccharine, which he believed was poisonous in large doses. After taking their tearful leave of each other, Noah drank the morphine while the others shared the saccharine. Noah soon lapsed into unconsciousness, but the others were left writhing in agony. Tortured by thirst, they were eventually forced to drink their own urine, which was unbearably sweet from the saccharine they had swallowed. Noah never regained consciousness, but the others survived, remaining in the bunker next to his decomposing body. They no longer had the strength to move it.

Shaindel then suggested cutting their wrists, but Ben-Zion's nine-year-old brother, Shlomo, refused. 'I don't care what the

Germans do to me,' he said, 'but I do not agree to cutting my wrists. I cannot see so much blood.'

His sister, Shulamit, disagreed. 'Little brother, don't you see there is no possibility to continue living in this world? Maybe in the next world, if it exists, we will continue to live.'

In the end, they did nothing, waiting for thirst and starvation to end their suffering, but on the eighth day, Shaindel began pleading with Ben-Zion to escape, leaving her and the other children behind. He argued, but she told him she had dreamed that her father had ordered her to make him go and had promised that if he did, he would survive.

On the ninth day, she eventually persuaded him. 'My son,' she said, 'leave us here and go. You must be brave and even cruel, if you feel your life is in danger, but I am sure you will survive this terrible hell. Remember it is not shameful to cry, but never stop laughing or believing in mankind and in love.' He never saw his mother or his siblings again.

After leaving the bunker, he was so weak that he fainted in the yard just outside the bunker and, when he came round, he had no idea how long he had been lying there. He decided to go up to the attic from where he could look out on the ghetto and see if it was safe to emerge. The house had been ransacked, there was no food or water, and he was so weak from hunger and thirst that it took him an age to climb the stairs. When he eased a roof tile aside and peered out, he saw that the auxiliaries were still searching, and had dragged out an 80-year-old man, Shaya Idel, wrapped in his prayer shawl. They kept jabbing him with their bayonets until it was soaked with blood and then laughed as they set fire to his beard and side-locks. Ben-Zion could smell the stench of burning hair and was unable to tear his eyes away, as they kept stabbing and kicking the old man until he lay still.

Some time later a German truck stopped in front of the house and some Jews Ben-Zion recognised climbed out. He called out to one of them, a blacksmith called Yitzchak, whom he knew well. They were a group of craftsmen who had gone to the roll-call on the field and been stripped naked and marched towards the execution site like everyone else, but the Germans had suddenly decided that they needed their skills, so eight men and three women, including a tailor, a cobbler, a carpenter and a barber, were separated from the rest and kept alive. They had now come to the ghetto to collect bedding from their abandoned houses.

Yitzchak told the German officer accompanying them that Ben-Zion was skilled with horses and asked if he could be spared to work in the stables for the cavalrymen stationed there. The officer agreed and they called to Ben-Zion to come out. When he did so, the German took one look at the emaciated, stooped figure in front of him and raised his pistol. 'I suppose,' Ben-Zion later said, 'my physical appearance after nine days without food and water, made me look more dead than alive and he wanted to finish me off.'

However, Yitzchak put a hand on the officer's arm and said, 'If you shoot him, then shoot me too.' He felt he had nothing to lose because his wife and children, one of whom was Ben-Zion's age, had already been killed.

The officer hesitated, then holstered his weapon and told the others to hide Ben-Zion among the pillows and blankets in the lorry so that the other Germans and the *Schutzmänner* would not see him as they left the ghetto. When they reached the cavalry barracks, Ben-Zion was delighted to find that his cousin Israel had also been spared to look after the horses.

Ben-Zion was given food and water, and then put to work, but he could not stop thinking about his family. Yitzchak told the base commander that they had heard about a young woman who was still alive and could cook and clean at the base, and he agreed to send a soldier and one of the *Schutzmänner* to bring her out of the ghetto. Ben-Zion was only too aware of the danger of revealing his mother's hiding place, but reasoned that even if they shot her and the children, it would at least be a quick death rather than the lingering torture of starvation.

By the time they reached the bunker, Ben-Zion's little brother had already died and when his mother refused to leave her daughter behind, both of them were immediately killed. Yitzchak had time to tell her that Ben-Zion was alive and she asked him to send her love and tell him that now he would understand her dream. Although Ben-Zion had no proof, he knew that Sawoniuk was the Nazis' most enthusiastic collaborator, and was convinced that he had killed Shaindel and Shulamit. Ben-Zion was now the only survivor in his family.

CHAPTER 3

The German cavalry at the base where Ben-Zion now worked were tasked with patrolling the riverbank and the surrounding villages and forests, hunting down escaped Soviet PoWs and partisans, but they also carried out interrogations of suspects. Almost every day, villagers would appear, bringing in young Jewish men and women who had managed to escape the massacre and gone into hiding in the forest. Without supplies or weapons, they were soon starving, but when any approached a village looking for food, they were almost always captured and handed over for the reward of a kilo of salt or sugar that the Germans offered for each Jew. The captives were tortured to extract information about others hiding in the forest, and then executed.

One day a former schoolfriend of Ben-Zion's was brought in. His ordeal continued for several hours, his screams audible throughout the base. When he died, Ben-Zion was ordered to bury his body. A board pierced by rows of sharp nails was fixed to the wall of the torture chamber and a rope hung from the roof. Tied at the wrists and ankles, the prisoner had been suspended from the rope and then repeatedly swung against the nails. The floor was covered with bloodstains and Ben-Zion could hardly recognise his friend, so badly torn were his face and body, but he wondered if he was any better off. He was still alive, but had no illusions about remaining that way, for he was sure that he and the other Jews would be killed as soon as they were no longer of use.

Most of his fellow workers were much older men and seemed resigned to their fate, but Ben-Zion was determined to escape, although he only told Yitzchak and two other men of his plans. He had once asked the German officer who had spared him what would happen to him and was told that he would be fine as long as the cavalry were at the base. Although it was unstated, the clear implication was that he would not survive long after that.

When he saw the cavalrymen rushing about one morning making hasty preparations to leave, he realised it was his moment to escape and broke a window in the cell he shared with the other Jews. He severed the barbed wire covering it with cutters he had stolen, then jumped out, followed by the three other men, and they ran to the nearby Christian cemetery. They climbed the wall and sprinted through the graveyard and across the town, twisting and turning through narrow alleyways. A few people saw them and shouted to raise the alarm, but before Andrusha and the other auxiliaries had spilled out of the police station and set off in pursuit, the fleeing Jews had reached the edge of the forest and disappeared among the trees.

They kept running before going to ground. They were free for the moment but their situation was dire. They had only the clothes they stood up in — already soaked by the heavy rain — and they could not approach the villagers for help, fearing betrayal for the rewards the Germans offered.

During the next few days, they crept out after dark and found a few beetroots and potatoes in the fields, missed during the harvest. They ate them raw because they did not dare light a fire and used some empty sacks stolen from the yard of an outlying farm as overcoats, tearing others into strips to make crude bindings for their bare feet.

They were not alone in the forests. As well as other Jews, there were remnants of the Soviet forces who had not been captured or killed, deserters, escaped PoWs, partisans, and socialists, communists and others on Nazi death lists who had gathered to wage guerrilla war against the invaders. However, Ben-Zion and his comrades tried to keep well clear of the others, fearing that deliberate betrayal by collaborators or informers, or carelessness or desperation caused by cold and hunger, might make them lower their guard and lead their enemies to them.

Armed fugitives could obtain food by threatening villagers and could even force them to give sanctuary for the night, but Ben-Zion's group had no weapons and faced a constant struggle for survival. As the autumn weather worsened, it became even more difficult to find food or shelter, even if only during the coldest hours of darkness. Sometimes they slept for a few hours in the cone-shaped haystacks farmers made to store winter feed for their animals, but they always had to be back in the forest before dawn, leaving no traces that might betray them.

At other times they slept in depressions in the undergrowth, covering themselves with branches, leaves and pine needles, and huddling together for warmth, with one of them always posted as sentry. They moved every few hours and never left the forest in daylight. They learned to speak in whispers and avoid stepping on dry twigs, and were always alert for suspicious sounds and sights. Faintly heard voices, the sudden flight or alarm call of a bird, or an animal crashing away through the undergrowth might be the only warning of approaching danger.

As the weeks passed, they became intimately familiar with every part of the woods and marshes, navigating by landmarks like a lightning-struck tree or an oddly shaped boulder, memorising ways through the densest undergrowth and even dragging logs and fallen trunks into the swamps to create secret pathways through them.

Other fugitives made permanent camps but, like burning green or wet wood that sent smoke rising above the canopy, remaining too long in one place heightened the risk of discovery. Driven by hunger, others left the forest by day to beg or steal food from farms and villages, but that greatly increased the chances of being spotted by patrols, betrayed by collaborators, or leaving tracks that could be followed to their hiding place.

After dark, Ben-Zion and his comrades lit fires to keep warm in the bitter cold. If they had no matches, they struck a piece of steel against a stone to make a spark that would ignite their kindling: dried mushrooms gathered from the forest floor, lichen, dry leaves and twigs. They would add dry windfall wood that burned with little smoke, but they also hung blankets or sacking from branches a few feet above the fire to diffuse it.

As winter set in and the temperatures fell even further below freezing, they dug a pit at each new site and made an underground shelter, its entrance disguised with branches, twigs and leaves. Shortage of water was never a problem because there were endless streams, ponds and marshes, and had it been any other season of the year, they could have eaten wild mushrooms, plants, berries and nuts, but they could find little or nothing. 'It was hard even to steal,' Ben-Zion later recalled. 'There were dogs in every village.'

They joined forces with another four Jews who had managed to escape from the ghetto. They all existed on a near-starvation diet for a few weeks, but fearing they would not survive the terrible cold and deep snows without adequate food, they began raiding farmers' 'clamps': stored potatoes, buried under a layer of straw and a covering of earth.

They put some of the booty in a freshly laid fire to roast, then unwound the sacking from their feet and held it up to dry while huddling as close as they could to warm their cold and wasted bodies. The half-burned, half-raw potatoes were the only food they had.

Whenever they left the forest, they took a winding route and one of them would hide on the way back, to see if they were being followed, before hurrying to catch up. However, a heavy snowfall one evening made concealing their footprints impossible and, later that night, they were ambushed.

Some were cut down where they stood but Ben-Zion managed to get away. Although bullets whistled around him, the tree trunks and dense undergrowth gave him protection. He ran until he thought his lungs would burst, then went to ground in a dense thicket of brambles and bushes. There were no sounds of pursuit, but his situation was now absolutely desperate. He was alone, his bare feet were bleeding badly and in danger of frostbite, and he was so wet and cold that he could not stop shivering. He risked discovery if he lit a fire, but knew if he did not that he would be dead before morning.

He brushed aside the snow until he found some dry wood. He had only three matches in his pocket and was so clumsy with cold that he wasted the first. The kindling caught with the second and he managed to coax it into flame, over which he huddled, gradually bringing a little warmth into his frozen body. 'As I sat by the fire,' he later said, 'I asked myself what I had done to deserve this hell.'

He survived the night and kept the fire burning throughout the next day, but knew that without food and shelter he could not survive for long. By nightfall he had decided that his only option was to risk seeking help from a man who had been an acquaintance of his family before the invasion. He did not know how he would be received, but he had now developed a strong streak of fatalism. If the man helped him, he would survive a little longer; if he betrayed him to the Germans or the *Schutzmänner*, Ben-Zion had decided 'I wouldn't even try to escape again. I had no physical or mental strength left.'

Even though the night was bitterly cold, he had to tear his sacking cloak into strips to bind his bare feet before setting out. He walked for hours through the darkness, in the teeth of a snowstorm so ferocious that he could barely see his way, but eventually reached his destination. He crept up to the man's house and banged on the window.

When the door opened, Ben-Zion was so hoarse and frozen that he could barely speak. He eventually managed to explain who he was, knowing that his unkempt hair, beard, and ragged, lice-ridden clothing would make him impossible to recognise. He was left shivering in the yard, but was then given an old overcoat, a jute sack to bind around his feet, a large loaf of bread, some sauerkraut and some boxes of matches.

For the next few days, he 'lived like an animal, without hope', roaming the forest until dusk and then finding a place to lie up. He gathered wood and warmed himself until his fire burned low, then scraped the embers to one side and slept on the heated earth. He awoke before dawn, chilled to the bone, brushed off what snow had fallen on him in the night, ate a morsel of bread and resumed his wanderings. He kept the remains of the loaf in a piece of sacking, delaying the moment he would either have to return to the village or seek out another source of food.

CHAPTER 4

As his hopes of survival were fading, Ben-Zion glimpsed a figure through the trees. When he caught up with him, he found himself face to face with his saviour from the ghetto. Yitzchak had also escaped the ambush. It was a life-changing moment. 'Now there was a point to living,' Ben-Zion later said. 'Together, all the hardships would be a little more bearable.'

They decided to risk returning to their potato store, on the off-chance that it had remained undiscovered. Creeping through the undergrowth, alert for the slightest sign of danger, they eventually reached the place and found the bodies of four of their comrades, riddled with bullets and burned almost beyond recognition. The ground was too hard-frozen to bury them, but they said *Kaddish* over them. To their relief, they managed to unearth some potatoes; the threat of starvation had been held off a while longer.

The following week they encountered the other two survivors from the ambush. Although their situation was still desperate, they drew additional strength from each other and hatched a plan to force local farmers to hand over some of the abandoned weapons and ammunition they had collected after the Soviet forces fled the Nazi invaders.

The fourth member of their group was a carpenter in civilian life, and he fashioned some dummy rifles that were convincing enough in the half-light for their purposes. They then set off for an isolated farmhouse near the forest.

In the middle of the night, they pounded on the door. When the farmer appeared, they jabbed the barrels of their wooden rifles into his ribs and threatened to kill him if he did not hand over his cache of weapons. He denied having any at first, but when they began dragging him away from his house as if they were going to execute him, he broke down, begged for mercy and led them to his barn. Minutes later, they were the proud possessors of three Russian automatic rifles, boxes of ammunition and hand grenades.

They now had the means to defend themselves and obtain enough food to stay alive. Few farmers gave food voluntarily, because anyone discovered helping the partisans was either shot or shipped off to a concentration camp, so most of their supplies were obtained at gunpoint. They would hold a pistol to the head of a farmer's wife and tell him, 'Whatever you have, we're taking and if you collaborate with the Germans, we'll be back.'

The Germans also made the local farmers pay them a tithe in grain, meat and dairy products. One of them was tasked with collecting the produce from each village and delivering it by horse-drawn wagon to the nearest military base or police station. They always did so at night, so they could be back home in time for the milking and other morning work.

Ben-Zion's group would intercept them and take whatever food they needed. Although fearful of reprisals, some were sympathetic, but others only gave up their produce when threatened. In either case, Ben-Zion's group would hand over a receipt for more food than they had taken, in order to convince the Germans that it had been handed over under duress, and allow them to keep more of their crops, reducing their hostility to the Jewish partisans if they came back for more.

They also used their weapons to compel villagers to hand over spare boots and clothes, and for the first time since they had entered the forest, they were warmly dressed and shod. They ate reasonably well, regained their strength, and became skilled with their weapons, ready to take revenge on the German oppressors and their collaborators. Every time they raided a village, they also obtained information on local troop movements and resistance activity. When they discovered that a large group of partisans, named after the Soviet Marshal Voroshilov, was operating from the area where they themselves were hiding, Ben-Zion's group began trying to seek them out.

Eventually they encountered a partisan patrol. They were well equipped, with warm clothes and boots, and Soviet weapons including automatic rifles, grenades, light and heavy machine-guns, and anti-tank weapons that needed two men to transport them. Their camp was protected by trenches, armed patrols and a watchtower that gave them early warning of any approaching danger, although few German troops willingly entered the densest parts of the forest and marshes, where the partisans knew every pathway and ambush point.

Ben-Zion and his comrades were eager to join them, but although they also knew the forest intimately, had their own weapons and were keen to fight the Germans, they were not immediately accepted. The partisans gave them the first hot meal they had eaten in months but then, fearful of informers and fifth columnists, cross-examined and beat them. They did the same to all potential recruits but Jews received especially harsh treatment.

Six more Jews, including another four from Domachevo, arrived the next morning and were subjected to an even more savage interrogation. 'We hadn't even finished our tale,' one of them, Saul Furleiter, said, 'when they began to beat us bloody with their clubs and whips, calling us spies, telling us they were going to dig our graves. Blood poured from all of us. My friend Srulke Rubinstein had his ribs broken.'

All the Jews were then given a perilous task to prove their worth: to return to Domachevo and burn down a number of warehouses on the outskirts, the house of the *Gebietskommissar* (the German district commander) and the dairy right in the middle of the town, which was supplying German bases with milk and butter. They had to do the *zadania* – the mission – unarmed, in case they were captured and their priceless weapons fell into German hands.

They would be accepted into the brigade only if they were successful. 'We understood they were sending us to our deaths,' Furleiter said. 'They gave us three days to complete the mission.'

It was clear that the leader of the partisan group did not care whether they lived or died, but Ben-Zion and his comrades were eager to take the fight to the hated oppressors whatever the risks. As another Jewish partisan, Frank Blaichman, said at the opening of the Jewish Fighters' Monument in Jerusalem 40 years later, 'It was not merely a struggle for survival; history had placed on us the task of avenging the blood of our families and millions of our people brutally murdered by the Nazis.'

Armed only with bottles of turpentine, they made the long trek back to Domachevo and, while the others prepared to destroy the warehouses and the house of the *Gebietskommissar*, the two youngest, Ben-Zion and a boy called Shlomo, crept right into the town, hiding in the shadows as a group of *Schutzmänner* passed within feet of them. They recognised the voices of Andrusha and some of their other former schoolmates.

When the sound of their footsteps had faded, the two would-be partisans forced apart two of the wooden fence palings surrounding the dairy and squeezed through the gap. There were several buildings in the complex – a milking shed, warehouses, store sheds, stables and the dairy itself – all built from wood. They dragged straw bales out of the stables across the yard and piled them against the walls of the dairy, then soaked them with turpentine. They ignited with a roar and the flames rapidly grew and spread to the other buildings. Burning brands and showers of sparks rained down around them and, highlighted by the blaze, they were spotted and fired upon. By a miracle, neither was hit, and they sprinted through the narrow, twisting alleyways and back streets of the town to evade their pursuers.

The rest of the group were only just preparing to set fire to the warehouses and the *Gebietskommissar*'s house when the dairy erupted. 'Suddenly there was shooting and yelling everywhere,' Saul Furleiter said. 'They shot rifle grenades, and everything was lit up. We had no choice but to retreat, and we barely escaped with our lives.' They rejoined forces and then began the 25-kilometre trek back to the partisans' base.

The fierce red glow in the night sky had announced their partial success long before they got back to the camp, but when the others admitted they had not destroyed their targets, the unit's commander, Golayev, at once ordered them to go back and complete their mission. The Germans would be more alert, but they had no other option. When they reached Domachevo, Furleiter and two of the others climbed through the window of a granary and set fire to the corn and wheat. The building was soon engulfed in flames, and although the *Gebietskommissar*'s house once more escaped destruction, the other targets were destroyed. The perpetrators fled under a hail of fire but returned safely to the camp.

Despite having demonstrated their bravery, Golayev, a well-known anti-Semite before the war, still refused to accept them as members of his brigade. Instead, he sent them to join another of the AL – *Armia Ludowa* – units named after the Red Army commander Marshal Zhukov, operating in a different part of the forest.

When they encountered a patrol from the Zhukov group, they were again disarmed and interrogated by the unit's commander, but were then welcomed as members, after swearing an oath 'to keep faith with the Soviet Union and commit myself to fight for Marx, Engels, Lenin and Stalin until my last drop of blood'. As the oath of loyalty suggested, most of the AL partisans were escaped Russian PoWs, supported by the Soviets, and the Jews got on much better with them than the Polish partisans of the AK – *Armia Krajowa* – also known as the Home Army, that was loyal to the Polish government-in-exile in London.

The Zhukov group's camp was a permanent one, deep in the forest. Surrounded by defensive trenches, it accommodated several hundred partisans living in shacks, huts and underground bunkers. Like an army, they were divided into battalions, companies, platoons and sections. Each section of 12 to 15 men had to clear the trees from their allocated area, excavate dug-outs and build tall triangular frames to screen their fires from outside eyes. There were workshops, a laundry, a central kitchen where cooks prepared hot food, and even a bathing area. Some women took the traditional roles of cooks and housekeepers, but others were fighters, joining raids, ambushes and sabotage missions, and proved just as ruthless and effective as the men.

The Soviet PoWs in the group tended to use their real names but many partisans hid their identities behind nicknames, so that if they were captured, they could not betray the real names of their comrades under torture, and thus enable the Germans to carry out savage reprisals on their families and villages.

The new recruits were each given a Soviet rifle and allocated to one of the platoons. Ben-Zion joined A Platoon, but found that many of his new comrades doubted the Jews' effectiveness and often made anti-Semitic jokes and comments. Their first mission was to raid a village for supplies. Half of them surrounded the village to stop anyone escaping to alert the nearby German base, while the other 40 went from house to house, confiscating food and clothing.

Ben-Zion and another partisan were told to patrol a few hundred yards from the village to watch for any German troops. When he heard faint noises in the darkness, he warned his comrade to take cover.

'Yid, are you panicking already?' was the response.

Undeterred, Ben-Zion belly-crawled towards the noise he had heard, using any available cover, and pausing every few seconds to watch and listen. Eventually he heard low voices and spotted German soldiers lying in ambush across the partisans' escape route. He crawled back the way he had come, alerted his comrade and then fired three shots in the air, the signal to abandon the raid.

They swiftly regrouped, but without the advantage of surprise, could not hope to defeat a large, well-armed force of German regulars, or easily evade them. The Germans were blocking the western route back to the forest. To the south and east was more enemy-held territory without a scrap of cover, including a town and another large German base. The northern approaches were guarded by treacherous marshes with deep hidden pools and mud like quicksand that could trap and drown a regiment. If the partisans tried to retreat that way, they risked being trapped between the swamps and the advancing Germans, but Ben-Zion and his group knew every inch of them. He volunteered at once to guide them.

Abandoning most of the supplies they had collected, they moved off silently, in single file, with Ben-Zion leading the way. Navigating by starlight, he found a safe route to dry ground, whereupon the platoon commander strode up to him and said, 'If it turns out that there were no Germans there, I will kill you.'

The words were barely out of his mouth when the Germans

realised that their prey was escaping, and opened up with every weapon they had. The partisans lost no time in moving on and, after marching all night, reached their base in the early hours of the next morning.

The unit's commander, Katkov, debriefed the platoon leader and then asked Ben-Zion for his version of events. He told him everything, including the death threat and anti-Semitic jibes. Katkov then addressed the entire unit, praising Ben-Zion's initiative and bravery, telling them that the Germans were murdering countless Jews and Russian PoWs, and demanding that they treat Jewish partisans as their equals. When he later overheard one of his men muttering about 'Getting rid of the Yid', Katkov warned them all that anyone going on a mission with Ben-Zion and returning alone without a credible explanation, would pay for it with his own life.

Stalin had sent orders to all partisan factions to make common cause to defeat the Nazis. As Larry Pomeranc, the son of another Jewish partisan in the group, remarks with a smile, 'Jews have always been great at fighting each other, but the order came down that whatever Jewish youth movement you grew up in, or whether you were Jews, Gentiles, or Muslims, and whatever your politics, you had to unite and fight the common enemy, Nazi Germany.'

Jews who had escaped from the ghettos and fled to the forests had to fight at first with whatever weapons they had or that farmers could give them – knives, pitchforks and shotguns – but whenever they killed collaborators or auxiliaries, they took their weapons and ammunition, and gradually became better armed. By mid-1943, many had also made contact with the Russian partisans, and became even better equipped and more formidable as the small groups eventually merged into brigades of 500 to 1,000 men.

As the tide of battle in the east ran ever more strongly

against the Germans, the partisans were increasingly well supplied by Soviet air-drops of rations, weapons and ammunition. Red Army officers were also parachuted in, sent by Moscow to organise them and formulate strategy and tactics.

Now established as a key member of his partisan group, for the first time Ben-Zion felt a growing confidence that the Nazis could be defeated.

CHAPTER 5

While Ben-Zion and his comrades were fighting in the forests of Belarus, Andrusha Sawoniuk was actively tracking down and eliminating Domachevo's remaining Jews and suspected partisans, supporters and sympathisers. A clerk who worked at the police station throughout the occupation said the Germans thought so highly of Andrusha that they requested him in preference to any of the other *Schutzmänner* when mounting operations and *Aktionen*. He was also trusted with a sub-machine gun, when most of his comrades were only issued with rifles.

Until 1942, the *Schutzmannschaft* had been an almost entirely voluntary force, but as the partisans grew in numbers and confidence, the Germans began conscripting large numbers of local men to carry out attacks on the partisans and reprisals against those believed to be supporting them. At first the reprisals were mainly targeted on individual persons or families suspected of partisan activities, although anyone who had come to Belarus from the east between the Soviet occupation in 1939 and the German invasion in 1941 was automatically suspect and marked out for 'special treatment': execution.

Before long wholesale killing and destruction became routine. Although reprisals were still notionally focused on villages believed to be partisan strongholds, they were launched on the flimsiest of pretexts. When they targeted a suspect village,

Schutzmänner killing squads went to every household where there were rumoured to be partisan supporters and executed all the members of the family, irrespective of age or sex. Even when a household had not been implicated in partisan activity, if any family member was not at home when the *Schutzmänner* burst in, all those present were often killed on the assumption that those absent were fighting with the partisans. The lack of any evidence of partisan support might still not be enough to save a village from destruction. A failure to report the presence of partisans in the area could be enough to trigger its burning and the murder of all its occupants. Those not killed were sent to Germany as slave labourers.

So extreme were the actions of some *Schutzmannschaft* groups – and Sawoniuk was one of the most notorious for the zeal with which he pursued Jews and partisans – it was reported that 'even the [German] security police had doubts about the methods employed', describing them as 'real enthusiasts for executions'.

If not on the scale of the industrialised slaughter carried out in the death camps, the killings and destruction perpetrated by the *Schutzmänner* were shocking enough. As historian Martin Dean remarked, 'Only a few kilometres from Sobibor and Treblinka, local policemen assisted in the mass shooting of their neighbours, within earshot of their own homes.'

After the inhabitants of a suspect village had been eliminated, their property and livestock were looted and then every building was razed to the ground. In just one *Aktion* against a supposedly partisan village, 289 people were shot, 150 farms burned down, 1,500 animals seized and huge quantities of crops and farm equipment either confiscated or destroyed.

As partisan activity increased, the Nazis divided the whole of Belarus into three categories: 'bandit-free', 'bandit-suspicious', and 'bandit-infested'. In either of the latter categories, all men found alone or in small groups were to be captured or shot. They also tried to create 'dead zones' around the forests where the partisans were based, with nearby villages depopulated and razed to the ground. In total 627 such villages were completely destroyed and their inhabitants murdered, often by being burned alive. This was described as 'the elimination of partisans'.

Incinerated villages were not to be rebuilt, and anyone found in them was to be shot. The Germans even attempted to set the forests alight, with troops using incendiaries and flame-throwers, but their vast extent and marshy terrain proved the partisans' salvation. Even in the heat of midsummer, the fires failed to spread far. Resistance activity continued to grow, and reprisals, including the destruction of people's homes, merely served to increase the number of new recruits.

Official figures reveal that by the end of the German occupation, in the whole of Belarus 209 towns and 9,200 villages had been destroyed, many of which were never rebuilt. The death toll was well over two million people. And, after the initial massacres by the SS and SD, most of those killed had died at the hands of the *Schutzmänner*, not the Germans.

CHAPTER 6

Ben-Zion's reward for his courage and leadership during the abortive partisan raid on the village was to be promoted to the partisans' elite *razvedka* – intelligence – division, exchanging his rifle for a sub-machine gun and also being given a horse. In the summer he kept it tied to a tree, and in winter it was housed in the unit's stables, partly underground and covered by a log roof concealed under a mound of windfall branches.

One of his regular tasks was to ride to the villages under German control, meet with informants and obtain details about troop movements and supply convoys that could then be ambushed. It was perilous work, for anyone caught would have his house burned to the ground and his entire family killed. To minimise the risks, Ben-Zion never met an informant in the same place twice, setting up rendezvous points in fields, forest clearings or alongside roads edging the forest.

His most valuable contact, Mitya, was a man he had worked with in the early stages of the occupation, installing and main-taining telephone lines for the Germans. Mitya was still doing so, but fearing reprisals from the Soviets for working with the enemy, he was also hedging his bets by passing information to the partisans. He had a special permit that allowed him to travel throughout the area and enter all military and police bases, putting him in the perfect position to note troop move-ments. If additional forces had been brought in, for example, that usually meant the Germans were planning a search and destroy operation in the forest. It was invaluable intelligence to the partisans, who could then ambush them or make a temporary withdrawal if the attackers' numbers were too great.

Ben-Zion was waiting for him at a telephone pole between two villages one day. He could melt back into the forest if anyone approached and the location gave Mitya an excuse to be there, checking the line. When he appeared, he said he had just passed a wounded Jewish boy, lying unconscious at the side of the road. Ben-Zion rode alongside him as he retraced his path. The boy looked very young, no more than eight or nine, was painfully thin and wearing torn and filthy clothes that were covered with blood. He had been shot in the chest and left for dead, but when Ben-Zion felt for a pulse, he found that he was still alive. He made a dressing with some strips of fabric, bandaged him tightly to stop the bleeding and, with Mitya's help, managed to lift him onto his horse. He held him against his chest with one hand and kept his weapon and the reins in the other as he rode slowly back to the camp.

Although Katkov told him the boy was too badly wounded to save, Ben-Zion refused to allow another needless death and persuaded the unit's Georgian doctor to treat him. Together they laid him on a table and cut off his clothes with a knife. There was an entry wound in the chest but no exit wound, and the doctor decided he had to operate at once. He cut through the chest muscles and found and removed the bullet, which had missed the boy's heart by millimetres.

He sewed him up again and told Ben-Zion that although the boy had lost consciousness because of blood loss, he now stood a good chance of recovery. However, the partisans were so short of medical supplies that the only further treatment the doctor could give was an anti-tetanus injection.

Worried that the boy might go into shock if he awoke surrounded by strangers, Ben-Zion stayed at his side throughout the night and all the next day, moistening his lips with water from time to time. He was very scared when he did regain consciousness, but Ben-Zion spoke to him in Yiddish, calming him and telling him he was with the partisans and safe from the Germans. He promised to stay with him until his wound had healed and told him there were several other Jews in the unit who would also protect him.

As he began to recover, the boy told him his story. His name was Benni Kalina, and he thought he was nine or ten – he was illiterate and didn't know his exact birth year. That made him about ten years younger than Ben-Zion, who perhaps saw in him an echo of Shlomo, the little brother he had lost. Benni was the youngest of seven children, six boys and a girl, and came from Meseritz, in the German zone after the invasion of Poland, so had been under Nazi control since September 1939.

As the killing of Jews began, Benni's father tried to save his youngest son's life by smuggling him out of the ghetto and giving him to a Christian family in a village 15 kilometres away to raise as their own. Benni never saw his parents or siblings again and he was so young when he was sent away that, years later, he could not even recall what they had looked like.

The Christian family risked death by harbouring a Jewish boy, but his true identity remained undiscovered, even when the Germans burst into the house one day and searched it for fugitives. He was kept at home to look after the family's cows, because his adoptive parents must have feared betrayal if a pre-viously unknown son suddenly appeared at the local school, but he was well treated and grew to love his new family. 'They were like my parents,' he later said. However, curiosity about his real family gnawed at him and, in the summer of 1943, he persuaded his adopted father to take him back to Meseritz for a few hours, in the hope of seeing them. 'You can enter the ghetto,' his new father said. 'I will wait outside and if you find anyone, you will come back and tell me what the situation is.'

Benni entered the ghetto just as an *Aktion* was beginning, the sixth and last sweep to remove the last few hundred of Meseritz's 18,000 Jews. Before he had even reached his family's home, Benni was seized and herded into the town square with hundreds of others. He tried to escape but a Polish policeman caught him and gave him a savage beating. Powerless to intervene, his adopted father could then only watch as Benni and the others, surrounded by Germans and police auxiliaries with baying dogs, were driven with whips and rifle butts towards the train station. There they were loaded into cattle trucks, so tightly packed no one could even sit down. The doors were slammed shut and bolted, and the train began its journey to the Treblinka extermination camp.

There was a small inspection hatch high up in the side of the truck, covered with barbed wire. After dark, three older boys managed to tear away the wire and, when they felt the train beginning to slow for a signal, they hauled themselves up and jumped out. A cousin of Benni's took hold of him and pushed him out of the opening, saying, 'Jump, Benni. I will jump after you.'

He tumbled down the embankment, then stood up scratched and bruised but otherwise unhurt. His cousin was nowhere to be seen but he ran after the three boys and they set off on foot together. However, their escape had been spotted and auxiliary police with tracker dogs soon found them and threw them in jail in the town of Bukov, where after interrogation, they were to be executed.

There seemed to be no possibility of escape, but among the other prisoners in their cell was the leader of an AK partisan unit. By bribery or coercion, his men on the outside had persuaded one of the Polish auxiliary guards to allow him to escape. The cell door had been closed but not locked, and that night the partisan leader simply walked out, with Benni and his comrades following. While his men fought off the soldiers and police, their leader made good his escape, but the members of the AK were notoriously anti-Semitic, and he told Benni and the others that Jews could not join his unit.

None of the other escapees, including the three who had jumped from the train, wanted to be hampered by the presence of a small boy, and they left Benni on his own. He managed to make his way back to the home of his adopted family but, terrified for their own lives if he was discovered, they encouraged him to leave again with four escaped Soviet PoWs who were heading eastwards, aiming to cross the Bug River and join one of the Soviet-backed partisan groups in the forest. The family persuaded the PoWs to take Benni with them by giving them food and their hidden weapons.

Walking only after dark, they covered 80 kilometres over the next three nights, crossing the river and threading their way through the barbed wire defences along its banks. Cold, wet and starving, but feeling that the worst danger was now behind them, they risked knocking on the door of a house at the edge of a village. The woman who lived there took them in, gave them hot food and allowed them to dry their clothes in front of the stove. She then went outside, saying she was going to fetch some milk. That was no particular cause for alarm because there was no refrigeration then and milk was often kept cool outside houses in wells, ponds or streams. She returned a few minutes later, gave them the milk and then disappeared into another room.

Soon afterwards, they heard the sound of motorcycles approaching the house. Benni jumped to his feet and dived behind the door but his comrades were still struggling into their clothes when it burst open and *Schutzmänner* stormed in and shot them dead. Benni ran out of the house, where more men were waiting. Although he was sent sprawling by a bullet in the chest, he managed to get back to his feet and keep running. Escaping his pursuers in the darkness, he took refuge in a haystack. He crept out at dusk and walked a few more kilometres before collapsing where Mitya and Ben-Zion found him the next morning.

Over the following months, Ben-Zion became a father figure to Benni. When he recovered, he was given a specially cut-down shotgun, and Ben-Zion kept him at his side as part of his scouting unit. Dressed as a shepherd boy, Benni's youth and diminutive stature enabled him to pass without suspicion as he walked through the fields, keeping an eye on military traffic. He spoke Russian, German and Polish as well as Yiddish and was not easily identifiable as Jewish, so he even used to chat to the Germans and gather intelligence from them. Ben-Zion taught him to recognise the insignia on tanks, trucks and railway carriages and report what he had seen, and the information was passed to Soviet commanders, who used it to plan their attacks.

Benni wasn't the only young Jew Ben-Zion helped. Thirteen-year-old Jack Pomeranc was with a group of partisans on the Polish side of the border when he was shot by an auxiliary while out searching for food. It was a clean wound but it became infected in the forest and he developed a high fever. His comrades had no medicines to treat him, but two partisans helped him to cross the ice-bound Bug River, and on the far side they encountered a patrol from Ben-Zion's unit. They brought Jack back to the camp, and when he saw the little boy, pale and close to death, Ben-Zion took him under his wing and nursed him back to health.

There were now eight Jews in the unit – five men and three women – with their own separate bunker covered with branches, leaves and often snow. They slept in there under sacks and whatever blankets they had, but it was so bitterly cold in winter that they still had to huddle together for warmth.

The Zhukov partisans carried out numerous daring attacks,

including a raid that freed 250 Jewish slave labourers who became willing recruits to the partisans' growing army. They also derailed trains and blew up the tracks, causing such devastation that in some areas the Germans had to patrol every section and post sentries on every bridge to try to keep the trains running. They blew up trains using primitive mines under the tracks, cut phone lines, and 'started demolishing all the bridges in the area,' Ben-Zion later said. 'We invaded a German camp and fought a pitched battle for six hours. We killed dozens of Germans and took about 120 German and Ukrainian prisoners and more than 100 wagons loaded with weapons, bullets and food.'

The partisans also sneaked into German bases and compounds to sabotage vehicles by putting sugar in their petrol tanks and ambushed supply trucks and convoys out on the roads. They then melted back into the forest, often using horses hidden nearby to speed their getaway.

The drainage ditches beside the roads, about a metre deep and two metres wide, made good trenches from which to launch their attacks. They would first shoot the machine-gunners on motorbikes at the head of the convoy, which forced the trucks behind them to slow down. They would then open up on them with machine-guns and anti-tank guns, aiming at the petrol tanks. A truck full of soldiers would often accompany a convoy but, under the hail of fire, would often be killed before they had even clambered down. In one ambush alone they killed 300 Germans and seized all their weapons and ammunition.

The Zhukov group also carried out a relentless search for informers and collaborators, unwittingly aided by the meticulous German bureaucracy. The Labour Department of each district kept records in the town hall showing payments that had been made to collaborators, including their real names. Partisans broke into their local town halls and stole the record books, giving them a list of every collaborator and informer in their area. Where possible, they were then captured alive and interrogated. They were first questioned separately and their stories compared, before being re-interrogated and confronted with the additional information their captors had gleaned.

Once the partisans were satisfied that there was no more useful information to be obtained, the collaborators were executed, sending a clear message that anyone who helped the Nazis kill Jews or partisans would also be killed. It was Old Testament justice: an eye for an eye. If someone had beaten Jews, he would himself be beaten, but those who had killed them or informed on them, leading to their deaths, were shown no mercy. Yet, despite everything the Nazis had done to his family and his people, Ben-Zion never spoke of hatred or revenge against them, only that it was necessary to fight them to prevent yet more Jews being killed. As another Jewish partisan said, 'We had lost our faith in the God our parents had believed in and had believed would save them in their hour of need, but we held on to our belief in justice.'

Beginning in late 1943, the Germans had launched a last major campaign to crush the partisans, but the Zhukov fighters withdrew deeper into the Pinsk and Pripyat marshes, areas of dense forest and swampland that extended for 300 miles east of Domachevo and 140 miles from north to south. It was impossible terrain for conventional warfare, close to impenetrable for German heavy armour but perfectly suited to their opponents' guerrilla tactics. Soon after the launch of Operation Barbarossa in 1941, the Germans had hatched a plan to construct canals to drain the marshes, 'cleanse them of their degenerate inhabitants', and repopulate the reclaimed farmland with German colonists and *Volksdeutsche*. However, Hitler abandoned the plan a few months later, fearing that it might instead create the Dust Bowl conditions that had devastated the US Midwest in the 1930s.

The Wehrmacht armies had passed to the north and south of the marshes when they invaded the Soviet Union in 1941. When some German units were forced to pass through the boggy terrain during their long retreat, they had to build causeways of logs across several swamps, and only light vehicles could use them safely. Attempts to crush the partisans around Domachevo had ground to a halt in there, and as the Soviet counter-offensive gained momentum after the battle of Kursk in the summer of 1943, the Zhukov group re-emerged to carry out fresh sabotage and hit-and-run attacks.

Large parts of Belarus were now no-go areas for German troops. The *Schutzmänner* were not well equipped to continue the fight, and the Home Guard formed from older Belarusians was in an even worse state. Its officers had no maps or compasses, their men did not have entrenching tools or wire cutters, their arms were a mixture of outdated and captured weapons and, since they did not even have rucksacks, they had to carry their spare ammunition and belongings in whatever bags they could find. While they and the *Schutzmänner* had no heavy weapons and only a limited number of light machine-guns, the partisans were now being equipped by their Soviet sponsors with heavy machine-guns, anti-tank weapons, artillery and even tanks.

On 23 June 1944, the Red Army launched a massive attack against German forces on the Eastern Front, named in honour of Pyotr Bagration, a Russian hero of the Napoleonic Wars. Soviet-backed partisans attacked railways and communications behind German lines while one and a half million Russian troops smashed through them. Over the following weeks they swept across Belarus, reaching the Bug River on 21 July and liberating Domachevo. By the time Operation Bagration came to an end the following month, 450,000 men had died and the Germans had suffered the worst defeat in their history.

The Zhukov Group's 270 surviving fighters, with Ben-Zion,

Benni Kalina and Jack Pomeranc still among their ranks, were at last able to emerge from the forest. 'There was great rejoicing among the partisans,' Ben-Zion said. 'Some went home, others wrote home. The few Jews among us knew there was no one waiting for us. We had nowhere to return to. So we decided to go and volunteer for the Red Army. As seasoned partisans we didn't have to do that; we could have stayed where we were, however we wanted to join the army and get our revenge.'

CHAPTER 7

Andrusha Sawoniuk's zeal in pursuing and murdering Jews and suspected partisans had led to him being involved in the killing of hundreds of people, and he was eventually rewarded by his Nazi paymasters with promotion to commandant of the Domachevo *Schutzmannschaft* after his predecessor, Vasiliy Trebunko, was killed in a partisan raid on the police station in November 1943. Andrusha's wife, Anna Maslova, a Russian midwife who had come to Domachevo to work in the hospital during the Soviet occupation, was badly wounded after being caught in the crossfire during the raid, and died soon afterwards. They had been married barely a year; Andrusha had worn his police uniform for their wedding and his fellow *Schutzmänner* had fired volleys in the air as he and his bride emerged from the Orthodox church.

After Anna's death, Sawoniuk swiftly remarried and took his pregnant second wife, Nina, with him in July 1944 when, knowing what his fate would be if he fell into the hands of the advancing Red Army, he fled Domachevo with the Germans. The retreat quickly turned into a headlong flight, with soldiers and officials plundering what they could before abandoning Belarus and any collaborators who remained there to their fate.

Fedor Zan remembered the day well, for he was forced to drive some of them in his horse and cart — one of the ten which the Germans commandeered to speed their retreat, and Zan saw Andrusha and Nina among the Germans in one of the others. As soon as the last one had crossed the River Bug, they blew up the bridge. Zan took them another 25 or 30 kilometres to the Polish village of Kiyovets, but then seized a chance to make his escape. Abandoning his horse and cart, he 'ran away to Borisy,' Zan said, swimming the river to reach the little hamlet on the outskirts of Domachevo where he lived.

Belarusian auxiliaries, Sawoniuk among them, and Home Guard members who had also fled with their paymasters, were assembled in East Prussia, and on 1 August 1944 they were re-formed into an auxiliary police brigade: the *Schutzmannschaft Brigade Siegling*, named for its commander, SS-*Sturmbannführer* Hans Siegling. Within a week, *Reichsführer*-SS Heinrich Himmler, responsible for finding fresh frontline troops to augment the battered Wehrmacht armies, had renamed Siegling's brigade the 30th Waffen-SS Grenadier Division. Curiously, the only other man who would one day be charged with war crimes in Britain, Szymon Serafinowicz, joined the same unit, though both later claimed not to have known each other.

Although German-officered, the 30th Division was otherwise composed entirely of Belarusian, Ukrainian and Russian collaborators, and the term 'Grenadier' was used to distinguish them from the divisions of 'pure' Germans, and the *Freiwilligendivisionen* [voluntary divisions] of *Volksdeutsche* ethnic Germans and 'Germanic' Dutchmen, Norwegians, Lithuanians, Latvians and Danes.

While the Allgemeine- (General) SS enforced the Nazis' racial policies, the Waffen- (Armed) SS had originally been elite 'Aryan' combat troops tasked with protecting high-ranking Nazis, chosen using strict racial and physical guidelines. Although this no longer applied, the recruitment of men regarded as 'subhuman' in Nazi ideology inevitably led to friction and the Grenadiers were treated very differently from their counterparts.

Nazi officers were obsessed with the possibility that their collaborators would turn their weapons on them, and mutinies by other non-Germanic troops, during which their officers were killed, had heightened those fears. Although the 30th Division nominally had armoured infantry and artillery sections, in practice there were no heavy weapons, the issue of machine-guns to Waffen Grenadiers was banned, and they were armed only with old and often poorly maintained captured rifles.

German SS troops were often hostile, calling them 'bandits' and 'Bolsheviks' and sometimes physically attacking them. They continued to wear their *Schutzmannschaft* uniforms, with only a double iron cross symbol on the right side of their black collars to show they were now Waffen-SS. Since there were no spares, they had to be worn even if ragged and filthy, and most men did not even have a change of underwear. Poor supplies of rations also led to them having to buy, beg or, more usually, steal food from neighbouring villages.

Reflecting his previous rank as a *Schutzmannschaft* leader in Domachevo, Sawoniuk was made a *Korporal* in the new unit, but the auxiliaries who had recently played a leading role in fighting the partisans in Belarus, now found themselves largely reduced to menial chores. Their dismal conditions and the abuse and humiliations heaped on them by their officers led to constant desertions. While they were based in East Prussia, many took their weapons and defected to the Polish *Armija Krajowa*. However, since those remaining had considerable experience of fighting partisans, Himmler ordered them to transfer by rail to south-eastern France in mid-August 1944, to help combat the French *Maquis* in the region who were making increasingly bold attacks on the supply lines and troops of the German 19th Army as they retreated before advancing US forces.

On 27 August 1944, only a handful of days after arriving in France, two complete battalions of Waffen Grenadiers mutinied, killed their officers and deserted to the *Maquis*. Two other battalions also deserted en masse, the majority fleeing across the Swiss frontier, where they were interned for the remainder of the war. The situation led the commander of the 19th Army, Field Marshal Walter Model, to complain to Siegling that his Grenadiers were 'completely unreliable. Division should be disarmed. The immediate transfer to the Reich for work assignment [forced labour] is necessary.'

By mid-September 1944 what was left of the 30th Division had been transferred to Alsace, where Siegling oversaw the removal of all 'useless and unreliable elements'. They were sent to carry out forced labour on strengthening the 'Western Wall', the fortification better known as the 'Siegfried Line'. Just over 6,000 men remained in the reorganised Division, but morale continued to be very low and discipline poor. Attempts to counter widespread drunkenness and violence by banning alcohol were only partly successful, even after offenders were threatened with being sent to concentration camps.

The Waffen Grenadiers were kept out of the front lines for several weeks, but on 19 November 1944, as Free French troops reached the banks of the Rhine and Germany's position grew increasingly desperate, the 30th Division was ordered back into action. Given their previous dismal record in combat, it was clearly a last throw of the dice, but they met with surprising early success and were even commended for their 'bravery and staunchness'. However, a French counter-attack the next morning drove them back and, within three days, the war diary of Model's 19th Army was again recording panic, mutiny and wholesale desertions from the 30th Division. Faced with tanks, the Grenadiers were, it said, 'running out of their positions without firing a shot . . . and are fighting partly against us'.

By then even their commander, Hans Siegling, was forced to admit that they were 'not capable of action anymore'. The remnants were transferred to Germany, where the Waffen-SS Grenadiers were disbanded on 31 December 1944, but Andrei

Sawoniuk was already long gone. Realising the inevitability of the Nazis' defeat, after serving with them for just three months, he had deserted on 11 November 1944, abandoning Nina in the process.

CHAPTER 8

Although Domachevo had now been liberated, there was no question of Ben-Zion laying down his weapons before the final defeat of the Nazis, and he fought with the Red Army as they moved on in pursuit of the fleeing Wehrmacht troops. This time he could not take Benni with him, but he left him with a family in a safe house just outside Domachevo, and promised he would return at the end of the war and adopt him.

Anyone over eighteen who had not already volunteered and was not staying behind as a Soviet functionary was told, 'We're going to Berlin,' and drafted into the Red Army. Many of the partisans who had survived for two or three years in the forests of Belarus were killed in the battles to take Brest-Litovsk and the other staging points on the way to Berlin.

As Ben-Zion's unit advanced, they liberated the Majdanek slave labour and extermination camp outside Lublin in Poland. Even though he knew that thousands of Jews had been shot by the Nazis, like almost all of his peers, Ben-Zion was unaware of the industrial scale of the slaughter. As Israeli historian Margalit Shlain noted, 'Even in late 1944, very few people knew what had been going on inside the camps, and those being sent there did not fully understand what they were going to. They knew about Nazi shootings and killings, but they didn't know about the camps.'

Ben-Zion now saw for himself the enormity of the Final

Solution. 'We were actually only in Majdanek for a few hours,' he said, 'but, for me, it felt like an eternity. I was in total shock. I can't forget what I saw to this day.'

As they approached the compound, surrounded by high, barbed wire fences and watchtowers, 'We didn't know it was an extermination camp,' one of his fellow Red Army soldiers, Bernhard Storch, said. 'We thought it was a military barracks and might have German soldiers there.' When they cautiously entered, they saw 'a tremendous mound of ashes but we still didn't know what it was. There was a tall chimney, so maybe a factory.'

Inside they saw 'what we thought were shower-heads in the ceilings. Then one of the officers came in and told us, "That's where people were gassed."'

The advance on the camp had been so rapid that the guards had no time to destroy the evidence of the horrors that had been inflicted there. As the Red Army soldiers explored further, they found the ovens where countless bodies had been cremated, still containing human remains and surrounded by pile upon pile of skulls and bones.

There were huts packed to the rafters with the possessions of murdered Jews, awaiting redistribution: suitcases, coats, dresses, jackets, trousers, prayer shawls, children's clothes, glasses, human hair and 'thousands of shoes, ladies, mens, and children's separately', all sorted into pairs. Ben-Zion's mind reeled at the thought that every single item had once belonged to a living person. The camp was shrouded in ash and oily flecks of soot, and the air was full of the stench of putrefaction. Days later, far from Majdanek, he could still smell it on his clothes.

His shocked gaze took in the dark, forbidding huts where yet more corpses lay. As he walked towards them, some stirred and the emaciated shadows of men, rags flapping around their skeletal frames, tried to sit up, still not able to believe that their incarceration was at an end. As he talked to them in Yiddish, one, 'a shadow of a man', reached out to try and touch him. 'I bent down towards him and he clasped my neck,' Ben-Zion said. 'He started to cry and told me, "Now I can die in peace, after seeing a Jew in the uniform of the Red Army, fighting against the Germans. I now know there is someone to tell what has happened here."'

Although the camp guards had tried to flee, many were captured by the Soviet forces. Most were summarily killed – a kinder fate than they deserved – but two were later put on trial at Lublin and sentenced to hang. Two Jewish partisans whose families had been exterminated at Majdanek were given the honour of placing the nooses around their necks.

Tens of thousands of Jews had been slaughtered there. 'There were a lot of Jewish soldiers and officers in the Red Army,' Larry Pomeranc says, and when they saw with their own eyes what the concentration camps were like after they liberated Majdanek, 'they were out of their minds looking for revenge.'

There was one all-Jewish partisan unit, led by Chiel Grynszpan, who had been a Polish cavalry officer. The Red Army gave them control of swathes of Eastern Poland and all the weapons they needed. They made Grynszpan the police commissioner of Lublin and then just said to him, 'You are now the commander of this region. Stay here, patrol the area, try to get back all the Jewish children who were given away to Poles, find the collaborators and the Germans who are in hiding, and do whatever you want with them. We have no pity for them.'

Ben-Zion's friend, Meir Bronstein, had found work with the Soviet regime and they had a chance meeting as Ben-Zion's unit was being moved to a different part of the Front. It was the first time they had seen each other since the massacre in Domachevo. As Ben-Zion later said, 'How could we manage to tell everything that had happened in that time, the whole lifetime that we had been through in the last two and a half years?' They had only an hour together before Ben-Zion's unit had to move out. In the chaos of war they again lost touch, but regained contact after another chance meeting in post-war Germany and remained friends for the rest of their lives.

As the Soviet forces crossed the frontier and began to advance into Germany itself, in Ben-Zion's words, 'the hour of revenge and payback came'. The agonies of 6 million slaughtered Jews, 16 million Soviet war dead, and countless millions more who had survived but whose lives would be for ever scarred by their ordeal, were now to be visited upon the nation that had caused them and, as long as their men remained disciplined in battle, Red Army officers turned a blind eye to anything else that occurred.

'In every place we conquered,' Ben-Zion said, 'we took our revenge on the German people for what their soldiers had done to us all in the years of the occupation.' Their blind hatred and fury were unleashed in an orgy of destruction, looting, rape, killing and burning.

The Red Army's advance was now unstoppable, and by the spring of 1945 they were at the gates of Berlin. The city was bombed relentlessly, artillery pounded its defences and buildings to dust, and thousands of tanks and tens of thousands of troops fought their way towards its centre. The Germans put up a desperate last stand, forcing them to fight from street to street and house to house, losing thousands more men in the process but, Ben-Zion said, 'It was our last battle too, and we were no less determined to win and be the first to raise the Red Flag above the Reichstag.'

On 8 May 1945, Soviet radio announced, 'To all army units, wherever they are. The Red Army has achieved a great victory. Berlin has fallen, Nazi Germany has surrendered.'

When their wild celebrations were over, Ben-Zion and his comrades left the ruins of Berlin and went back to Brest-Litovsk on a train packed with looted valuables. Every soldier was allowed to take as much as he could carry, but most took useful items rather than German marks, which were regarded as worthless. 'Who could have imagined then that the German money would regain its value?' Ben-Zion later said. 'Whoever did take the banknotes, got rich quite quickly.'

He took some civilian clothes to wear after being discharged from the army and was also given a new Red Army uniform, a pair of shoes, a pair of boots and some money. Then he hoisted his kitbag onto his shoulder and set off for Domachevo. The trains were not yet running again because the tracks blown up by the partisans had not been repaired and the rusting remains of countless German engines, wagons and carriages lay alongside them. His attempts to hitch a lift were no more successful, for the roads had also been so extensively bombed and shelled that no traffic could get through and, in the end, he had no choice but to walk all the way.

Belarus as a whole had suffered worse than any other occupied region at the hands of the Nazis. The cities were in ruins and thousands of villages had been put to the torch. The death rate of Jews was among the highest in Europe, roughly 80 per cent of the pre-war numbers, and half the population had either been killed, sent to slave labour camps or – the relatively lucky ones – forced out of their homes and expelled from the country. Three million people had been left homeless.

When Ben-Zion reached Domachevo, he went first to the forest, where he said prayers over the mass grave of the Jews, and shed tears for his lost parents, brother, sisters and friends. He was the only member of his family to survive the war, one of just 13 out of over 4,000 Jews of Domachevo who had not been slaughtered. 'I sat down near the grave,' he later said, 'and for several hours could not get up. I heard voices and felt like someone was pulling me into the grave; I felt as if I was paralysed. After some hours a few Soviet soldiers passed by and helped me to get up and with them I reached my town.'

He found what a Soviet report described as 'a heap of ruins':

350 houses and 1,000 farm buildings had been burned to the ground. Such was the destruction that he could not even recognise where his home had been until he saw a poplar tree that his grandfather had planted in their yard, somehow still standing among the ruins. Ben-Zion used to climb it when he was a boy. His grandfather had once told him, 'I will not survive, but this tree will.'

When he went to the safe house where he had left Benni, the couple who lived there, with tears in their eyes, could only tell him that he had gone out one day and never come back. Ben-Zion searched the town and the surrounding villages, asking everyone he met if they had any news of Benni, but there was no trace of him.

Domachevo was now once more part of the Soviet Union, with the River Bug forming the border with Poland. The newly appointed Secretary of the local Communist Party, Cholodov, the former commander of a battalion in Ben-Zion's partisan unit, promised him and the other Jewish partisans jobs and houses in the town if they would stay and help to rebuild it. However, Ben-Zion told him that he could not remain where every place and every thing evoked a bitter memory of all he had lost.

Cholodov then offered to send him to his own family home in Russia, telling him that he would 'be like a son to me' and they would send him to university there. Ben-Zion thanked him but said, 'Russia is not my homeland, even though I fought for it. My people have stood up to fight for their own country, the Land of Israel, in Palestine. That is where I want to go. I want to fight there for my own country.'

Cholodov eventually accepted defeat and, after leaving instructions to contact him at once if Benni ever returned, Ben-Zion left Domachevo for the last time in company with four other Jewish survivors. They took advantage of the Repatriation Act, allowing anyone with a Polish birth certificate to move

A souvenir postcard of Domachevo in the 1920s or 1930s, then a bustling resort town, where the majority Jewish population lived in relative harmony with their neighbours.

After the Nazi destruction of Domachevo and the massacre of the Jewish population, the survivors, including women and small children, fled to the forests with whatever clothes they could find or improvise. Some partisan groups protected large encampments of refugees.

A map that was part of a secret report produced by Einsatzgruppe A, showing the number of Jews executed (symbolised by coffins) in Russia, the Baltic states and Belarus by late 1941. Estonia is described as now 'Judenfrei'. The caption near the bottom reads 'The estimated number of Jews still on hand: 128,000.'

Partisans using a precarious causeway of logs to cross a marsh
in one of the vast Belarusian forests.

Members of Yehiel Grynszpan's all-Jewish partisan group.

A group of Jewish resistance fighters. Their ill-matched kit and shortage of weapons were typical, as was often their youth, such as the boy at centre.

Many Jewish women and children fought for the partisans in the forests. Note the very young girl at front centre, holding a submachine gun.

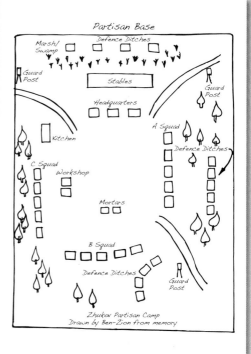

Sketch map of the Zhukov partisan camp in the forest near Domachevo, drawn from memory by Ben-Zion Blustein.

Within the map:

Partisan Base

Marsh/Swamp

Defence Ditches

Guard Post

Stables

Guard Post

Headquarters

A Squad

Kitchen

Defence Ditches

C Squad

Workshop

Mortars

B Squad

Defence Ditches

Guard Post

Zhukov Partisan Camp
Drawn by Ben-Zion from memory

Jewish partisans in Belarus burying two of their comrades. Many others killed in combat had to be left unburied, abandoned where they fell.

The watch towers and fence at Majdanek concentration camp.

The crematoria and gas chamber seen through the barbed wire at Majdanek.

Red Army soldiers in the ruins of the Reichstag in Berlin 1945.

Andrei Sawoniuk in army uniform
during the war.

Sawoniuk photographed in 1948,
just after his arrival in Britain.

Ben-Zion and Clara Blustein in 1946.

Benni Kalina in Israel in the 1950s.

Aerial view of Domachevo in the late 1990s, showing Pushkin Street 'The Road of Death' leading to the massacre site. The scars left on the town by the Nazis have never healed.

from the Soviet Union to Soviet-occupied Poland, to cross the River Bug and make their way west.

Although the war was over, the AK partisans had not disarmed but gone underground and were now fighting the Soviets. Virulently anti-Semitic, they were also targeting Jews who had survived the Holocaust only to find themselves once more being persecuted and attacked. After witnessing an attack in Parczew where three Jews were murdered by AK thugs, Ben-Zion and his friends were desperate to leave the country.

Knowing that the new Polish regime was deporting large numbers of *Volksdeutsche* from Silesia, the *Bericha* Movement – the Jewish underground organisation smuggling Holocaust survivors to Palestine – made use of that mass exodus as cover for Jews escaping across the border. When Ben-Zion contacted *Bericha*, he and his friends were given forged German passports and, with 30 others, put on a train packed with *Volksdeutsche* refugees.

However, Polish guards had been alerted by an informant that there were Jews on the train, and at the border they ordered Ben-Zion and the others to disembark for interrogation. It was a terrible moment. Believing themselves to be on the way to freedom in the West, they were now facing the prospect of returning yet again to oppression and persecution, but they stood their ground and one of them, who spoke fluent German, insisted they were a group of Germans returning home after spending the war years in the Soviet Union. After a tension-wracked few minutes, the guards backed down and allowed them to enter Germany.

Having crossed the border with the Red Army only a few months before, it must have been strange indeed for Ben-Zion to re-enter the home of the Jews' hated oppressors but, like Poland, he saw Germany as being just a way station en route to his true freedom.

They were taken to a refugee camp outside Hanover and, once more identified by informers as Polish Jews, were locked up there. But not for long. With one of his comrades, Ben-Zion managed to break out that night and escape. They made their way into the city and the next morning were able to contact a Jewish organisation. It alerted a rabbi with the British Army, who went back to the camp with them and secured the release of the others.

By the summer of 1946, Ben-Zion, his comrades and his friend Meir Bronstein were living at a United Nations refugee camp in Munich. There he met 17-year-old Clara Ayoun, five years younger than him. She had spent the war years in Siberia and only recently been reunited with the surviving members of her family at the camp. Ben-Zion and Clara were married in November of that year and their son, Shalom, was born the following August. They remained in Germany until 1948, but five months after the declaration of the State of Israel on 14 May of that year, the Jewish Agency arranged for them and other would-be migrants to travel by train to Bandol on France's Mediterranean coast.

Ben-Zion said an emotional farewell to Meir, who had opted to remain in Germany, where he was making such a good living on the black market that he was known as 'Black Meir'; he told his daughter it was because he had black hair. He and Ben-Zion had grown up together and survived together but, although they kept in touch by mail, they would not see each other again for 50 years.

A few nights later Ben-Zion and the other migrants were driven into Marseille in a convoy of covered trucks and smuggled aboard the *Galilee*, which sailed while the port authorities looked the other way. The ship was overloaded, there was not enough food or water, and rough weather made the nine-day voyage even more gruelling, but this time, Ben-Zion said, 'Our suffering was worth it. Finally we had left Europe, soaked with

Jewish blood; our hearts beat with hope for a new life, in our own country.'

At dawn on the ninth day, they could see Mount Carmel. 'As if someone had silently ordered it, we all rose to our feet. Anyone who could, pushed his way up to the deck and marvelled as the beautiful city of Haifa appeared before us. I was choked with tears as I hugged Clara, holding the baby . . . I felt I had come home.'

After a brief spell in a migrant camp, Ben-Zion found a room for his family in an abandoned building. He was conscripted into the Israeli Army the following year and fought in several battles against the Syrians in the north, but was then transferred to the more peaceful far south of the country. A soldier's pay was minimal, and in order to make extra money he began waking at two in the morning and going to work for a nearby company manufacturing cement blocks. When reveille was sounded in the camp at 6.30am, he rushed back to wash and change into his uniform, ready to be on parade for roll-call with his comrades.

When he went home on leave, he used some of the money he had earned to buy a red tricycle for three-year-old Shalom. 'I can still see my boy tearing off the wrapping paper and discovering the tricycle,' he said. 'He was so excited, he began to shout and cry from joy, and Clara and I cried too. That whole evening, he could not leave the tricycle alone and he eventually fell asleep clutching it. All the expensive presents I would buy in the future for my son and grandson did not match up to that gift and the happiness it brought us.'

When he was discharged from the army in 1951, he found work as a builder's labourer, and soon acquired the skills to become a self-employed plasterer and builder. He saved enough money to buy a small but light and airy apartment in the lower-middle-class suburb of Givatayim, just outside Haifa, where their daughter was born in 1952, named Nechama for his lost, much-loved, elder sister.

His family was not wealthy, but after the long years of suffering and struggle, 'I was happy with my lot in life. I knew how to value my good luck: I had a family, a roof over my head, a clean bed and a pillow for my head.'

CHAPTER 9

Using his Polish birth certificate – Domachevo had been part of
Poland when he was born and his native tongue was Polish – and
lying about his recent past, claiming to have just escaped from a
German farm where he had been working as a forced labourer,
Sawoniuk had managed to switch sides and enlist in the Polish
II Corps on 27 December 1944. Commanded by Lieutenant-
General Wladyslaw Anders, it formed part of the British Eighth
Army. Sawoniuk was helped by the fact that many Poles who had
been forced conscripts into the Wehrmacht were also joining
the Corps around this time. Had any of his new comrades been
from Domachevo, he would have been exposed and killed, but
he was not recognised.

His Polish Army record noted that he had served from 1
August to 11 November 1944 in the 'German Army according to
his own statement', and described him as 'an infantry rifleman'.
He had stated his civilian occupation as 'mill worker', presumably to back up his false claim to have been a forced labourer
in Germany. Curiously his surname was initially recorded as
'Grzadkowski', but at some point that was crossed out and
'Sawoniuk' substituted. Whether that was simply a clerical error,
or he had been afraid to reveal his true identity at first, but had
then been reassured by the number of other volunteers who had
served with the Wehrmacht, is not known.

Sawoniuk was passed fit for active service on New Year's

Day 1945. Assigned to the 10th Hussar Regiment of II Corps, he served with them in Egypt and Italy. That he was less than a model soldier is evident from the comments of his superiors. His level of intelligence was described as 'average' and his general assessment was 'less than satisfactory'. Under 'Qualities or Faults', the best the commander of his squadron, Captain of Horse Skowronski Zygmunt, could find to say about him was that he was 'phlegmatic'. He added that Sawoniuk 'requires supervision in his work, no initiative, reckless, superficial, unreliable, likes to drink, constantly dissatisfied and insubordinate'.

The Polish II Corps had played a major part in the battles of Monte Cassino and Ancona in 1944, but after Sawoniuk joined them, he appears to have avoided any direct involvement in combat, even though the Corps was heavily involved in the Bologna offensive in April 1945. By then German troops defending the city were debilitated, demoralised and facing a numerically superior and better-equipped enemy, now enjoying virtually undisputed command of the skies. Although 38 Polish soldiers were killed as they began the attack, they lost their lives not to German weapons, but to 'friendly fire' from American bombers. Over the next 12 days, while British and American troops fought on the flanks, the Poles broke through the German centre and steadily advanced towards the city.

Whether Sawoniuk played any role in the fighting is doubtful. His service record showed that he had been detached on a tank weapons course in mid-February and took a 'motor vehicle driving course' in mid-March, but the space under 'Time spent at the front, participating in action' was left blank in his record, nor was there any mention of wounds, and his only decoration was the Star of Italy, awarded to all soldiers who had served in Italy under British command, however minimal their involvement.

When Bologna fell on 21 April 1945, it proved to be the last battle for II Corps. It was withdrawn from the front line the next day, a decision at least partly prompted by fears about Polish morale, following the Yalta Conference to decide the future shape of Europe. There, without any consultation with Polish politicians, Churchill, Roosevelt and Stalin had agreed that the Soviet Union would annex the whole of east Poland – the area they had occupied in 1939 under the Molotov–Ribbentrop pact. The Poles were to be given some former German territory in the west as partial compensation, but there was widespread fury at this brutal example of realpolitik, and when the Third Reich surrendered, rather than laying down their arms, the Polish AK partisans merely switched to fighting the new Communist regime.

In September 1945, with the war in Europe long over, Sawoniuk had two brief detachments to the Third Regiment of Silesian Uhlans, though for what purpose was not recorded, and remained a member of the 10th Hussars until 23 September 1946, when he was transferred to the Polish Resettlement Corps 'with the effective rank of Hussar'. Funded by the British government, the PRC allowed Polish exiles who had served with the British Armed Forces and did not wish to return to Communist Poland to settle in Britain. Its aim was to help them make the transition to a country few if any of them knew, while maintaining some control over them until they had adjusted to the British way of life.

A Home Office 'Aliens Report' on Sawoniuk at the time of his entry to Britain on 27 June 1946 shows that he claimed to have been a forced labourer on the German railways until 1941 and was then sent to work on a German farm until he was liberated in 1944, whereupon he joined the Polish II Corps. Those claims were palpably false but remained undetected by the hard-pressed British immigration officials at the time.

With the rest of the Polish II Corps, he arrived in Britain by boat, docking at the Port of Glasgow. He was then sent to a military camp at Petts Wood in Surrey and, after being demobbed, moved first to East Sussex and then to Dulwich in South London, where he worked for the building department at St Francis Hospital for seven years.

Soon after the war he had bigamously collected a third wife, a Dutchwoman, Christina van Gent, who divorced him in 1951. In 1958, the same year that he became a naturalised British citizen, he married for a fourth time, to an Irishwoman, Anastasia, and they moved to 'a pretty home' in a quiet residential street in Peckham.

However, Sawoniuk's inability to sustain any relationship for long soon led to cracks appearing in this one too. They had a son, but he seems to have become estranged from him – he took his mother's surname – and they divorced in 1961, when the boy was only a few months old. His wife remained in the family home and her relations later told a reporter that Andrusha was 'a virtual stranger to them and was not a part of their close-knit family group'. There were allegations in both divorce cases that Andrusha had been violent and abusive, though there were no police records to confirm that. His mental state was also fragile enough for him to have undergone electroconvulsive therapy at the Maudsley Hospital in 1956.

He began working for British Rail at London Bridge Station the same year, first as a porter, carrying the bags of wealthy customers or local holidaymakers struggling off trains from the resorts of Kent and the South Coast. He then worked as a member of a railway cleaning team and was promoted to team leader before becoming a ticket collector. British Rail was operating a 'whites only' recruitment policy at the time, and even publicly advertised the fact. It was not reversed until the early 1960s, and might have been a factor in Andrusha's choice of employer.

In 1975, he moved into a one-bedroom council flat at 31 Cadbury Way, on the newly built Rouel Road Estate in Bermondsey, just off the Old Kent Road. He continued to work for British Rail, mostly at London Bridge Station, before transferring to Peckham Rye for the last few years before his retirement in 1986. Over the years, tens of thousands of passengers must have handed their tickets to him without any idea of his background. Always careful to keep a low profile, he never became a member of any of the railway unions, to the surprise of their officials.

Michael Hookway, a former ticket office supervisor at London Bridge Station remembers Sawoniuk very well, 'Not for his jovial or pleasant manner, quite the opposite in fact, being morose, unable to make eye contact, surly and reluctant to hold any sort of conversation.' Most of the staff calling at the supervisor's office to pay in the money they had collected at the ticket barriers would have a few words with Hookway while he checked their cash and ticket books, but 'with Sawoniuk, silence prevailed. I always felt that there was something strange about him, because of his extraordinary reluctance to engage with other staff.'

When he came to Britain, Andrusha had anglicised his Christian name to Anthony and was known as Tony to those workmates he did speak to but, confident that his path from Domachevo to London had been too complex for any investigator to unravel, he still went under the surname of Sawoniuk.

CHAPTER 10

Many years were to pass before Ben-Zion discovered what had happened to Benni Kalina. Although he had left him in the safe house in Domachevo and promised to return at the end of the war to adopt him, Benni was unable to simply sit and wait for that to happen, and became increasingly obsessed with the woman who had betrayed him and his comrades. The other partisans told him that her house was part of a *Volksdeutsche* village. Many of the menfolk were in the German Army, and the remainder, including the woman's two sons, were in the police. It was now obvious to Benni that she had alerted a neighbour while she was outside, ostensibly getting milk and, with the other police and auxiliaries, her sons had then stormed the house, shot his comrades and badly wounded him.

Although still only 11 or 12, the war had made Benni old beyond his years, and he decided to go back and confront her. Armed with the cut-down shotgun he had used with the partisans, he left the safe house early one morning, without saying a word to the couple Ben-Zion had asked to look after him, and walked the 15 kilometres to the woman's village. He first hid in a place from where he could keep watch on the house and learn her routine. Having seen that her sons visited her regularly, he chose a time when she was alone in the house and knocked on the door. When she opened it, he said, 'Do you remember me?'

She was puzzled and said, 'No.'

He told her he had been a partisan in the area, and said, 'The house looks familiar and I want to know what happened to my comrades.' As he studied her face, he could see the realisation dawn. She then admitted that Benni and his comrades had been in her house but claimed she didn't know how the soldiers and police had discovered they were there.

'I know exactly who you are,' Benni said. 'I know that both your sons are policemen, and that you left the house and told them and the Germans. My friends were killed, I was wounded and I am the only survivor.'

'She started to tremble,' Benni recalled, 'and said that it wasn't true, but I was completely sure of myself. I said to myself, I have to do something, and I took out my gun and shot her.'

He dragged her body into a back room of the house and left it there but, rather than fleeing the scene, helped himself to some food from her kitchen and settled down to wait. He stayed in the house for two days and nights, watching and waiting through the daylight hours and into the evening, and then snatching a few hours' sleep before resuming his vigil at dawn the next day. Finally, on the third day, the woman's sons, still wearing police uniforms, arrived to visit her. As they walked in through the door, he shot both of them in the chest at point-blank range. They slumped to the floor and he stood over them until he was sure they were dead. He felt no remorse or regret; in his mind, the three deaths were a just revenge for the killing of his three comrades. He waited in that charnel house until nightfall, then slipped away and walked back to Domachevo.

When he got back, he met some of his former comrades from the partisans and told them what he had done. They were not shocked – they had killed plenty of informers themselves during the war – but under the Soviets, the rule of law had now been reimposed and scores could no longer be settled in the old way. They told him that he had to get away or he would be arrested for murder. He took their advice and fled before the Soviet police could find him.

Not knowing if Ben-Zion was alive or dead, he then walked 80 kilometres to his old home town of Meseritz and, 'finding nothing there', he caught a train to Warsaw and eventually travelled on to Lodz, on the dividing line between the Soviet and American zones. There he was found by a Jewish organisation that was rescuing orphaned survivors of the war and sending them to new homes in the West. They offered him the chance to go to England or America but, Benni said, 'As a boy I had known about Palestine. I knew what Israel was and I wanted a home.' Three months later, he was one of a group of children sent to Youth Aliyah at Nahalal in Israel, an organisation housing children 'at risk of being abandoned to the streets'.

He soon ran away and tried to enlist in the army but was rejected because of his youth and sent back to Nahalal. However, when the War of Independence broke out in 1948, he ran away again, lied about his age and joined the Golani Brigade of the Israeli Army. Never having been to school, he was illiterate but 'when they asked how old I was, I said 1930. I had no idea what 1930 or 1932 or 1935 meant. I didn't know when I had been born, but I understood that 1930 would mean I was old enough to volunteer.'

Drawing on his experience with the partisans, he fought in a series of battles in Upper Galilee, Kibbutz Degania, the Golan Gate and Masada, and was again wounded, this time in the leg, but continued to serve until the end of the war. After his discharge, he settled down to civilian life, working as a small farmer in a communal village. He married when he was still only 17 – his wife was two years older – and they had three children.

He often thought about Ben-Zion and wondered what had happened to him, but never really expected to see him again and never told anybody, not even his wife, about what had happened to him before he came to Israel. Of his earlier life with his real family before the war, there was nothing to tell because, as he said later, 'I remember nothing; it's like I was born at sea. I don't even have anything to imagine.'

When Ben-Zion had first questioned him in the forest, Benni told him that he had been born in 1933. 'However, I don't know if that is true,' he later mused, 'because, in that case, I should have been able to remember something of my family. Maybe I was actually younger than that. I don't really know, just like I don't know the fate of my family. Were they murdered in Treblinka or in Majdanek? Or were they killed one night in Meseritz, when more than 3,000 Jews were buried in a mass grave? Meseritz was a town of somewhere between 18,000 and 20,000 Jews. Only a handful remained.'

Ben-Zion had developed regular work as a self-employed builder, and was often away from home throughout the week, constructing accommodation blocks at kibbutzes in the newly occupied territories. He was devoted to his wife and growing family, but his experiences had not made him suspicious of, nor hostile to strangers and outsiders, and he remained open and friendly to everyone, believing that people are born good and it is their life experiences that make them the person they then become. His grandson, Ben, described him as 'a quiet person who only talked when he had something specific to say, but when he did, everybody listened'.

In Jaffa he met people from Benni's home town, told them his story and asked about him, but no one seemed to know anything. Although Ben-Zion never forgot the boy, he could find no trace of him.

Holocaust survivors often found that Israelis who had not

come from occupied Europe themselves struggled to comprehend the enormity of their experiences and would even ask the semi-accusatory question, 'But why did you not fight?' Some went further than that, dismissively talking about them as 'sheep' and, Benni said, treating them as 'second-class citizens, not respected'.

Primo Levi, a survivor of Auschwitz, had talked of the vital need to testify to what had happened there but, because the reality was so alien to the experiences of those who had not been victims of the Nazis, there was also a terrible fear of not being believed. Many who did speak about their ordeal were shattered to discover that even their fellow Jews did not believe them.

One Holocaust survivor, Miki Goldman, later to be a key witness in the Adolf Eichmann trial, had been given a punishment of 80 lashes in a Nazi concentration camp when he was just 13. After the war he was called a liar by Israelis who did not believe a child could have survived such punishment. That, Goldman said, was the 81st blow, and the most bitter and painful one of all.

Survivors could often find sympathy and understanding only among their fellows, and groups sprang up all over Israel where those from a particular town or area of Eastern Europe could unite and share their experiences, knowing that at least there, they would be met with understanding, not criticism.

Benni avoided such gatherings until the mid-1960s, when, for the first time, he went to a meeting of survivors from Meseritz. When he introduced himself, one of the others said, 'Look, I don't know you, but your name is familiar. A guy called Ben-Zion Blustein was always asking if anyone knew anything about you. He was a partisan and said he saved your life. He lives near Jaffa and I have his address.'

Benni turned up at the house the next day. Ben-Zion was still at work, and when he came home and saw someone waiting for him outside his house, he didn't recognise him at first. The last time he had seen him, Benni was a boy of 10 or 11 and he was now an adult with a moustache. He looked 'a little like Charles Bronson' and, according to Benni's son, Meir, sometimes acted like him too. Benni didn't want to say straight away, 'Listen, it's me, Benni Kalina,' so he pretended he was there looking for work with Ben-Zion's building firm.

Ben-Zion was 'tired, hungry and short-tempered, wanting only to bathe, eat and rest. I could not understand why this man kept giving me strange looks,' but when Benni spoke again, he recognised his voice and burst into tears. 'It's my boy, Benni Kalina!' he said. 'It's the wounded boy I found in the forest. I've been looking for him all these years and now I've found him.'

Ben-Zion's son, Shalom, had often heard his father crying out in his sleep, for the horrific events in Domachevo still haunted his dreams, but the first time he ever saw him weep was when Benni turned up at their house. Ben-Zion introduced him to Clara and the children and he shared their evening meal. 'We were all so happy and crying at the same time,' Benni said.

He wanted Ben-Zion to come and meet his family and see his small farm straight away, so the very same evening, they drove there in Ben-Zion's truck. On the way, Benni asked him not to mention the Holocaust, nor talk about the ghetto, the partisans or anything to do with the war in Europe. 'No one at home knows what I went through during the war.'

Ben-Zion was startled. 'You haven't told them? Why not? Why hide everything from them?'

'Don't you know how we immigrants and Holocaust survivors are treated here? I've hidden my past because I don't want my children to be traumatised by what I went through.'

Ben-Zion bowed to his wishes and was introduced to

Benni's wife and family as a friend from the Israeli Army. From that day on the two men were inseparable. Ben-Zion helped him find a new apartment for himself and his family, and taught him to be a plasterer, and they then renovated homes together.

Many years later, when Scotland Yard detectives called on Ben-Zion and interviewed him in the 1990s, they asked him if he would be willing to give evidence against Andrei Sawoniuk in a trial at the Old Bailey in London. One of those detectives, Charlie Moore, says that at first, 'It took a lot of softly, softly work by our Israeli interpreter, Miri Drucker, to persuade Mr Blustein to make a statement, but each time we saw him after that he became more determined to right the wrongs of that despicable period.'

One of his main reasons was because he thought that if Andrusha was brought to trial, he might finally find out if, among his many other crimes, he had killed Ben-Zion's mother and younger sister. However, he still hesitated about agreeing to travel to London to be a witness because, worried about the impact on his health, his wife, Clara, did not want him to do it, but Benni urged Ben-Zion to testify. Benni's parents and all his siblings had been slaughtered in the Holocaust and, says his son, Meir, he was a firm believer in justice and revenge.

As they sat sharing their lunch among the stacks of timber and sacks of cement and plaster for the house they were renovating, Benni fixed him with his gaze. 'You have to testify,' he said. 'You must do it, not only for your own mother, your stepfather and your brother and sisters, but for my family, and for all the Domachevo Jews whose voices were silenced forever by the Nazis. They have no one else to speak for them. I got my vengeance by shooting the woman and her two sons who betrayed me and murdered my friends. You can avenge the deaths of your own family and friends, and your whole community by bringing that monster Sawoniuk to justice. The world needs to be told what happened, and if you don't do it, who will?'

CHAPTER 11

The path that would eventually lead to Andrei 'Andrusha' Sawoniuk facing justice at the Old Bailey was a long and tortuous one. Although he had fled Domachevo in 1944, before agents of the Soviet Extraordinary Commission into War Crimes arrived in the town in pursuit of 'traitors to the Motherland', Sawoniuk's many crimes were vividly recalled by the survivors there, and the investigators immediately opened a file on him: 'All Union Search File No. 1065.' There was such a shortage of paper in the immediate post-war period that the reports compiled about him were written on the back of torn-up military maps.

Witness statements gathered by the NKVD – the forerunner of the KGB – described Andrusha as 'a most bloodthirsty person – many people died at his hands'. One of his former comrades remembered him as 'the most active policeman' in enforcing the Nazi policies and said that he 'went to other executions of his own accord'. Fourteen other Domachevo *Schutzmänner* were prosecuted by the Soviets over the next four years, but Andrusha continued to elude them.

Unaware of his flight to the West, the investigators went to extraordinary lengths in their attempts to capture him, sending 16 different NKVD and KGB covert agents to Domachevo over the course of the next dozen years to hunt for traces of him. One agent, codenamed 'Kopito', was tasked with extracting information on Andrusha's whereabouts from his distant relatives and his few remaining friends, but drew a blank. Another agent posed as a hairdresser, no doubt hoping that one of her customers would let something slip in conversation, but was no more successful. Yet another went undercover in Domachevo for nine months, posing as a peasant farmer, but he too failed to unearth even the smallest clue to Sawoniuk's whereabouts. The NKVD files covered 30 handwritten pages about him, and kept increasing as further information and statements were gathered, but he had left no discernible trace.

The first hint that he might be alive and in Britain came when the KGB interrogated a man called Kozlovsky, who had been a colleague of Sawoniuk's in the Domachevo *Schutzmannschaft*. He told his interrogators that he had seen Andrusha in Egypt just before he was due to travel to Scotland with the Polish Free Army for resettlement. The KGB treated the suggestion that he might now be in Britain with caution and there was no corroboration of it until 1951, when for the first time since he had fled Domachevo seven years earlier, Andrusha broke cover to send a letter and parcel, postmarked London, to his half-brother Nikolai. The KGB routinely intercepted mail from the West and the Sawoniuk file, which had been gathering dust, was at once reactivated.

Nothing further was added to it for 30 years until 1981, when another Belarusian exile the Soviets had been tracking, Stephan Androusyuk, sent a letter to his sister in Domachevo. 'You will never guess who I saw the other day,' he wrote, after spotting Sawoniuk's characteristic shambling gait in Marylebone High Street in London. 'Andrusha Sawoniuk! He was walking in that same way!'

Once more the letter was intercepted by the KGB and the information was added to the Sawoniuk file. Agents tried to establish an address for him, perhaps with the intention of assassinating him, but they failed to do so, and with the Cold

War still poisoning relations with the West, no information about him was passed to the British authorities.

Since the Nuremberg trials of Nazi leaders in the immediate aftermath of the Second World War, it had been generally accepted that, like slavery and piracy, jurisdiction over war crimes and crimes against humanity was universal under international law. Poland, Hungary, Yugoslavia, Greece, Russia, France and Israel had all conducted further trials of Nazi war criminals over the succeeding years, but Britain had not. Speaking soon after Nuremberg, Winston Churchill, now much more interested in prosecuting the Cold War rather than Nazi war criminals, had called for 'an end to retribution. We must turn our backs on the horrors of the past and look to the future.'

In a debate in the House of Lords in May 1949, Lord Henderson stated that His Majesty's Government did not intend to pursue 'any further trials of people accused of crimes against the laws and usages of war'.

That remained government policy for 40 years but, in 1986, a dossier compiled by the Simon Wiesenthal Center on 17 ex-Nazis believed to be living in the UK was delivered to the British authorities. Two years later, as part of Mikhail Gorbachev's policy of *glasnost* – openness – the Soviets handed over a list of 97 Nazi war criminals believed to be in Britain.

In theory, any war criminals that the British authorities were able to identify could have been extradited to face trial in their countries of origin or those where their crimes had been perpetrated, but in fact, there was no extradition treaty between Britain and the Soviet Union, which included Belarus, and little appetite to introduce one, since it might have forced British residents or citizens to face the dubious justice of the Soviet courts.

However, a War Crimes Inquiry was established under

Sir Thomas Hetherington, a former Director of Public Prosecutions, and William Chalmers, the former head of the Crown Office in Scotland. Reporting in July 1989, their central recommendation was for legislation to extend the jurisdiction of the domestic courts to try acts of murder and manslaughter committed as war crimes. Those crimes were 'so monstrous that they cannot be condoned', and failure to take action would 'taint the United Kingdom with the slur of being a haven for war criminals'.

Just as the US Prosecutor Telford Taylor had argued about the establishment of the International Military Tribunal that oversaw the Nuremberg trials, the Hetherington Inquiry was effectively stating that the issue was not whether it would be outrageous to prosecute Nazis for their war crimes, but rather that it would be outrageous not to do so.

However, fearing that they might otherwise be opening the door to retrospective prosecutions of British soldiers for acts committed in wars or so-called 'policing actions' in former colonies, the framers of the War Crimes Act were careful to restrict it to offences committed in Germany or German-held territory during the Second World War.

The Bill eventually presented to Parliament stated that, 'Proceedings for murder, manslaughter or culpable homicide, may be brought against a person in the United Kingdom irrespective of his nationality at the time of the alleged offence if that offence –

(1) was committed during the period beginning with 1 September 1939 and ending with 5 June 1945 in a place which at the time was part of Germany or under German occupation; and constituted a violation of the laws and customs of war.

(2) No proceedings shall . . . be brought against any person unless he was on 8 March 1990, or has subsequently become, a British citizen or resident in the United Kingdom, the Isle of Man or any of the Channel Islands.'

A furious debate ensued, with Margaret Thatcher and Sir Edward Heath finding themselves – not for the first time – on opposite sides. In meetings with the Israeli government, Thatcher had committed herself to action on war criminals, but Heath, an artillery officer during the war, claimed the Act would simply lead to 'show trials' of old men. Perhaps surprisingly, Lord Shawcross, Britain's lead prosecutor at Nuremberg, was also opposed, saying that it 'violates the great traditions of English Law'. Tiptoeing around the edge of anti-Semitism, the former Lord Chancellor, Lord Hailsham, accused Mrs Thatcher, whose Finchley constituency included a substantial Jewish population and who was very strongly pro-Jewish and pro-Israeli herself, of 'giving in to a special interest community'.

Other opponents argued that the considerable interval of time between the crimes and a suspect being brought to trial would make physical evidence impossible to find, witness testimony questionable and even identification of the suspect doubtful. Some also quoted with approval Lord Reading's comment that 'justice delayed is justice denied', and claimed that the Act was retrospective, selective and motivated not by any desire for justice, but for revenge.

Urged on by Mrs Thatcher, supporters of the Act argued that its opponents were guilty of conflating retribution with vengeance, and cited the Geneva Conventions that had already extended the principles of the law to 'usages established among civilised peoples, from the laws of humanity and the dictates of the public conscience'. There could therefore be no dispute that murder and manslaughter of a civilian population constituted offences against the laws and customs of war, and the Chief Rabbi, Lord Jakobovits, was in no doubt that a failure to pass the Act would 'make it certain that for millions of victims, there can be and there will be no justice'.

Three times the House of Commons passed the Act by 2:1

majorities – and three times the Lords rejected it by similar margins. It eventually became law in 1991, after Margaret Thatcher had been replaced by John Major, and then only after the Commons used the Parliament Act that gave the House primacy over the Lords, to force it through. Passed in 1911 and amended in 1949, in the face of earlier Lords' rebellions, it was only the fourth time the Act had ever been invoked, and the first since the 1949 amendment.

Specialist War Crimes Units (WCUs) were set up at the Crown Prosecution Service and Scotland Yard, as part of the Metropolitan Police Serious and Organised Crime Group, and detectives began to look into the Wiesenthal Center list and the names supplied by the Soviet Union. Among the latter was the file on Andrei 'Andrusha' Sawoniuk: 'No. USSR 57: Assisted the Nazi fascists in the killing of innocent civilians.' No witness statements were attached to the Soviet files but they included dates of killings in which he had allegedly been involved and the names of people in Domachevo who could testify to his crimes. Until that moment, no Western intelligence agencies had ever heard of him.

The Metropolitan Police detectives assigned to the WCU had been sceptical about their work at first, thinking, as an adviser to the War Crimes Inquiry said, that 'Mrs Thatcher had just got a bee in her bonnet', but when they examined the files, they realised 'these were people who had committed thousands of murders', and began serious attempts to find them.

Detective Chief Superintendent Eddie Bathgate had been given command of the unit, with a £3 million budget from the Home Office to cover an initial three-year investigation. Since the Home Office, rather than the Met, was picking up the tab, the WCU even had to pay rent on their office on the 5th floor of Scotland Yard.

The WCU did not try to recruit men with language skills, experience in archival research or other potentially useful talents for this unusual investigation. They were just, one member says, 'ordinary detectives who had the job thrust upon them'.

The unit eventually included nine detectives – the DCS, a Detective Chief Inspector, three Detective Inspectors, a Detective Sergeant and three Detective Constables. One of them, DC Charlie Moore, was recruited largely because on a previous case he had developed skills with HOLMES – the computerised Home Office Large Major Enquiry System brought in after the chaos of the Yorkshire Ripper enquiry. The clumsy 'Large Major' in its title was presumably used so that the acronym would echo the legendary detective.

The only surprising question that Moore was asked at his interview for the unit was, 'Are you Jewish?' 'They didn't want any Jewish investigators,' he says, 'because of fears that they could not be impartial investigators of Holocaust crimes.'

They were supported by six administrative personnel, and historians and researchers, notably the Chief Historian, Dr Martin Dean, who spoke German and Yiddish, and a Russian speaker, Alasdair MacLeod, who both proved invaluable at tracking down information in foreign archives. Interpreters were also used to translate documents from Polish, Hebrew and several other languages.

The WCU's initial tasks were to plan a strategy and assess what specialist skills would be needed and, Moore says, identify 'what diplomatic and bureaucratic hoops we were going to have to jump through to get access to the people and documents we needed'.

The first priority was to find out whether the suspects were still alive, and they began searching the NHS and Social Security records, which were not computerised then. Many of the suspects – they were all men – could not be traced or had already died, but with a list of those who were still alive, the detectives tried to identify where they came from and what they were alleged to have done.

It was no easy task because 250,000 Poles had come to Britain after the war, and sifting through them to separate blameless immigrants from potential war criminals was a mammoth undertaking, further complicated because, even though they had been in Britain for 40 years, a surprisingly large number had never learned to speak English.

'We were a very small team,' Moore says, 'and it wasn't long before we discovered the enormity of the challenge we were facing. When police are investigating a murder, the first forty-eight hours are crucial. Today you would be cordoning off the crime scene, ensuring it was not contaminated, searching for clues often invisible to the naked eye, lifting fingerprints and attempting to get a DNA profile for the killer. You would be seeking out ballistic evidence and blood spatters to identify the firearm used and pinpoint the angle and distance from which a weapon was fired. But here we were starting investigations into allegations of war crimes that were over half a century old. So we began with the name of a suspect and worked backwards to find evidence and witnesses.'

Here the historians and researchers were crucial in obtaining access to archives in Eastern and Western Europe, Israel and elsewhere. They found files that identified suspects and their crimes, and some of the witnesses who might testify against them, and also picked up references to more records, often in different countries. Many of the allegations were vague or hearsay, and others proved to have been purely malicious, but there was compelling evidence against a number of suspects.

In the absence of physical evidence, the War Crimes Unit's emphasis had to be on identification and, using the material the historians had produced, the detectives then began gathering statements from people who had grown up with the suspects or lived in the same village or town, and would still be able to recognise them despite the passage of time.

Three two-man teams were formed, each handling initial

investigations in separate, formerly Nazi-occupied regions: one in Belarus, one in Ukraine, and one in the Baltic states of Lithuania, Latvia and Estonia. Eventually their searches spanned the globe, including Germany, Austria, Poland, Denmark, Sweden, Russia, Abkhazia, Israel, Canada, the United States, South Africa, Australia and New Zealand. As Charlie Moore remarks with a grin, 'The air miles were brilliant.'

One of the first potential witnesses he interviewed was actually living in Britain, in Streatham, and he has never forgotten his encounter with her. She showed him the tattoo from Auschwitz on her arm and told him that she had been forced to clean the latrines in the French prisoner-of-war camp next to the concentration camp. Although the PoWs were on very short rations, they knew that Auschwitz inmates not being killed outright were being starved to death, so they often left a turnip for her. She hid it until she returned to her barrack room, where she washed off the effluent and ate it raw. Somehow, she survived until the camp was liberated.

Many of the interviewees were still living in Eastern Europe and almost all the others had originated there. 'Often the only police they were familiar with,' Moore says, 'did not exactly have a reputation for sensitivity and compassion. We had to go in as police officers from a foreign land that they had little or no knowledge about, and win their trust. Then we had to persuade them to turn back the clock over fifty years and try to recall minute details of the most unspeakable atrocities. Many of these people had not even shared those horrific memories with their own loved ones, and here we were trying to reopen the wounds. One witness was sobbing uncontrollably. His wife had never heard his account before.'

A woman told Moore she and her young daughter had been forced to strip and, with other naked men, women and children, were made to stand on the edge of a pit. Knowing what was about to happen, she placed her hand over her daughter's eyes so she wouldn't see the men preparing to shoot them. When the machine-guns fired, they tumbled into the pit, but she was not killed. Her only wound was a bullet hole through the hand she had been holding over her daughter's eyes, but it killed her child, shot through the head. The woman lay cradling her daughter's body until dark, then crawled naked out of the pit and crept into the forest, where she was found and taken in by the partisans.

CHAPTER 12

WCU detectives soon amassed a bulging file of allegations against Sawoniuk, but tracking him down in Britain proved impossible at first because of one simple but absolutely crucial error. In order to search the Met Police database, the Immigration and Naturalisation Service archive in Croydon or the NHS and Social Security files in the national records office in Southport, the first three letters of the surname had to be entered correctly. When the Soviet list of war crimes suspects had been handed to the British government in 1988, it included the name 'Andrey Savanyuk' – the transliteration from the Russian spelling. However, he had used the Polish version of his name – Sawoniuk – when entering Britain after the war. That error led to an unsuccessful search of databases for names beginning 'SAV' instead of 'SAW'.

It was to be another five years before the WCU's Chief Historian, Martin Dean, found the Polish version of the name in a file in the Stasi archives in East Germany in 1993. That discovery led him to other documents in Polish, Russian, German and British files. The Polish archives revealed allegations made by witnesses in the trial of another former Domachevo police chief, Konstanty Korneliuk. Belarusian KGB files included a statement by one witness who had seen him and another policeman dragging Freydka Bender and her two daughters out of the attic of a house in the ghetto. It was confirmed by a second witness, while a third, Anton Martynovich Kharkhut, saw Sawoniuk shoot them with a rifle in 'Shilovo wood, one kilometre from Domachevo'. Kharkhut had to bury the bodies.

Another witness, Michal Danilovich Kozlovski, saw five men who had been kept alive to work for the Germans being taken by Sawoniuk and two other policemen, 'all of them armed with pistols, into the outhouse in the station yard and then I heard irregular shots. I could not see who was actually doing the shooting'. Yet another witness had seen Sawoniuk and another policeman shooting a 60-year-old Jewish woman.

The files also detailed the Soviet trials of other members of the Domachevo police, some in Poland but the majority in Belarus. Those, Martin Dean says, gave the WCU 'more and more evidence against Sawoniuk before we'd spoken to a single witness ourselves'. The files also contained a photograph of Sawoniuk and several of his fellow policemen, all wearing *Schutzmannschaft* uniform, and revealed the existence of a 214-page dossier compiled on him by the KGB. 'The race was now on to find this file.'

Both Dean and the head of the War Crimes Unit, DCS Eddie Bathgate, made repeated requests to the Belarusian Procurators (the equivalent of the Crown Prosecution Service), emphasising that without it, a prosecution in the UK was very unlikely. The Belarusians should have been eager to help the investigation, Dean says, because it had 'always been a big propaganda thing, trying to embarrass the West by showing that they were harbouring all these war criminals'.

However, the snail's pace of Belarusian bureaucracy, and perhaps a lingering suspicion about Western motives, meant that months dragged by before he was given access to the Central Card Index held by the Ministry of Interior in Minsk. Within minutes he found a card for Sawoniuk, giving the reference to the Search File. It included the statements of witnesses – most of them now dead – recording a series of murderous incidents.

One 'barely legible statement' Dean found described Sawoniuk as a 'butcher-executioner' who took a direct part in all the executions.

Dean also found files naming Sawoniuk in the records of the Polish Army, the Polish Resettlement Corps, UK immigration, and the German records of the 30th Waffen-SS Division, which, among other things, gave his rank – *Korporal* – in the *Schutzmannschaft*. Dean's research also brought him to the uncomfortable realisation that, 'It wasn't five or ten war criminals who had come to Britain via the Polish Army; there were actually hundreds of them.'

Among the files were the names of seven other local policemen from Domachevo who, like Sawoniuk, had come to the UK after the war, only one of whom was still alive. He was traced and interviewed and he confirmed Andrusha's wartime role as a member of the Domachevo *Schutzmannschaft* and later its commandant. He was ruled out as a potential witness, however, as his own service in the auxiliaries might have made his evidence appear unreliable.

Having examined all the available evidence, Martin Dean's formal recommendation to the WCU was emphatic and unambiguous: 'The allegations made against Andrei SAWONIUK received primarily from the files of the former Soviet and other Eastern European governments are so numerous and of so serious a nature that this case deserves thorough investigation. Moreover, the allegations appear to be substantiated by documents from Western archives such that they cannot be dismissed as an elaborate KGB plot left over from the Cold War.' (Emphasis in the original.)

A fresh search of the NHS and Social Security files at Southport, this time using the correct three-letter indicator 'SAW' now finally revealed Sawoniuk's British identity and address in Bermondsey, just down the road from the WCU's office at Scotland Yard. As Dean remarks, 'It was lucky we found him when we did because they were already saying to me, "We don't want any more names," because we were generating hundreds that they had to investigate.'

To build their case against Sawoniuk, Charlie Moore was one of the detectives who visited Domachevo and the surrounding towns and villages again and again, sometimes for days, sometimes weeks at a time, to identify and interview potential witnesses. They were always accompanied by a Belarusian Procurator and interpreters who spoke Russian, Belarusian, Polish and Ukrainian.

Moore was touched by the hospitality he and his colleagues were offered by the local people, who invited him to their houses, and although they had very little, were eager to share whatever they could. Moore was startled to see empty coffins propped up in some of their living rooms, and discovered it was a local tradition to make their own coffins ready for when they died.

Almost all of them kept a backyard pig that they would feed on scraps and windfalls, and then slaughter in the autumn. 'They would say to us, "Come back in September when we've killed the pig,"' Moore says, with a smile. Jill Murray, a case clerk with the Crown Prosecution Service before joining the WCU, actually did. She had the job of looking after the witnesses when they came to Britain, and went to Domachevo in the autumn to meet them and get some idea of their circumstances and the help they would need. 'When we knocked on one witness's door,' she says, 'his wife answered it wearing a blood-soaked apron, and we could hear the most terrible noises from the room behind her. She said to the interpreter, "Would you mind coming back in an hour, my husband's just killing the pig."'

People were 'queuing up outside the town hall who couldn't wait to tell us about Sawoniuk,' Moore says, and interviewing them all was a painstaking process. None of them spoke

English, so interpreters would translate the detectives' questions and the witnesses' answers, and typists would transcribe and print them. The witness then signed a version in their language while the interpreters signed a declaration that the English translation was a true and accurate one.

The detectives had found a picture of Sawoniuk in the 1940s, and they put it in an album alongside photographs of random people of a similar age. If someone claimed they had seen him carrying out a murder, they would be presented with the album and asked if they could pick him out.

As more and more witnesses were interviewed, the number of murders that Sawoniuk was alleged to have committed kept on rising. As Fedor Zan said to Moore, 'He's killed more people than you've got hairs on your head.'

Martin Dean says that another indictment of Sawoniuk could have been produced, based purely on the evidence in the KGB files, none of which was used in the Old Bailey trial. Moore believes that Sawoniuk killed at least 200 men, women and children, though the evidence in many of those cases was too tenuous to be put before a court.

The rigour of the CPS lawyers in sifting and discarding evidence that had been so laboriously gathered, but which they felt was insufficiently strong to put before a judge and jury, must have been agonising for the members of the WCU. As Dean says, 'It's frustrating when your own side are doing that before you even get to trial, and you worry that you may run out of ammunition.'

The primary focus of the investigation was on Sawoniuk's crimes against Domachevo's Jews, and that was sometimes frustrating to the witnesses who, Moore says, often asked him, 'Why do you keep asking us about the Jews? He killed lots of other people too.'

One man testified he had seen Sawoniuk force a 12-year-old boy to dig his own grave, then shot him dead and got another boy to fill it in. Moore and another detective managed to track down the witness but, although he gave them a detailed account of what he had seen, he was not willing to go to London to testify.

They also interviewed an old woman whose son had been murdered by Sawoniuk, on suspicion of being a partisan. He had suddenly appeared at a family gathering outside her barn and opened up with his machine-gun, blowing the boy's brains out. Although the woman was delighted that Sawoniuk was finally going to face trial for his crimes, she refused to go to London to testify against him. Several other potential witnesses were also either unwilling to travel to the UK, or were too frail, physically or mentally, to do so.

Nonetheless, by the time they had completed their investigations, the WCU had assembled a powerful case against Sawoniuk. When detectives and uniformed police turned up unannounced and holding a search warrant at Andrusha's run-down council flat in Bermondsey at 10.10am on 21 March 1996, he was stunned into silence.

A search of the flat at once produced documents that he had retained as mementos throughout all those years, including a photograph of him in his Polish II Corps uniform and giving his army number – 30008062 – and a travel permit relating to his marriage to Christina van Gent in 1947. Before leaving, they told him to present himself at Southwark police station for a formal interview in ten days' time and advised him to find a solicitor.

The police raid had been greeted with shock by Sawoniuk's neighbours, watching from behind their net curtains. He was a familiar figure to them, but his troubled family life and Nazi past were unknown. Although some called him 'Tony the Pole' or 'the German', most just knew him as Tony. He could be seen most mornings, walking stick in hand, shopping at Tesco on the Old Kent Road, the Co-op or Marks & Spencer, but otherwise he kept himself to himself and 'seemed content to live a quiet retirement'. He was so reclusive that Commander Mulvihill, sifting through witness statements from the WCU, described him as 'a model of anonymity'.

One neighbour called Andrusha 'mild mannered and friendly', and Marion Henry said, 'I have been here as long as anybody and Tony has always been a nice bloke,' but another described him as 'rude and a prat'. Few of his other neighbours on the estate knew him but all said that he had never made any attempt to be friendly. A woman living opposite him said, 'He didn't make conversation with anyone around here,' and according to members of the Tenants Association, he never participated in any community events or meetings, despite being one of the first people to live on the estate.

Later that day, Andrusha turned up at the offices of a firm of solicitors on Southwark Park Road in Bermondsey, opposite a pub known locally as 'The Blue'. It was pouring with rain, and he looked such a bedraggled figure that the receptionist took him for a tramp. She thought he had come straight from the pub across the road and was probably drunk. So when he asked to see a solicitor, she told him to leave his contact details and said someone would be in touch.

He gave her his address and handed over a card he had been given by the War Crimes Unit, telling her he was being 'accused of killing some Jew boys', but insisted on seeing a lawyer straight away and raised his voice as he did so. When she continued to tell him that he would have to wait, he began to shout at her. The receptionist who, solicitor Steve Law says, was 'a South Londoner', well capable of handling 'insistent visitors', then told him to 'clear off'. Martin Lee, one of the firm's partners, came down to see what the commotion was about, but by that time the furious Andrusha had stormed out.

When the receptionist told Lee what had happened and showed him the card Sawoniuk had left, he at once recognised the unique importance of the WCU, and sent every member of his staff out immediately with orders to scour the surrounding streets until they found him.

He had not gone far and, when he returned, he was greeted with considerably more warmth than on his first appearance and offered a drink. Contrary to the receptionist's assumptions, it turned out that he was a diabetic who now neither drank nor smoked, so Lee sent for a cup of coffee instead and settled Sawoniuk in his office for a preliminary chat. Andrusha gave him a rough outline of what the detectives had said to him and agreed to appoint Lee as his solicitor.

Over several meetings, Lee and a junior solicitor got to know Andrusha a little better. In marked contrast to some of the figures he would be encountering when the case came to trial, he may have seen them – one from a working-class background – as kindred spirits. Whatever the reason, they found Sawoniuk to be a courteous client, never missing an appointment with them, and Lee describes him as 'friendly, and at times even jovial, with a good sense of humour'.

That was not a description that any of his contemporaries in Domachevo, nor even on the Rouel Road Estate, would have recognised, and Lee also acknowledges that Sawoniuk was a very lonely man. In all the time they were representing him, neither solicitor ever saw him with friends or heard him mention any, and nor did there ever appear to be any visitors to his Bermondsey flat.

His only relationship seemed to be with his son, and it was uncertain how close they were. He may well not have known what his father had done during the war until it was revealed in the newspapers after his arrest and perhaps had decided to disown him to protect his own young children.

Sawoniuk's solicitors continued their efforts to find positive aspects of his background that might be used in mitigation but it was a thankless task because he was, Steve Law says, a 'closed book' and never shared anything personal with them.

On 1 April 1996, and again two days later, Lee and his client presented themselves at Southwark police station, where, recorded on audio, Sawoniuk was interviewed at length by officers of the WCU. They first had to advise him of the charges levelled against him, covering a series of murders committed in the Nazi-occupied territory of Belarus between 1942 and 1944.

It is difficult, if not impossible, to shock policemen, because their daily contact with some of the worst aspects of human nature inures them to even the grisliest of crimes, but Lee remembers the young policeman who had been tasked with writing out the charges, beginning to shake as the details of the 20 counts of murder were read out, one by one.

During the interviews at Southwark, Sawoniuk flatly denied the allegations. 'No one can put a finger on me that I killed a Jew,' he said. 'The people who gave you that evidence are liars. The people over there will tell you anything for a couple of bob.'

He denied he knew any of the witnesses, said he had not been in Domachevo in September 1942, having been sent to Germany as a forced labourer earlier that year, had never been a member of the *Schutzmannschaft*, and there had never been a locally recruited police force at all, only unarmed lookout men. He even claimed that there had been no ghetto in Domachevo and no restrictions had ever been imposed on the Jewish population under the German occupation.

After the initial interviews, detectives travelled to Belarus, Ukraine, Russia, Poland, Holland, Israel, South Africa, the USA and Australia, questioning over 400 potential witnesses and assembling 90,000 pages of evidence. Most witnesses were as old as Sawoniuk himself, who was 77 by the time his trial began.

Defence solicitors had also been busy with their continuing efforts to collect evidence in favour of their client, including a visit by Martin Lee to the NKVD archive in Brest, Belarus. He was expecting, and in fact hoping, to be offered no help, as a lack of co-operation would have enabled him to apply to have the proceedings thrown out as 'an abuse of process', since documents essential to Sawoniuk's defence could not be produced. However, the officer who greeted him, although a sinister-looking character of whom Lee's interpreter was patently terrified, could not have been more helpful, saying, 'You can have whatever you want.' The archives proved to contain meticulous files on numerous accusations of murder and violence against Sawoniuk, as a result of which he had been designated as 'an enemy of the state'.

Whether there was enough hard evidence to merit charging him under the War Crimes Act was still questionable, and it may have been his misfortune to have been located at a time when there was a growing political will to demonstrate Britain's willingness to act against war criminals. In addition to the new legislation and the handing over of the Soviet and Wiesenthal dossiers, the 1995 Srebrenica massacre, the UK's adoption of the Rome statute of the International Criminal Court in 1998, and Tony Blair's New Labour government, elected in 1997 and willing to embrace action – even military action – on moral grounds, had all created a climate in which such a trial was possible. Sawoniuk's defenders could argue that he simply happened to be the one caught in the crosshairs at the wrong moment.

In March 1997, Sawoniuk was formally arrested and charged by the War Crimes Unit of the Crown Prosecution Service with five counts of murder. A reporter from the *Southwark News* doorstepped him at his Bermondsey flat, but the encounter was brief. Speaking in 'an East European accent', Andrusha shouted, 'How did you find me? I have nothing to say. No! No! No!' and slammed the door in his face.

As his solicitors and the barrister given the brief, Bill Clegg, prepared Sawoniuk's defence, they found their workload much heavier than normal. 'If the crime had taken place in England,' Clegg says, 'Scotland Yard would have already carried out the investigation. They would provide you with leads and you might use a private investigator to follow up anything they hadn't done or wanted further insight into, but in this case, we effectively had to do our own investigation work, which didn't help. For example, we had to physically go and look at the scene, which actually hadn't altered much in the intervening sixty years. There were no plans or photographs you could rely on.'

As Clegg was soon to discover, the temperament of his client was another thing that could not necessarily be relied upon. The first time that he met Sawoniuk in chambers, Clegg found him to be 'belligerent about us and the charges, and he had a very short temper'. He often shouted at Clegg when they were in conference, which did not build confidence about how he would perform in the hostile atmosphere of a courtroom. Solicitor Steve Law took a slightly more charitable view of his client, describing him as 'un-coachable. He was his own man and did things the way he wished.'

The defence team was not entirely in agreement about the strategy to be pursued, but as the barrister making their arguments in court, Clegg would have the casting vote. They were agreed that Sawoniuk should be presented as a very minor player in the Nazi scheme, but his solicitors wanted to make more of his upbringing, first under a right-wing Polish government, then Communism and then Nazism. They wanted to argue that, as an isolated and impressionable youth, his understanding of social norms had been corrupted and he had effectively been brainwashed, but Clegg disagreed.

On 29 May 1998, at Bow Street Magistrates' Court, Sawoniuk was committed for trial but released on bail – unusual in a murder trial, but perhaps understandable given the circumstances. After hearing evidence from witnesses who had arrived from Belarus and Israel for the hearing, the magistrate, Graham Parkinson, allowed four of the five charges to go forward but dismissed one because the supporting witness had been unable to travel to London to testify. All the charges related to murders committed in the three-month period between the German *Aktion* that massacred the Jews of the Domachevo ghetto on 19 and 20 September 1942 and the end of that year. In total the charges covered a score of murders, but since English law requires just one alleged murder on each count, the four charges related to four individual killings: two specific Jewish men and two unidentified Jewish women.

Documentary evidence would play a negligible role. The interval of time and the destruction of records in the chaos of war and its aftermath meant that even Sawoniuk's recruitment into and service with the *Schutzmannschaft* could not be documented. The evidence of his involvement and the killings with which he was charged would rest entirely on witness testimony.

CHAPTER 13

The proceedings of what some tabloid reporters were already calling 'the trial of the century' had actually begun with the empanelling of the jury the day before the formal opening of the case. As the traditions of English law required, the Sheriff of London summoned 75 persons from the Jurors' Book to appear at the Old Bailey from Monday 8 February 1999 onwards. The Undersheriff then selected the panel of jurors at random from those names, in a process known as 'balloting', like shuffling a deck of cards and dealing out 12 of them, together with a few extra ones to act as reserves.

Had the trial been held in the United States, the prosecution and defence counsel would have subjected potential jurors to a rigorous process known as *voir dire*, attempting to identify and eliminate any who, from conscious or subconscious bias, might be prejudiced for or against the defendant, or even because the attorney had formed an instant, instinctive dislike to them. No such challenges were permissible under English law – in order to exclude a juror, *prima facie* evidence against them had to be produced and that was a vanishingly rare event – so, as one of the prosecution legal team remarked, the jury they got was 'just the luck of the draw'.

However, anxious from the start to avoid any suggestion of bias, Mr Justice Potts did tell the jurors, 'If either you or your family suffered as a result of German actions against Jewish or other races or religions, then it may be better if you served on a different jury, or if for any other reason you do not feel that you would be able to give an objective or dispassionate view of the evidence, could you please indicate this to the jury bailiff?'

No one did so.

Potential jurors were also told that they would be leaving the country to view the area where the crimes were alleged to have occurred, and asked if they:

- Have a current British passport?
- Are prepared to fly on a scheduled flight?
- Can be absent for the specified period from home?
- Are prepared to be inoculated by injection if their current vaccinations are not up to the recommended level for travel to this part of Europe?
- Have any medical or other reason that would disqualify them from travel?

Once more, none of the eight men and four women spoke up and the trial went ahead with an unaltered jury. They were required to bring their documents in to be checked the following morning and, when they did so, one passport proved to have been issued the previous day, suggesting that, after jury selection, its owner had made a frantic journey to the Passport Office to avoid missing out on the trip to Belarus. They were all left rubbing their arms after being given jabs against hepatitis, typhoid, diphtheria, tetanus and polio. There was one other potential health hazard in Domachevo, which could not be inoculated against: it was in the fallout zone from the 1986 Chernobyl nuclear disaster and the ground was still likely to be contaminated to some degree.

The next morning, Tuesday 9 February 1999, dawned dank and bitterly cold. Steve Law picked Sawoniuk up at his flat. The trees were covered in frost along Upper Thames Street and the Embankment, and flurries of snow were falling by the time the cab dropped them off outside the Central Criminal Court.

Had Law and Andrusha glanced at the newsagent's kiosk on Ludgate Circus, they would have seen the first instalment of a new monthly partwork, *Hitler's Third Reich*, on sale for £1.50. The blurb invited readers to 'witness the terrible secrets of Germany's evil empire'. Those wishing to save themselves £1.50 would only have had to walk one hundred yards to the courtroom where some of those terrible secrets were about to be revealed for free.

The Central Criminal Court was much more familiarly known as the Old Bailey, after the street in which it stood, running from Ludgate Hill up to Holborn Viaduct. There had been a court of law on the site for centuries, next to the notorious Newgate Prison, but the familiar, four-courtroom building, capped with the dome and the iconic golden female figure holding a sword and the scales of justice, had been completed in 1907, after the old jail had been demolished. South Block, the extension housing the other eight courts, was not opened until 1972.

Law tried to hurry Sawoniuk inside but, as usual, despite the cold, a crowd of spectators and demonstrators had gathered — some protesting against things unrelated to that day's proceedings — along with a phalanx of reporters, photographers and TV crews. As soon as he was spotted, a fusillade of camera flashes lit up the gloom and glinted on the road surface. Some of the crowd booed and yelled abuse, and reporters crowded around, shouting questions as Law struggled to steer his client through them unscathed. Andrusha, his face set but his eyes showing his fury, brandished his walking stick as he was hustled inside.

The grand original entrance to the Old Bailey was no longer in use and, having run the gauntlet outside, Law and Sawoniuk had to enter through the concrete portals of the new building. A battery of CCTV cameras monitored the exterior and interior, and everyone had to pass through airport-style metal detectors and then be searched by security staff. Terrorists, murderers and organised crime bosses regularly faced trial there.

Sawoniuk and Law climbed the steps to the lobby. If the inscription above the old entrance – 'Defend the Children of the Poor and Punish the Wrongdoer' – had been intended to reassure even the humblest citizen of their rights under the law, the scale and grandeur of the Grand Hall can only have intimidated them. Its dome echoed that of the nearby St Paul's Cathedral. Its lavishly decorated marble, ornate plasterwork and allegorical paintings made people crossing the vast space fall silent, hushed by the sombre atmosphere, leaving only the echo of their footsteps. A series of axioms – part exhortation, part warning – were inscribed above the archways, including, 'Right lives by law and law subsists by power' and 'London shall have its ancient rights'.

There were marble statues of English monarchs, including Queen Victoria and Charles I, but none of the defendants who had passed through the courts down the years, such as Oscar Wilde, Dr Crippen, William Joyce – who as 'Lord Haw-Haw' had broadcast Nazi propaganda into Britain during the war – Ruth Ellis (the last woman to be hanged in Britain), Jeremy Thorpe, the 'Yorkshire Ripper' Peter Sutcliffe, and Ronnie Kray, who had famously remarked to the judge, 'If I wasn't here, I could be having tea with Judy Garland.'

Court No. 1, where the Sawoniuk jury had been empanelled the previous day, and where the pre-trial formalities had been completed, was the largest of four courts in the old part of the building. It was richly decorated with ornate plasterwork, oak panelling and green leather seats embossed with the royal crest of Edward VII – the monarch at the time of its decoration – picked out in gold. A huge circular roof-light illuminated the room. Before the introduction of electricity, mirrors had been placed above the dock, reflecting natural light onto the face of the accused, as if it would reveal his guilt or innocence. Discreet fluorescent lamps had later been fitted to facilitate proceedings on even the dullest of winter days.

Although Court 1 had been used the previous day, the trial itself would be taking place in Court 12, on the third floor of the new building. If Sawoniuk had glanced up at the wall as Law was escorting him along the corridor connecting the Grand Hall to the new building, he might have caught sight of a shard of glass embedded in the plaster high above him – a memento of a 1970s IRA bomb detonated in the street outside. The blast had blown in the windows, mercifully not killing anyone, but maiming and injuring many with flying glass. When the damage was repaired, that fragment had been left as a permanent reminder.

The new building was much less lavishly decorated than the old part and, like the others there, Court 12 was panelled in plain oak, with a green wool carpet and modern, green-upholstered chairs, and was artificially lit. From his vantage point, the judge looked out over 'counsel's row' – the benches where the lawyers all sat at right angles to him, with the prosecution closer to him and the defence further away, beside the dock, which was glazed to above head height. The white-tiled walls of the narrow staircase, which led down from the dock to the labyrinth of cells in the bowels of the building, could just be glimpsed.

The barristers and solicitors sat facing the jury, on green, tip-up leather seats, and had only a narrow wooden shelf in front of them to hold their papers. The jury box – two rows of six seats – was against the right-hand wall from the judge's viewpoint, with the press benches beyond it, and the dock was on his left, positioned so the accused would face the judge and his accusers in the witness box. The dock was encased in toughened glass, both as protection for those on trial and those sitting in judgement from attack by the defendants. A row of benches at the back of the courtroom was reserved for privileged spectators, distinct from the public gallery, which held 30 people. Reached by a separate entrance and staircase, it was effectively on the floor above the court, looking down into the room.

The queue for seats for high-profile cases like this one often began forming in the small hours, and for notorious trials like that of society osteopath Stephen Ward in 1963, at which Christine Keeler and Mandy Rice-Davies were the star attractions, the queue had started the previous afternoon, with people sleeping on the pavement all night to be sure of a seat. For Sawoniuk's trial, the first spectator, a grey-haired man, had arrived at four in the morning. He declined to give his reasons for being there to an inquisitive reporter.

As was his custom on the first morning of a trial, the defence counsel, Bill Clegg QC, had arrived early, making use of what was known as the 'Lord Mayor's Entrance' in Warwick Square to avoid the waiting crowds at the front. He had plenty of time for breakfast, a cup of coffee and a glance at a newspaper in the 'Bar Mess' – the barristers' private cafeteria officially known as the 'Advocates' Dining Rooms' – on the fifth floor. Prosecution counsel, Johnny Nutting QC, arrived a little later, and, just after ten o'clock, they both went down to the fourth floor Advocates' Robing Room to change out of their street clothes and don their wigs and gowns, before taking their places in court.

Counsel and court reporters, who all knew each other of old, exchanged greetings and caught up on the gossip. Clerks from the barristers' chambers hurried in, pushing metal trolleys laden with court papers – at least a dozen bulky lever arch files, bulging with documents. Priscilla Coleman, a Texan regarded as the doyenne of court artists, was also there early, making preliminary notes for sketches of the defendant and any unfamiliar leading figures. Photography was prohibited in the courtroom, as was drawing. Instead, she had to hurry out to the press room while the impressions were still fresh in her mind. Even then, she might be subject to further constraints to protect the identity and security of a witness, instructed, perhaps, only to show someone in three-quarter profile, or to draw them from behind. She often had to work at a frantic pace but, on this morning, she had been able to make reasonably leisurely notes about Andrusha's appearance, because he had already taken his seat well before the judge made his entrance.

The 77-year-old Sawoniuk wore a blazer, neatly pressed trousers and shiny shoes. His white hair had been recently trimmed, and his spectacles, through which his watery, blue-grey eyes peered myopically, looked new. He still had a strong Eastern European accent, with a few Cockney phrases he must have picked up working on the railways thrown in for good measure.

He was deaf in one ear, nearly blind in one eye, suffered from diabetes, heart disease and high blood pressure, and walked with a limp. Despite that catalogue of ailments, he was square-jawed and solidly built, and seemed a more physically robust character than his medical history suggested. His walking stick also looked more of a theatrical prop than an actual necessity, for he had been seen striding out and even breaking into a run, brandishing it like a club rather than a means of support.

After photographing him arriving at court a few times, *Sun* photographer Ray Collins formed the strong impression that Sawoniuk was exaggerating his disability to win the sympathy of the jury. So he called the picture desk and suggested they should send another photographer to catch him leaving his home. A freelancer, Darren Fletcher, was duly despatched. On his arrival outside Sawoniuk's flat, he found a TV crew already in place. When Andrusha spotted them, he made off in the opposite direction at first, but then reappeared. 'He threw a few things at us,' Fletcher said, 'then came down a ramp and suddenly came lumbering towards us, swinging his walking stick over his head. He clearly wasn't as incapacitated as he pretended.'

However, as a concession to a defendant of his age and infirmity, Sawoniuk was excused from being in the dock and instead was allowed to sit alongside his solicitor on the back row in the well of the court. Steve Law remained next to him throughout the day, making sure his client understood everything being said, though Sawoniuk's deafness meant that he followed most of the proceedings from the transcript on the LiveNote autocue in front of him. In a trial that was already breaking new ground in several ways, this was another: the first time that a simultaneous transcript of court proceedings had ever been displayed.

Andrusha stared straight ahead most of the time, rarely shifting his gaze towards the jury box or press benches, or the public gallery away to his right. When he did catch sight of a row of Orthodox Jews there, he said to Law, 'Look at all those Jew boys.' Intended as an aside, his partial deafness made him speak loudly enough to be clearly audible to others sitting nearby.

Law flinched. 'You shouldn't say that.'

Sawoniuk shrugged. 'Why not? They call me Nazi boy.'

CHAPTER 14

A hush fell on Court 12 as three loud raps on the oak door at the rear corner of the judge's bench announced the imminent appearance of His Honour, Mr Justice Potts. As the Clerk of the Court intoned, 'Be upstanding in court,' everyone rose, accompanied by the sound of creaking chairs and shuffling feet, while the Clerk continued the time-honoured command. 'All persons who have anything to do before my Lords, the Queen's Justices at the Central Criminal Court, draw near and give your attendance. God Save the Queen.'

After a pause just long enough to raise the tension another notch, a door at the back of the court opened and Sir Francis Humphrey Potts, bewigged and resplendent in the scarlet robes of a High Court 'red judge', swept in and took his seat. 'Case Number T980662 in the Central Criminal Court, in the matter of Regina v Anthony Sawoniuk' was now under way.

Mr Justice Potts, balding and bespectacled, with a complexion that suggested he was no stranger to a good dinner washed down with a fine claret, was a farmer's son from Penshaw, near Sunderland in the north-east of England, and his origins were occasionally audible in the faintest trace of a Wearside accent, especially when under stress.

He was approaching retirement age, and knew that this would be one of the last major trials over which he would

preside. He had a reputation for being a courtroom marti-
net – known behind his back as 'Porridge Potts', because
of the stiff sentences he imposed – but he was determined
that these proceedings would be scrupulously fair, giving no
grounds for a mistrial or an appeal.

As a result, he extended every courtesy to the defendant
and the witnesses, and the exchanges between him and the
two leading counsel were models of restraint and old-world
politeness, bordering at times on self-parody. 'He was
extremely accommodating,' Bill Clegg says, 'and didn't refuse
anything he was asked for. He was very anxious to demonstrate that the court would be as sympathetic as possible to
the ages of all the participants in the case.'

Johnny Nutting agrees. Potts 'was such a safe pair of hands
and played the case as straight as possible, to reduce tensions
and so there could be no criticism'.

Well before the trial, Clegg had made an attempt to stay
the proceedings as an abuse of process, because, he con-
tended, the crimes with which his client was charged had
taken place so long ago that it would be impossible for him
to receive a fair trial by the standards of English justice. He
would be unable to find documents or witnesses who could
have exculpated him, since they had either died or were no
longer traceable after so many years.

Potts rejected those arguments. Whether the lack of
witnesses and documents was more detrimental to the
defence than the prosecution was entirely speculative, and
the reliability of the prosecution witnesses would be tested
by rigorous cross-examination. He agreed that the trial of
war criminals would inevitably pose special difficulties, but
English law – the War Crimes Act 1991 – required him to
conduct it.

In pre-trial hearings, Clegg had also objected to 'allegations of crimes committed by the defendant but uncharged',

being put before the jury. That submission was also rejected, allowing the Crown to call numerous witnesses to testify to Andrusha's alleged cruelty and brutality in a series of incidents that were not the subject of charges. The Crown also had statements by another eight witnesses whose testimony was not considered essential, or who were too ill or infirm to testify, or had died between the launch of the investigation and the proceedings. Had they been included, the jurors would have heard even more allegations of his violence, including an attack in which a woman was repeatedly kicked while lying on the ground.

Once the judge had taken his seat, the jury entered. They had all sworn an oath or made an affirmation to 'return a true verdict according to the evidence', and they were now ready to play their part in one of the most extraordinary dramas that even the Old Bailey had witnessed. Since the dock stood empty, they may not have realised at first that the defendant they were there to try was already in the courtroom.

The Clerk of the Court first read out the four specimen charges of murder, beginning with Count 1. 'Statement of offence: murder, contrary to Common Law. Particulars of offence: on a day between 19 September 1942 and 27 September 1942, Anthony Sawoniuk, a person resident in the United Kingdom on 8 March 1990, in Domachevo, Belarus, a town under German occupation, murdered a Jewess in circumstances constituting a violation of the laws and customs of war.' That charge was entirely dependent on the testimony of Alexandre Baglay, from the hamlet of Borisy on the outskirts of Domachevo.

Count 2 related to the murder of a Domachevo Jew called Shlemko, between 19 September and 4 October 1942, and relied on the testimony of Ivan Stepaniuk, another resident of Borisy.

Count 3 concerned the murder of another unknown Jewish

woman, between 19 September and 4 October 1942, the killing witnessed by Fedor Zan, another Borisy resident.

Count 4 related to the murder of a Jewish man, Mir Barlas, between 4 September and 31 December 1942. The sole witness to this was Ben-Zion Blustein, who had lived in Israel since the war and was the only one of the four key witnesses not to come from Borisy.

A formal plea of not guilty to all four counts had been entered at the committal hearing the previous year and, after the charges had been read, the prosecution counsel, Johnny Nutting, rose to begin presenting the case for the Crown. A tall, Old Etonian, with a manor house in Wiltshire and a 20,000-acre Scottish estate, as well as his flat in Albany, just off London's Piccadilly, he numbered the Queen among his clients and, according to Bill Clegg, had a black-tie dinner with his wife every Friday night. He had actually succeeded to the Baronetcy of St Helens in Booterstown in the County of Dublin during the proceedings, entitling him to be addressed as 'Sir', but Sir Humphrey asked him to defer using the honorific until after the trial was over. 'Let's not confuse the jury,' he said. 'We can't have two Sirs.'

A patrician, establishment figure like Nutting might almost have been hand-picked to raise Sawoniuk's hackles, but as the only barrister to have previously prepared a prosecution under the War Crimes Act, he was the obvious choice. That case was against 86-year-old Szymon Serafinowicz on a charge of murdering three Jews while he was also a *Schutzmannschaft* commander in Mir, Belarus, in 1941–42. Astonishingly, once more, his name had been misspelled in Scotland Yard's records, and even though Serafinowicz was listed in the phone book and had lived at the same address in Banstead, Surrey, since 1956, it took detectives 18 months to identify and locate him. By then he was suffering from dementia and died in August 1997, six months after a jury ruled that he was not fit to stand trial. Of the 97 names handed to the British authorities by the Russians, Sawoniuk was the only other to face prosecution.

Bill Clegg was an old foe of Nutting, and although his origins were far less gilded – he was a grocer's son and a grammar school boy – away from court where they were invariably on opposing sides, the two were good friends. Clegg was similarly well qualified to represent Andrusha, since he had acted for Serafinowicz in that first case. Explaining how he came to defend such apparently unsavoury clients, he talks about the 'cab rank rule. If you're offered a trial and you're available and it's your specialisation, you have to accept it. This ensures that no matter how horrific the crime, there will be a barrister. But it's a curious thing defending people for murder. You have to divorce yourself from your emotions.'

In an English court, barristers are required to remain standing behind the rostrum and not prowl the courtroom, gesticulating like attorneys in American crime dramas, and while making his opening statement, Johnny Nutting stood rigidly to attention, like an officer reviewing a march-past. He began by referring to the four separate counts of murder listed in the indictment. 'On each occasion, say the Crown, this defendant executed Jewish men and women, whose only offence was to be Jewish and who had escaped the main massacre of several thousand Jews when the ghetto in Domachevo was liquidated. The evidence indicates, in our submission, that the defendant was not only prepared to do the Nazi bidding, but carried out their genocidal policy with enthusiasm.'

The Crown planned to call a succession of witnesses, but only two of them could claim to have actually seen Sawoniuk committing the murders with which he had been charged. Others would say that they had seen him maltreating Jews, or watched him force-marching Jews towards the killing ground, heard shots and then seen Sawoniuk returning alone, or been told by him that he had killed a Jew, but whether a jury would regard any of that as evidence of murder beyond a reasonable doubt was open to question.

It was not unprecedented for a defendant in an English court to be facing charges of murder of persons unknown, but it was certainly very unusual, and Nutting acknowledged that while two of the counts of murder were of unnamed individuals, 'In the policy of genocide pursued by the Nazis, the names of individuals were of no account. It was identity as a Jew which sealed the fate of thousands, millions of men, women and children.'

Sawoniuk was on trial for his own crimes, not those of the Nazis perpetrating the 'Final Solution', but the wider context of the murders: the Holocaust – or the *Shoah* (catastrophe) as it is called in Hebrew – was already being evoked by the prosecution, leading the defence solicitors to fear guilt by association for their client.

Nutting also found a way to draw the jurors' attention both to the fact that Sawoniuk had been an enthusiastic volunteer for the *Schutzmannschaft* and that he had denied it when first interviewed by Scotland Yard, saying, 'The defendant does not now – I underline the word "now" – dispute that he served as a policeman in Domachevo.'

He went on to detail a string of lies that Sawoniuk had told detectives when they were first questioning him, in interviews that had been filmed and recorded. 'Members of the jury, what he told the police must have been deliberate lies. Why he told lies will be a matter that you may have to consider as part of your judgement in this case.'

Nutting admitted that his case would rest on eyewitness testimony over half a century after the event, and said that, in an ordinary criminal trial, it would be perfectly possible for witnesses' recall of events to be faulty after such an interval of time. However, he insisted that in this case, the witnesses' memories could be trusted because, 'They describe events which are literally unforgettable; incidents which, once witnessed, would remain fixed in a man's memory for the rest of his life.'

Andrusha sat motionless and silent, other than an occasional muttered aside to his solicitor, throughout Nutting's lengthy opening statement. Although he was charged with murder, he was not seen as a flight risk, and therefore remained on bail rather than on remand. At the end of that first day and of each subsequent one, with his walking stick held off the ground, he gave a short bow to the judge, and his junior solicitor, Steve Law, then escorted him out of the court. There was a short debrief with his counsel and solicitors after the court rose, a pattern that was repeated on each subsequent day, but 'it was not necessarily particularly forensic,' Clegg says. 'We'd just meet and review events at the end of the day, give a resumé of anything that had been good, bad or indifferent, and discuss our approach to the witnesses who would be on the stand the following day.'

After that, Law walked with Andrusha to a waiting taxi and took him back to his flat. As Clegg remarks with a grin, 'The solicitor arranged a minicab to take him to and from court every day. It was a useful precaution to make sure he got there without hitting anybody first!'

When Andrusha had first moved into the estate in Bermondsey, it was a fairly quiet area and his neighbours were mainly lower-working-class families and long-term residents. Over the years it became progressively more run-down and increasingly populated by low income or unemployed single parents, transients and troubled families.

Law had no sympathy whatsoever for Sawoniuk's anti-Semitism, but he couldn't help feeling a little sorry for him when he dropped him off at his flat, because the publicity surrounding the trial meant that from the first night onwards, a crowd of yobs in what had become a very rough area of London was always gathered outside the building, waiting to yell abuse and insults at him.

CHAPTER 15

The morning of the second day of the trial was again bitterly cold, with fog shrouding the Old Bailey and the gilded figure of justice on top of the dome only occasionally visible through the mist. Unsurprisingly, the opening of the trial had been given saturation coverage in the British media and the proceedings resumed with the jury excluded while judge and counsel discussed a report in the *Evening Standard* and an item on the BBC TV *News at Six* that included footage of Fedor Zan walking through the forest outside Domachevo and demonstrating where he said he had seen Sawoniuk carry out the murder that formed Count 3 of the indictment. The judge wanted time to reflect on whether this amounted to a contempt of court, but he was clearly seething, and when a BBC lawyer presented himself, Potts told him that 'on the face of it, that seems to be an intolerable interference in the processes of this trial . . . the British Broadcasting Corporation had better watch their step.'

When the jury was readmitted to the courtroom, he acknowledged the level of media interest in the case and told the jurors, 'It would be foolish for anyone to assume that you do not watch television or read the papers. All I want to say is that you have taken, each of you, an oath to try the case on the evidence, and therefore please concentrate on the evidence you hear in court.'

Johnny Nutting then spent the remaining part of the day giving the jurors an exhaustive and – from the glazed expressions on one or two of their faces as the afternoon wore on – exhausting commentary on numerous large-scale maps and aerial and other photographs of Domachevo and the surrounding area.

Day 3 of the trial, Thursday 11 February, was the sort of dull and wet winter day that barely seems to get light at all, before darkening towards dusk again. Rain showers were stippling the grey waters of the Thames as the taxi carrying Sawoniuk and Law inched its way through heavy traffic over London Bridge, then followed the north bank of the river towards the Old Bailey.

In Court 12, Johnny Nutting resumed from where he had left off the previous day, completing his painstaking explanations of the maps and photographs that the jurors were poring over, before calling his first witness, Christopher Browning. A professor of history at a university in Washington State, he was an acknowledged world authority on the Holocaust, having written four books and 60 academic papers and articles on the subject, and had previously been called as an expert witness at war crimes trials in Canada and Australia, as well as Britain. Browning's brief was not to speak to the charges against Sawoniuk, but to explain the historical background of the Nazi regime, the beliefs that had led to the 'Final Solution' and the role of the police in implementing it in the occupied territories of Eastern Europe.

Nutting's strategy in this was obvious. He wanted the jury to see the 'Final Solution' propounded by Hitler and the other Nazi leaders, the massacres committed in the occupied territories, the killings in Belarus and the particular murders alleged to have been committed by Sawoniuk in Domachevo as all part of the same pattern. Nazis committed murders,

Sawoniuk was a Nazi – therefore Sawoniuk committed murders, QED.

Browning was a well-upholstered figure with a high forehead, gold wire-rimmed glasses and a habit of speaking out of the side of his mouth, as if everything he said was in confidence. Having outlined the evolution of Nazi policy towards the 'Jewish problem', and Hitler's belief in the need for *Lebensraum* (living space) in the East for the population of an expanding German Empire, Browning turned to the invasion of the Soviet Union. Hitler had made it clear to his generals, he said, that it would not be a conventional war like the invasion of France, but 'a war of destruction' involving not only territorial conquest, but a crusade against Communism and a racial war against the Jews. Captured Communist functionaries were to be executed on the spot. German soldiers were required to 'act ruthlessly' against agitators, partisans, Bolsheviks and Jews, and were exempt from court-martial for any actions they took against civilians. They were also authorised to carry out 'collective reprisals': the destruction of villages near the site of any attacks on German troops. The effect, Browning said, was to give German forces and their collaborators blanket immunity from the consequences of any actions against civilians, however extreme. The only sanction they would face would be for failing to be ruthless enough.

Nutting then led Browning on to the role of the auxiliary police in Domachevo. Joining the *Schutzmannschaft* was voluntary, Browning said, and the incentives were: 'first of all, pay; secondly, rations for both the policeman and his family; thirdly, exemption from forced labour in Germany'. Their duties included ordinary police work, military activities like guarding valuable sites, patrolling and fighting partisans, and the 'enforcement of Nazi occupation policy'. He identified three crucial areas of that: 'First would be the requisition of food. All peasants growing food had to make deliveries to the German occupiers. This would be enforced by the native police. The second would be the requisition of forced labour in Germany . . . The third area of what I would call enforcement would be the killing of Jews.'

Browning said that orders allowed German soldiers and Order Police to delegate *Schmutzarbeit* (dirty work) to the local police. That order was left to German officers on the ground to interpret, but in at least one case it led to Germans shooting adult Jews, but requiring the local police to shoot children.

Nutting then pressed him on whether it was possible for local police to resign, and Browning cited a report from the police commissioner for the region that included Domachevo, saying that he had granted the request of 'various police to resign or withdraw because of health or family reasons'.

His testimony was briefly interrupted so that Fedor Zan could be sworn in as a witness. When the court adjourned to Domachevo the following week, he would be showing the jurors where he had allegedly seen Sawoniuk commit the murder detailed in Count 3. On this occasion his long trip to London was required for no more than a two-minute appearance. He swore the oath on a Russian Orthodox Bible, speaking in 'a mixture of Ukrainian and Belarusian' with an interpreter alongside him. After being reminded by the judge that he would still be under oath when the court reconvened in Domachevo the following Tuesday, Zan withdrew, possibly to take advantage of the hot water in his hotel for a lengthy bath.

When Browning resumed his testimony, he detailed how, from the start of August 1941, the Nazi policy of eliminating the adult male leadership of Jewish communities had been expanded to include women and children. The ghettos had been created to keep the Jews incarcerated until their mass extermination could be achieved, and apart from the Jewish craftsmen whose skills the Germans needed, those still alive at the end of 1941 owed their survival to a winter so severe, even by Belarusian standards, that it was impossible to dig large burial pits, and the fact that the sheer numbers of Jews in the occupied territories made it impossible to shoot them all that quickly.

The massacres resumed as winter gave way to spring, and in September 1942, Domachevo's ghetto was liquidated. What the Nazis termed 'the Jew hunt' for those who had avoided the mass slaughter then began, in which the *Schutzmannschaft* played the major part. 'They, of course, know the local terrain,' Browning said. 'They are the ones who are familiar with where people would hide.'

Johnny Nutting had hoped to complete Professor Browning's testimony that day, but on behalf of his client, who 'felt rather ill when we rose' the previous day and 'gets more exhausted toward the end of the week', Bill Clegg was successful in his request to the judge to end proceedings for the day at 3.15pm.

Professor Browning wrapped up his testimony by 11am the next morning, Day 4 of the trial, having taken the jurors up to the point where the Red Army liberated Domachevo in the summer of 1944 and the German occupation came to an end. He had been in the witness box for more than four hours over the two days.

One long-serving legal correspondent said that he had never known the prosecution go to such lengths to ensure the jury understood the background to a case. Johnny Nutting says he felt that context was necessary because 'none of the jurors had been born when these crimes took place, but I deliberately restricted Chris Browning to a very few documents because I wanted the jury to be listening to a history lesson, not have their noses buried in lots of pieces of paper, and I wanted him to be short and absolutely compelling'.

Steve Law still questions the relevance of Browning's testimony about the Nazis' grand schemes to the trial of a lowly individual, and believes it created a very unfavourable context for Sawoniuk's defence. 'If a Yardie was put on trial in the UK,' Law says, 'they would not bring in an expert to give evidence about Yardie culture in Jamaica.' Like the visit to the massacre site in Domachevo, he feared that Browning's testimony about the Holocaust would inevitably colour the jurors' views during the remainder of the trial.

When Bill Clegg rose to cross-examine Browning, he did not make the mistake of directly challenging the testimony of such a renowned authority on the Holocaust. 'We weren't Holocaust deniers; we weren't saying it hadn't happened,' Clegg says. Instead, he began by getting Browning to agree that Belarus had been a desperately impoverished region, with its subsistence farmers 'ranked as amongst the poorest people in Europe'. He then turned to the Soviet invasion in 1939, seeking Browning's agreement that there had been widespread executions and deportations into what Clegg described as 'slavery' in Siberia.

An academic historian to his fingertips, Browning took issue with that loose terminology. 'If we mean slavery in the sense of people who can be bought and sold – the American slave system – no. If we mean slavery in terms of uncompensated labour under forced conditions, yes.'

It might have appeared to the jurors that Clegg was trying to minimise Nazi atrocities by showing that the Soviets had been equally culpable, but it soon became apparent that his intention was different, to build a picture of Sawoniuk as a helpless pawn, an uneducated, unqualified, unemployed nonentity in a town where, whichever authoritarian regime happened to be in control, his actions were circumscribed, his options almost non-existent and the penalty for defiance was exile, forced labour or death. As Mr Justice Potts noted to himself – one of many pencilled annotations he made as he reviewed his copies of the transcripts every evening of the trial – 'Clegg making case for hardship – extenuation in AS's case.'

Clegg then briefly turned to the documents available to historians like Browning, emphasising the large gaps in the historical record caused by wartime destruction and further exacerbated by the passage of time, before returning to his main theme: the miserable lot of the Belarusian peasant farmers. He led Browning through their plight after the German invasion, caught between partisans hiding in the forest and demanding food from them, and the Germans collecting a tithe of their farm produce and ruthlessly punishing any collaboration with the partisans.

Clegg was then at pains to establish that the actions of the local police force were crucial in safeguarding food supplies, protecting outlying farms from attacks and guarding economic resources. In emphasising the defensive roles of the *Schutzmannschaft,* he was attempting to minimise the sense of their involvement in killings, of course, but Browning was not so easily led. He agreed that they were offering some protection to the local population against the partisans, but added that when 'the calculation and expectation was that the Germans were going to win the war, they were, in effect, placing their bets on that side'. That changed, and they then had to contemplate ways to survive under a Soviet occupation. 'Those calculations of what was in their own interest were both immediate and economic,' Browning said, 'but also related to a long-term political guess as to where they would end up.'

'You really attribute that degree of political sophistication to—' Clegg began, not trying to hide his amused disbelief, but he was at once interrupted by a withering put-down from Browning.

'I do not think calculating "Are the Germans or Russians going to win?" is a sophisticated calculation.'

Clegg next asked Browning to comment on a diagram showing the considerable number of links in the Nazi chain of command from Hitler at the top, through Himmler, Heydrich and the regional and district SS commanders, all the way down to the Order Police in Domachevo and, at the lowest level, the locally recruited *Schutzmannschaft*. Once more he was attempting to emphasise the lowly position of Sawoniuk, and once more Browning was less pliant than Clegg might have hoped.

'So the *Schutzmannschaft* are the bottom of the chain of command?' Clegg said. 'Their members would not be decision-makers?'

'Not decision-makers in terms of policy. At the very lowest level they would still have to make decisions in terms of how general policy would be implemented. Because, of course, there is so little supervision, clearly they had to have some discretion and room for making decisions if they were to operate.'

'Well, they would always, would they not, be under German command?'

'No. I believe that quite often they would go on patrols or search through the ghetto after the liquidation. It is not at all necessary that they would be under German command.'

The exchanges between the two men were becoming increasingly testy and, after drawing something of a blank there, Clegg next turned to the equipment used by the auxiliaries. Browning agreed that they were badly clothed and equipped and in many cases were dressed in rags, and with inadequate footwear.

'Their feet were tied up with string and rags,' Clegg said. 'This is the great police force we are talking about, is it not?'

'I do not know who has called them a great police force,'

Browning said. 'They had inadequate footwear, yes.' He agreed that the auxiliaries were armed with 'surplus captured weapons rather than top-of-the-line German weapons, which were kept for the German Army', but when Clegg turned to rations, and said, 'Is it not right that many policemen had to be discharged because there was insufficient food to feed them?' Browning disagreed. 'No. I do not know of the discharge of policemen for that reason.'

However, this time Clegg had a document to back him up and triumphantly quoted from a report by the police chief in Brest-Litovsk who complained that he had 'selected 60 men for auxiliary police duties and fully 32 of them had to be dismissed because of completely inadequate provisioning with food'.

Browning accepted that but once more modified Clegg's broad-brush assertion that the auxiliaries 'are not being paid. They are not being fed. They are not being clothed. They are not being armed.'

There was no evidence to show whether they were paid or not, Browning said, and while not every auxiliary in Domachevo had a weapon, they did have 40 rifles between them.

Clegg's last point of attack was whether Sawoniuk's recruitment into the *Schutzmannschaft* had been voluntary or coerced. He tried to establish that local mayors were under pressure to find enough recruits for the auxiliaries and that failure to do so would have had unpleasant and possibly fatal consequences. Once more Browning refused to be drawn into speculation about things for which there were no reliable sources.

'Now, if the local mayor had not been able to provide anyone to serve in the local police force, that would have made him very unpopular with the new German administration, would it not?' Clegg said.

'You are asking me to speculate. I do not know what the repercussions would have been.'

'No, but using all your experience of the way that the occupying Nazi war machine operated, if . . . the Gestapo come round and say, "Where is your police force?" and your response is, "Oh, we could not find one," things would not be looking very bright for that mayor, would they?'

'If he were anxious to ingratiate himself with Germans, that would not have been very successful.'

'If he was anxious to live, it would probably not be a very good approach, would it?'

'I do not know that that would have resulted in execution, particularly if the order from the Germans was to find reliable men and he said he couldn't find reliable men.'

By now, Clegg's normally jocular, clubbable courtroom manner was under some strain. 'Well, it may be that the perception at the time of the mayors who received that order was less generous than yours?'

'Well, you are asking me to speculate on things for which I have no documents.'

Clegg then tried to suggest that young men had had no option but to join the *Schutzmannschaft*. 'Did you ever watch a film called *The Godfather*?' he said. 'Do you remember a phrase in it, I think uttered by Marlon Brando, when he said he was going to make someone an offer that they cannot refuse?'

'Yes.'

'Well, there were a lot of offers that could not, I suggest, be refused in rural Belarus following the German invasion.'

'That is possible,' Browning said.

Perhaps emboldened by that rare agreement, Clegg once more overplayed his hand. 'If an orphaned teenager were asked to join the local police,' he said, 'you may describe him as a volunteer, but can we just think what other alternative employment the teenager might have open for him as a career under the German occupation, if he has no farm, or family of his own. He would almost inevitably, would he not, be one of those sent into slavery in Germany?'

Browning disagreed. The policy of sending unemployed young men for forced labour was not implemented until 1942, and Sawoniuk had joined the *Schutzmannschaft* within days of the German invasion in June 1941.

'You keep using the word "volunteer",' Clegg said. 'It is a choice between slavery or parading in rags, without arms and no boots, trying to guard the local population against the partisans, among other things. That is the sort of options these people had, was it not?'

Browning agreed that there were no easy choices in Nazi-occupied Belarus, but insisted there were other options for a young man like Sawoniuk.

Clegg's attempts to get him to agree that the duties of the auxiliaries would not necessarily have been explained to recruits when they joined were similarly unsuccessful. 'If you were joining the police, it was clear, as you would say, that one of your tasks would be to enforce the policies of the occupier,' Browning said, 'and from very early in July, in at least Brest, people were being killed by the thousands. That is the closest major city to Domachevo. So the capacity of the new occupation regime to carry out mass murder was clear from a very early point.'

Clegg would have wished for a different message to have been left in the jurors' minds as Mr Justice Potts adjourned for lunch.

The sparring between Clegg and Browning continued when the court resumed after lunch. Clegg stated that there was no evidence that any of the Domachevo auxiliaries had received any training, but Browning offered the correction that nor was there any evidence that they had not.

Clegg then argued that their old rifles and small amount

of ammunition would have been 'wholly insufficient to play a significant role in the killing of so many people'.

Browning retorted that auxiliaries were given extra ammunition before *Aktionen* against the Jews, and 'one thing one can do with old rifles is to shoot unarmed people at point-blank range. That is certainly a more effective use of that kind of weapon than fighting armed partisans.'

After a few more questions, Clegg decided to stop digging on that point. 'You cannot exclude the possibility that the *Schutzmannschaft* might have done something. If we leave it like that, Professor, I am perfectly content.'

Mr Justice Potts, growing restless at Clegg's line of questioning, then intervened. 'I know it is terribly difficult, Mr Clegg, [but] we have to keep our eye on the evidence given.' He pointed out that Browning had testified, based on evidence he had found, that *Schutzmänner* participated in the *Aktion* in Domachevo on 19 and 20 September 1942. 'Is it really profitable to go further and speculate what might or might not have happened with this witness?'

'I do not think the witness is confining himself to the record,' Clegg said. 'That is the trouble.'

However, the judge's intervention did succeed in lowering the temperature of the exchanges, as Clegg then moved on to the period after the Red Army's arrival in Belarus and the fate of those who had been policemen under the Germans. Browning agreed that, if caught, they were liable to execution or to lengthy terms in Soviet labour camps.

'Somebody . . . may well have a very strong motive in denying the fact that he was a policeman, would you not agree?' Clegg said.

'Someone within the Soviet sphere would have had, yes, a considerable motive to not reveal his past,' Browning said.

'Or anyone who was fearful of being sent back to somewhere within the Soviet sphere?'

'Yes.'

'I have no further questions,' Clegg said, but Browning's time on the stand was not yet over, for Johnny Nutting now exercised his right to re-examination, wanting the jury to be aware that nothing Browning had said 'relied on any of the eyewitness testimony that has been collected by the police in this case. Can we take it therefore that your evidence is based solely on the historical documentation?'

Browning agreed and Nutting then asked him to explain the nature of primary and secondary documents. 'Primary documentation are the documents written by the German authorities at the time,' Browning said. 'For a secondary source, you are trusting the ability and competence of the historian to have relayed the record properly. The primary documents, the historian is reading the raw material for himself or herself, and it is the primary documentation that I have used for my preparation for the trial.'

Nutting then went on to rebut several points that Clegg had been at pains to try to establish during his cross-examination. Browning said that poor workers and peasants were unlikely to have been deported to Siberia during the Soviet occupation, and that forced labour under the Nazis did not begin until the early summer of 1942, nor conscription into the auxiliary police until 1943. He also referred to a document and a photograph demonstrating that in June 1942, although there was still a shortage of shoes, *Schutzmänner* were not 'in rags and tatters', as Clegg had alleged, but had new uniforms and good food provisions.

After reminding the jurors of the need to 'avoid even accidental exchanges about the case' while they were in Domachevo the following week, Mr Justice Potts then adjourned the trial for ten days, until Tuesday 23 February. The court would reconvene in Belarus the following week to allow the jurors to visit the crime scenes, and it would not sit on the following Monday as a concession to the key prosecution witness, Ben-Zion Blustein. He was flying in to London from Israel on the Sunday – El Al never flew on Saturdays because it was *Shabbat* – and he would need, Nutting said, a day to recover from his journey before giving his evidence.

CHAPTER 16

The jurors, lawyers and court officials all flew out of Heathrow on the Sunday afternoon. Among the media party accompanying them was *Sun* journalist Ian Hepburn. In his 34 years as a crime reporter, he had covered a succession of major stories including the Birmingham Bombings, the Yorkshire Ripper, the murder of TV presenter Jill Dando and the disappearance of Madeleine McCann, but looking back now, the most memorable of all, he says, was undoubtedly the Sawoniuk murder trial and the visit to Belarus.

He almost didn't make the trip. After attending the judge's media briefing in the canteen of the Old Bailey, he rang his Head of News, who was unimpressed that the trip was going to take a week, and was only likely to produce a single colour piece. 'I'm always being accused of being indecisive,' he said. 'So I'm going to make a decision here and now. You're not going. Come back to the office.'

Hepburn's immediate thought was, What a waste, but on second thoughts, decided it wouldn't be too harsh a sacrifice. It was likely to be 20 degrees below freezing, everyone going to Belarus had to have multiple vaccinations and there was also the unsettling knowledge that when Chernobyl, 300 miles away, exploded in 1986, the prevailing wind had blown the radiation cloud right over Domachevo.

However, when he walked through the door of the

newsroom in Wapping, East London, he was greeted with the words: 'I've changed my mind. You're going.' After a hasty trip to the British Airways medical centre for an armful of jabs, with a wallet full of zlotys, roubles and dollars in his pocket, and an overnight bag bulging with thermal underwear over his shoulder, Hepburn joined the flight from Heathrow to Warsaw.

When the pressmen boarded, they found that the jury of eight men and four women were already in their seats at the rear of the aircraft, cordoned off from everybody else and guarded by eight court ushers and protection officers wearing yellow hi-vis waistcoats. 'We had been told in advance that the jurors' integrity was paramount,' Hepburn says, 'and we were to keep our distance, not speak to them and not take any pictures from which they could be identified.'

After landing in Warsaw, a convoy of three coaches took them to a hotel in the centre of the city, where most of the media broke away to find a bar before finishing the night in a candlelit restaurant in the catacombs of the old town. One notoriously short-fused journalist was with them. 'Charming and a good friend when sober,' Hepburn says, 'but in drink he could be a bloody nightmare.' As the night wore on, he got progressively more drunk and 'began slagging off everyone. He then leapt up, threw a wad of zlotys on the table to cover his share of the bill, and stormed out. Unfortunately, he hadn't got his head round the Polish currency, and left enough cash to pay for everyone's meal. I think that's called karma.'

With the jury and their minders in the lead coach, the judge and legal teams in the second and the media bringing up the rear, they set off for the Belarusian border the next day, and spent the night in Brest-Litovsk enjoying the dubious pleasures of the Intourist Hotel, before travelling on to Domachevo the next morning, Tuesday 16 February 1999.

Driving through a blizzard, with police escort vehicles leading the way and local police in fur hats at each crossroads holding back traffic, the convoy eventually ground to a halt in the heart of the town. The coaches disgorged their passengers, escorted by more heavily armed police in camouflage fatigues, while old men and women muffled against the cold watched in bewildered silence as the jurors inspected the locations where the crimes detailed in the four indictments had taken place.

Concerned about losing the light before the tour had been completed, the judge urged them to eat their lunch on the bus taking them between locations, and to take as short a break as possible before moving on. When they entered the forest, they had to walk in single file because of the thick-lying snow. At the back of the long, straggling procession, a photographer began whistling the theme tune to *The Great Escape*, and others joined in. It was out of earshot of the judge and jury, but not of the communications officer from the Lord Chancellor's Office. With a face like thunder, he ran back through the snow and shouted, 'For God's sake, show some respect. This is a court in session.'

The whistling died away and they followed in dutiful silence as Fedor Zan led the jurors along the route he had taken from his sister's house to the place where he said he had seen 15 women murdered 57 years before. As Hepburn wrote at the time: 'The judge, Mr Justice Potts, was then a boy of ten. The prosecutor, Mr John Nutting QC, was a four-week-old baby. And defence counsel Mr William Clegg QC, born 5 September 1949, wasn't even a twinkle in his father's eye.'

Along the way, it became apparent that map-reading was not high on the list of required skills for members of the legal profession. Deciding where they were in relation to the map they were using led to some lengthy pauses and tentative exchanges between the judge, the Court Usher and the two leading QCs that were faithfully recorded in the court transcript.

Mr Nutting: 'We have come up here and I think we are in here and what we will do is go across there and so we are approximately here.'

Court Usher: 'And we are going this way?'

Mr Nutting: 'We are going this way. I think we are going to go up here and we will deviate somewhere up there, so we are somewhere in here. About.'

Mr Justice Potts: 'This looks like the . . . where do you think this is on the map? Come forward. Perhaps we can consult.'

Mr Nutting: 'We haven't got the other map, have we? The one with the better definition? It's probably on the coach.'

Mr Clegg: 'I think it must be.'

The Court Usher then said, 'My Lord, the jury would like to know, please, approximately how many yards or metres it is from where he heard the screams to where we are now?'

Mr Justice Potts: 'Ah, by what route? By the path he took or by the way the crow flies?'

Court Usher: 'Both please, if possible. As the crow flies, my Lord.'

Mr Justice Potts: 'We need a crow.'

As Potts duly noted to himself on the transcript of the day's proceedings: 'Not without humour, this section.'

By the time the jurors had been marched through the forest and been shown the main massacre site and numerous other significant locations, in deep snow and bitter cold, their enthusiasm for visiting further sites in the town was waning rapidly. When they were offered the chance to view the *bania* and the school, the Court Usher told the judge, 'The jury indicate they are content they have seen everything they want to see themselves, as long as you are content.'

'They want to go home?'

'Yes, please.'

Judge, jurors, counsel, court officials and press all clambered back on their buses, most of them with sighs of relief. It was unlikely that any would be tempted to return. As their clouds of black diesel fumes drifted away on the wind, the spectators made their way home through the gathering dusk and the town was left to slip back into its post-Soviet torpor.

The judicial party and its camp followers again spent the night at the Intourist Hotel, where the unfortunate jurors were held virtual prisoners, though the judge did take pity on them and host a drinks party that evening. Otherwise, they were confined to their own floor, watched over by court staff mounting a round-the-clock guard to deter intruders.

As *Times* correspondent Alan Hamilton remarked, 'Who they were expecting to intrude was unclear. The only visible threat came from the elegant, lanky prostitutes who plied openly for trade in the hotel's bar and lobby and roamed the hotel corridors, knocking on bedroom doors. Whatever they might have wished to discuss with the jurors, it was unlikely to have been the finer points of the trial.'

Mr Justice Potts called the jurors together in the Executive Lounge at Warsaw Airport on the Thursday morning, to thank them and to issue a warning not to discuss anything once back home with their families other than superficial information about the weather and their journeys to and from their destinations, emphasising that 'once you start talking about it, then you are in very grave danger of having your views, your judgement, affected by people who really have not seen it all'. He reminded them that they had 'just had part of the case' and closed by wishing them all a very good flight back to the UK.

CHAPTER 17

The court reconvened on Tuesday 23 February on a cold but sunny morning. Johnny Nutting's mood was more the former than the latter, having been shown an article that had appeared in the *Daily Mirror* while everyone had been in Domachevo. With the jury excluded, Nutting put it to Mr Justice Potts that the piece suggested there had been 'some kind of a wrangle' over his remuneration. It had then 'inaccurately recited some of the details of the fees involved. It is quite possible that the effect of such an article would both demean and belittle leading counsel in the eyes of the jury.'

It was not a state secret that QCs were well paid, but the impact on the jurors – several of whom might have been earning very modest wages – of discovering the actual eye-watering amounts paid to the prosecution counsel in the case, might well have caused them to look on him less kindly, and that might, Nutting implied, affect their attitude to his client too.

In fact, the article had not mentioned 'a wrangle', but had claimed that Nutting was charging taxpayers £120 an hour to travel to and from work. It could have been worse still for him because the journalist had evidently not thought to enquire if Nutting was claiming for travel from his apartment just off Piccadilly – a few minutes' journey from the Old Bailey – or his Wiltshire manor house, a three-hour drive away, or even his country estate in the Flow Country in the far north of Scotland. However, the *Mirror* had established that '£350,000-a-year Mr Nutting' had claimed £3,243 as his expenses for visiting Belarus, outraging a source at the Crown Prosecution Service, who said, 'The fees just for his travelling are incredible. This is a hugely expensive gravy train. No one would argue Mr Nutting is not one of Britain's finest lawyers. However, the bills for his services are astronomical.'

The Labour MP for Battersea was quoted as adding, with a certain amount of hyperbole: 'I would have thought it was cheaper to send the Queen in her gold carriage. I find it quite mind-boggling. I suspect that people are sometimes a bit cavalier with taxpayers' money regarding legal aid.' Since Andrusha was on legal aid, the entire cost of his defence and the trial was being borne by the taxpayer.

However, Bill Clegg was quick to rise and express similar indignation, perhaps fearing that his own fees would be the next up for scrutiny, and Sir Humphrey, with a lucrative career as a silk of his own before ascending to the bench, was moved to concur. When the jury was then admitted to the courtroom he cautioned them that, if they had seen the article, it should not be allowed to distract them from the 'issues that you have to decide' and that, in any event, 'much of what is suggested in the article is simply false'.

Having got that out of the way, the first witness to be called was Ben-Zion Blustein, the only Jewish witness against Sawoniuk. When Scotland Yard detectives had first interviewed him in 1996, according to his son, Shalom, 'they were quite startled by his detailed recall of events and places – he remembered every detail. He even drew a map of Domachevo from memory, and when we went there later, although most of the wooden houses had been taken down, the stone houses were still standing and all of them were in exactly the places he had drawn on the map.'

During their investigation, detectives had flown Ben-Zion from Israel to Domachevo so that he could walk the streets with them and pinpoint the sites of key events. He travelled with Clara, Shalom and grandson Tomer. None of them had ever seen his birthplace, and it was the first time Ben-Zion had been there in over 50 years, making it an emotional and at times overwhelming experience for him. Tomer had brought a cine camera and made an hour-long home movie of the visit.

Accompanied by two detectives, an interpreter and a couple of Belarusian minders, they walked slowly through the streets, with Ben-Zion pointing out familiar buildings, or, more often, the empty sites where they had been. 'I recognised the entrance to the town,' he said then, 'but a lot of the town itself had changed. I tried to see the trees that my grandfather planted many years ago but they were not there.' When he did see places and buildings that he recognised, he became so animated at times that he was talking faster than his interpreter could translate from the Hebrew for the detectives.

Ben-Zion and his son were wearing brand-new sheepskin coats and cream cashmere scarves, in marked contrast to the drab and well-worn clothes of the Domachevo natives who stopped to watch them pass by. Clara, in a fur coat, a cashmere headscarf and dark glasses, held back a little, letting her husband lead the way, but when his emotions got the better of him and his eyes filled with tears, she went straight to his side and spoke softly to him.

Ben-Zion had learned Russian during the Soviet occupation of Domachevo and had also spoken it while fighting alongside the Soviet partisans in the forests, and Clara was even more fluent, having spent five years with a family in Siberia when she was a teenager. When they saw two old *babushkas* sitting on a bench despite the bitter cold, they walked up to them and asked if there were any survivors of the war years still living in Domachevo. They said there was one woman and that they would go and fetch her.

A few minutes later they returned, escorting Galina Puchkina, dressed like them in a bulky overcoat and plain headscarf. She peered through her glasses at Ben-Zion, then walked straight up to him with a broad smile on her face and gestured at his white hair. 'You were so handsome and a brunette back then,' she said in Russian. 'Now look at you!'

'So were you,' he said, and they both laughed. She took his hands in hers and kissed him on both cheeks and on his forehead. Both of them had tears in their eyes. She had been a classmate of his in their schooldays and a friend of his sister, and was, Ben-Zion said, 'the most beautiful girl I had ever seen.' They began an animated conversation, recalling friends lost in the war, and she told him of others who had died in the intervening years and the very few who still survived. The years and the hard life she had lived had left their mark on her but there was still a sparkle in her eye, and her voice was surprisingly youthful.

She walked with them as Ben-Zion showed the detectives the place where his stepfather had been buried, near the poplar tree his grandfather had planted, although there was no trace of it now. He pointed out the site of the dairy that he had burned down with the partisans, the ruins of the blacksmith's forge and the flour mill where the Germans had hitched the Rabbi of Lubartov and his followers to a wagon like carthorses and whipped them down to the river. He then led them to the well in the centre of the village, which had a galvanised bucket on a rope that the townspeople still used to haul up water. He showed them where the ghetto had been, the police station and the German barracks and stables, and led them down to where the old bridge was marked by a row of wooden stumps showing above the water, a few yards from the iron bridge that had been built to replace it. Finally they walked to the sand-hills, where among the tall trees that now grew there were the mass graves of thousands of Jews and the monument the Soviets had erected: 'To the victims of the German fascist terror 1941–45'.

The last time Ben-Zion had ever said *Kaddish* was when he stood over the mass grave before leaving Domachevo in 1945. Although both his grandfathers had been rabbis, after all that had happened to his family, friends and community in the war, he'd turned his back on his religion. 'I decided then,' he said, 'that I didn't believe in God,' and, with the exception of his son's wedding, for 50 years he had refused even to set foot in a synagogue. Now, as he stood once more at that gravesite, he found that he again wanted to say the prayer for the dead. Clara gently straightened his collar, and he, Shalom and Tomer stood side by side and said *Kaddish*. Ben-Zion then stood alone by the monument, reciting the names of all his lost family members and friends.

Before they left the site, he addressed the detectives directly, pausing frequently as the interpreter translated from the Hebrew. 'On 20 September 1942,' he said, 'they took all the Jews out of the town, beyond this hill. Immediately they began beating them up and ordering them to undress. First of all, they suspected the Jews were carrying valuables, but the second reason was that, when you leave people naked, they don't run any more, they don't try to escape. After they had been stripped naked, the blacksmith was the only one who tried to run. He ran off towards Kobelka but they shot him dead. Then they started bringing up groups and shooting them. You have to imagine, people, families, mothers with children. It was cold, they were naked, just waiting their turn to die. That was the end of the Jews of Domachevo. That is what I wanted to say.'

His old schoolfriend Galina Puchkina had stayed with

them throughout their visit, chatting to Ben-Zion while Clara talked in Russian to her friends. She told Ben-Zion that she had been married, although her husband was now long dead, and she had an adult son who she looked after because he was 'slow'.

Before leaving, Ben-Zion took her to one side, well away from everyone else, although Tomer continued to film him from a distance. 'How can I help you?' he asked.

She refused to discuss it at first but he insisted. Eventually she answered, 'Well, if I had a cow, I could milk it, feed my son with the milk and butter, and perhaps sell some to my neighbours too.'

'And how much would a cow be?'

She told him and he handed her some money. 'Well, here's enough to buy two cows.' Then, with more tears and kisses, they parted, though for the rest of his life he sent her $200 a month, to help her be more comfortable in her old age.

When Ben-Zion arrived at the Old Bailey to give his testimony, Clara and Shalom were alongside him. He was immaculately attired in a black overcoat, the same cashmere scarf he had worn on the visit to Domachevo, a grey suit, silk tie and button-down shirt. Now 74 years old, his thinning grey hair was combed back. The map of his life was etched in the lines and folds of his face, but he remained a powerful-looking figure, directing a piercing gaze from beneath his bushy eyebrows.

A murmur ran round the court as he made his slow way towards the witness box. This was the emotional heart of the trial, the testimony of the only witness who could speak to the events in Domachevo from the perspective of its vanished Jewish population, and every eye was focused on him as he took the oath, speaking in Hebrew, with his hand resting on the Old Testament. He also gave his evidence in Hebrew, translated by an interpreter standing next to him.

He was clearly tense, but also very focused, visibly trying to suppress his emotions. For the first time in over half a century he had now come face to face with the man who had once been his friend but had long been his hated enemy. His eyes sought out Sawoniuk in the courtroom and he stared at him for a long moment before looking away. 'He instantly recognised him,' Shalom said. 'He had aged but it was clearly the same person.'

Ben-Zion was a hugely significant witness, not only because of his first-person testimony, but also because he had lived in Israel since the end of the war and was therefore highly unlikely, as Sawoniuk had been claiming, to have been part of a KGB conspiracy or, as Clegg apparently intended to suggest, to have joined the villagers of Borisy in trying to frame Andrusha.

The emaciated survivor in Majdanek had said to Ben-Zion, 'Now I can die in peace . . . I now know there is someone to tell what has happened here,' and he was testifying not just to bring Sawoniuk to justice but to pay homage and give voice to those who could not speak for themselves. He undoubtedly saw it as his mission to make the jury, the court and the world understand the extent of the suffering of his family and his people. 'He felt a great deal of responsibility towards those who had died and suffered,' Shalom says. 'Including his own family and friends.'

Ben-Zion's distress was obvious as he relived those traumatic events – so long ago, and yet still so fresh in his mind – but he did not falter during the two days he spent in the witness box. His account was intensely moving, emotional and impassioned, and several of the jurors were in tears while he was speaking.

Had Sawoniuk been facing charges of mass murder or genocide, Ben-Zion's testimony could have been even more wide-ranging. However, he was being tried on four specimen charges relating to four different murders, and Ben-Zion had personal knowledge of only one of them. So, under the dry rules of evidence, much of what he wanted to say would be inadmissible.

Johnny Nutting led him through his testimony, first setting the scene of his childhood in Domachevo before the war. 'I had known Sawoniuk since I was nine or ten,' he said. 'He bred pigeons, and as children we used to play and run. In the summer months we used to wash in the stream near his house. Therefore, I used to meet him almost daily . . . But when he became a policeman, he became a man of power, a master, a lord, and I was a Jew. He used to behave cruelly whenever he wanted and with whomsoever he wanted.'

Nutting then turned to events following the Nazi invasion, the restrictions, maltreatment and random killings of Jews and the involvement of the *Schutzmannschaft*. Ben-Zion talked about the killings of Mendel Rubinstein and Herschke Greenstein – the barber who had been forced to bury his three sons after the SS had shot them, even though one of them was still alive.

The first mention of Andrusha in the context of beatings and killings came when Ben-Zion recounted what happened to Rachel Ipsun Schneider – 'a girl of my own age. She studied in the same class I did.' She worked in the fields by day, and when Andrusha and another auxiliary searched her as she returned to the ghetto one evening and found a few potatoes she was trying to smuggle in, they gave her a savage beating and dragged her off to the police station.

Ben-Zion also claimed that 'on more than one occasion' he had seen Andrusha escorting groups of Russian prisoners of war to the site where they were executed, the *boyiska* that had once been the sports field. It was also the place where the inhabitants of the ghetto had been assembled and searched for valuables while their homes were looted.

He had been testifying for over four hours, with just a brief break for lunch, when Mr Justice Potts adjourned proceedings for the day.

CHAPTER 18

Ben-Zion resumed his testimony the next morning, the sixth day of the trial, and Johnny Nutting at once began to question him about the massacre on the eve of the Day of Atonement in September 1942. He said that soldiers and police auxiliaries were already surrounding the ghetto when dawn broke on the Sunday morning. The Jewish elders – the *Judenrat* – were then told by the Germans that there was a rumour that a number of Jews had managed to escape from the ghetto and flee into the forest. All the Jews were therefore now to assemble on the *boyiska* for a roll-call. 'They announced if any member of any family does not appear at this parade, they would liquidate the whole family.'

He described how his mother had said she did not believe the Germans, and the whole family, including Ben-Zion's younger sister Shulamit, who was ten, and his little brother, Shlomo, who was seven, hid in the bunker that his stepfather, Noah, had built beneath the yard. Ben-Zion's elder sister, Nechama, was now married and lived elsewhere with her husband.

Ben-Zion had to pause, his eyes brimming with tears and his voice cracking as he tried to speak. One of the women jurors was wiping her eyes with her handkerchief and two of the others again looked close to tears. Watching from the benches at the rear of the court, Clara and Shalom sat like stone, staring straight ahead, feeling his anguish but unable to help him.

'At this stage in my testimony,' he said at last, 'it is the most difficult time in my life. I dream about this for nights on end, and I think about it almost every day. When I was requested to come to this trial, I had a great dilemma whether to appear. This trial is about fifty years too late. I knew it would be hard for me to be here and especially to talk about this time.'

As he fell silent again, Bill Clegg permitted himself a faint shake of his head, perhaps hoping to encourage the judge to curtail Ben-Zion's displays of emotion. In fact, Johnny Nutting intervened. 'Would Mr Blustein forgive me if I interrupt him? I am sure that we can take it that his memory of what happened in the next few days is very emotional indeed. If he could bear with us and describe as best he can what happened for the rest of that day, and shortly what happened during the course of the next eight days, we would be very grateful to have his testimony.'

Ben-Zion nodded. 'I will try and let you know everything that you have asked of me, but I think it essential that the court should know I knew it would be hard for me.'

Mr Justice Potts leaned forward. 'Mr Blustein, we understand how you feel about these matters but it is essential, if you are to give evidence, that you listen to the questions that are put to you and answer them directly.'

Nutting then asked Ben-Zion what he had heard from the ghetto during the course of that day. 'We heard lots of shooting, we heard shouts and cries, and we could understand what was happening there. On the same day, the eve of the Day of Atonement, on a rainy day, they forced all the people to—'

Potts interrupted him. 'Mr Nutting simply wanted to know what you heard. Do you understand, Mr Blustein? I think it very important, if you do not mind, just to answer the question and leave it to Mr Nutting to ask another one, if he thinks it right.'

'That evening, after the shooting had stopped,' Nutting said, 'did you hear any sounds indicating that those who had left that morning had returned to their homes?'

'No one returned.'

Ben-Zion spoke of the eight days in which his family hid in the bunker, the death of his stepfather and the attempted suicide of the rest of them. It was, as the judge noted to himself that evening, 'very moving'. With frequent apologies for interrupting him, Nutting tried to gently hurry him through parts of his testimony that, while equally moving, had no relevance to the charges against Sawoniuk.

Ben-Zion described the attack on the 80-year-old Jew, Shaya Idel, bayoneted and beaten by auxiliaries including Andrusha, and of seeing two Jews, Aharon Kronenberg and Mir Barlas, who had been captured, interrogated and badly beaten by the Germans at the cavalry base before being handed over to the auxiliaries, including Andrusha, to be killed. Ben-Zion had never seen either man again.

A few days after Mir Barlas had disappeared, Ben-Zion said, Sawoniuk came into the stables where he was working. 'Andrusha said to me that Barlas was very courageous and we will soon meet up there, he said, pointing upwards.'

'In other words, in the next world?' Nutting said. He then asked about a subsequent time when Andrusha had come into the stables.

Ben-Zion replied: 'He said to me, "Don't think that because you are living here today, you are going to live forever. As soon as the Germans leave here, they will hand the Jews over to us and we will massacre you, just as we have massacred many up to this day."'

If true, it was damning testimony. In the silence that followed, Clegg reached for his notepad and wrote furiously, perhaps hoping to convey to the jurors that he would be challenging Ben-Zion vigorously when the time came for his cross-examination.

He would not have long to wait. Nutting led Ben-Zion briefly through the story of his escape from the base, his time living in the forest and the liberation of Domachevo by the Red Army in July 1944, but his last question was simply, 'Did you ever see your mother or your brother or your sisters again?'

'No.'

As Nutting was about to give way to Clegg, Ben-Zion said, 'I wanted to say that from the whole town, where there were originally four thousand to five thousand Jews, there remained twelve Jews and one woman.'

Nutting sat down at 12.40pm, leaving Ben-Zion to face about 20 minutes of cross-examination before the court broke for lunch. Whenever he had previously spoken of his experiences, whether to his family, in interviews for the Yad Vashem World Holocaust Remembrance Center in Israel, in conversations with his friend and biographer Margalit Shlain, or at schools, colleges, army bases and gatherings of survivors, his audience had been silent and sympathetic, often moved to tears, and he had never been challenged about his veracity. Now, at the conclusion of his testimony, he was to be subjected to a gruelling cross-examination by a defence counsel intent on damaging his credibility by challenging his recall and disputing almost every statement he had made.

Whatever his private feelings might have been, Clegg's job was to defend his client to the best of his considerable ability, and Ben-Zion was the first of the four key prosecution witnesses whose testimony had to be damaged and credibility undermined, if Clegg was to secure a not guilty verdict.

Ben-Zion's testimony was vital to the Crown in establishing Andrusha's character and pattern of behaviour, and placing the specific charges he was facing in the broader, more general context of his systematic violence and cruelty. Another witness, Ivan Stepaniuk, would also speak to that, and give evidence pointing to Andrusha's guilt, but Alexandre Baglay and Fedor

Zan were the only Crown witnesses who could claim to have actually seen Sawoniuk committing murder. Clegg would have to attempt to demolish their credibility, too, when the time came, but for the moment, Ben-Zion was in his sights.

He began in relatively disarming fashion, exploring what the Jews had heard about Nazi massacres before the invasion and the heroic tales about some of the survivors. The first sharp edge was not apparent until he referred to Ben-Zion's statement that the trial was taking place 50 years too late. 'It is enormously difficult to think back over fifty-eight years and remember the detail of all the events that happened, would you agree?'

Ben-Zion greeted that with a flat 'No. I want to say that an event can happen to an individual and after a few days he can forget it, but when an event happens, when they kill parents, children, friends, and you wake up one day and you are the only one in the world . . .' He paused and, once more, some of the jurors were visibly holding back tears. 'Night after night I am there with them, and day after day I think about them, such things it is impossible to forget. I tried some time ago to remember the people who lived in the ghetto and I was successful almost ninety per cent to remember and record the names of all the people. These are things which I will not forget to my last days.'

Clegg tried again. 'No one would suggest that however long you lived, you could ever forget the terrible events in the ghetto when your family died. But surrounding that terrible incident, there were many other events in your daily life that will obviously be far more difficult to remember now than they would have been fifty or fifty-five years ago?'

'Things that I wanted to forget I do not remember, but things that were so important to me I will never forget, and I want to point out that many years, almost night after night, I would talk to my mother. I would tell her every day everything that happened to me. Such things a man can never forget. I also thank God that he gave me a good memory that I can remember all these things and I have come to this trial as a witness, as a mouth, for the tens and maybe hundreds who were killed by this man, to be their voice at this trial. I am not seeking revenge. I trust that the English legal system is fine enough to find the most suitable penalty.'

'Well, we are enquiring at this stage not about penalty but about what happened,' Clegg said hurriedly, 'and it is about that that I wish to ask you.'

It was hard to imagine how the cross-examination so far could have gone much worse and it must have been Clegg, not Ben-Zion, who was now longing for the court to adjourn. He turned to the relatively uncontentious topics of Domachevo before the war, what Ben-Zion knew of Andrusha and his family and how many Russian Orthodox families had lived in and around the town.

At one o'clock he enquired of Mr Justice Potts whether it would be a good moment to adjourn for lunch, and he must have been relieved when Potts agreed. If the cross-examination had been a boxing match, Ben-Zion would have been well ahead on points, for Bill Clegg had yet to lay a glove on him, but there was a long way to go and he was confident that he still had enough material to shake Ben-Zion and make the jury see him in a different light.

Clegg continued to labour in the early part of the afternoon session, first in an unsuccessful attempt to get Ben-Zion to agree that the police auxiliaries might have been conscripted, and then engaging him in lengthy exchanges about whether and at what stage the police had uniforms.

Ben-Zion's replies grew increasingly dismissive. 'This thing did not interest me and I do not know about it . . . It does not make any difference to me . . . It is not my duty to watch out when they did wear and when they did not wear.'

The subject of police uniforms was a line of questioning Clegg would repeat with several other witnesses, but, if there was a point to it, it was one he had either lost sight of or discarded by the time he came to make his closing statement, because he did not refer to it then.

It is probable that his strategy was to wage a war of attrition, wearing Ben-Zion down – or wearing him out – with meandering exchanges about police recruitment and uniforms before attempting to pin him down over inconsistencies and contradictions in his testimony compared to interviews conducted over the course of the previous 55 years.

Clegg had more success when he eventually turned to the subject of the murder of the Jews. He established they were not the only victims of the Nazis – though, as Ben-Zion pointed out, 'The Jews they killed because they were Jews; the rest they killed because they were afraid that they were against their authority.'

Clegg then asked him about the specific killings of Mendel Rubenstein, the barber Herschke Greenstein, and the Rabbi of Lubartov and his followers. In every case, Ben-Zion conceded, he had not witnessed the murders. 'I did not see, but I wish to point out this was a small town. What happened in one house, the whole town immediately knew about.'

'Mr Blustein,' Clegg said, perhaps feeling the tide was at last turning in his favour, 'I am not suggesting now, nor will I be suggesting later, that these people were not killed by the Germans. I have no reason to doubt that they were. I am merely establishing that which you have seen yourself and been a witness to, and that which you have learned about afterwards.'

Clegg passed briefly over the massacre and its aftermath before going on the attack about a police search of the house while Ben-Zion was in hiding. Here Clegg had some real success in pointing to contrasts between what Ben-Zion had told British detectives in 1996, what he had testified in pre-trial hearings in the magistrates' court and what he had said in his testimony the previous day.

He had originally said he recognised the voice of the auxiliary police commander Vasily Trebunko, known as Vashka, because he had been singing a Russian song to himself while searching the house with other policemen, but in different statements he had said he heard Andrusha humming along, or shouting outside the house.

Sensing an opening, Clegg kept hammering the same point for over half an hour and, under the barrage of questions, Ben-Zion was drawn into exaggerating his claims. 'I think the moment they left, Vashka called out to Andrusha, "Let's go." I am not certain but I think so. "I did not find anything. Let's go."'

'If they had called each other by their Christian names, it would have made identification easier,' Clegg said, baiting the hook. 'Did that happen?'

'Yes. I say once again I am not certain I heard. I think so. I heard Vashka saying to Andrusha, when he finished the search, I think he said, "Come, let's go."'

'So did they or did they not use each other's names?'

'I say if I remember, I think I heard him say, "Andrusha, let's go. I haven't found anything." I think so.'

Mr Justice Potts was not in favour of counsel gurning and grimacing to register disbelief in what a witness was saying, but the eyebrow that Clegg raised as he paused and glanced towards the jury was too subtle a gesture to provoke any judicial ire.

The judge adjourned the trial for the day soon afterwards but, before he did so, Nutting rose and his silken phrasing left no one in doubt of the steel that lay beneath. 'Mr Clegg is an old friend, and he is the sort of advocate who is the last person, as I know only too well, to take a false point in relation to a statement.' He then went on to imply that was exactly what he had done by taking a quote from Ben-Zion's statement to the police out of context. After some discussion, Clegg agreed to read the full text when the court reconvened the following morning. Ben-Zion had now been in the witness box for almost two full days and it was clear that Clegg was nowhere near the end of his cross-examination.

CHAPTER 19

The seventh day of the trial, Thursday 25 February, offered no respite for Ben-Zion, who returned to the witness box to face another relentless interrogation by Bill Clegg. As Mr Justice Potts noted on his transcript, it was 'a long continuation where Clegg tries to establish inconsistencies in BZ's testimony'. His strategy was now clear, to draw the jury's attention to those inconsistencies, even over quite trivial matters, in the hope that it would encourage them to take a sceptical view of his reliability as a witness on much graver matters too.

In response to the exchange with Nutting at the end of the previous day, Clegg first read out in full the part of the statement Ben-Zion had given to police about Andrusha and Vashka searching the house: 'I heard the voices of Andrusha and Vashka, whose voices I knew very well. I also heard them calling each other by name.'

Clegg then spent some time probing the differences in that account and Ben-Zion's various other statements, before moving on to the killing of the 80-year-old Shaya Idel. Here he was trying to get Ben-Zion to admit that, although he had said the Germans had left the town after the massacre, they had been involved in the killing of Idel, since he had used the word 'soldiers' not 'policemen' when talking about the incident. Ben-Zion insisted he meant that the police had bayoneted the old man.

'Are you saying to us you never saw a soldier stab him?' Clegg said.

'No. What I want to explain – maybe it is hard for you to understand – when I saw this sight, I felt so bad I sat down. It was not a show for me that I could stand and look at it and ask myself whether I saw this soldier stab or whether it was a policeman. What I have told you is that he was amongst them. This case is about Andrusha and he was among them.'

Clegg pressed him. 'You have never before in your evidence to this court used the word 'soldiers' to describe policemen, have you?'

'For me a policeman and a soldier is the same idea. That is what I meant.'

Clegg asked him if he was sure he was not saying that just to explain the difference in his testimony.

'Never,' Ben-Zion said. 'For me that is holy.'

'Can I make it clear that my suggestion is that Andrusha was not one of those in the street with your neighbour?'

'I said he was. You can say what you want.'

Clegg then turned to the statement that Ben-Zion made to the Soviet NKVD in 1944. Clegg read out the section, signed by Ben-Zion, in which he acknowledged, 'I have been warned about the consequences of giving false evidence in accordance with Article 136 of the Criminal Code of the Byelorussian Soviet Socialist Republic.' He then demonstrated that Ben-Zion had indeed given false evidence to the NKVD investigator by claiming that he and his family had hidden in the forest from the time of the German invasion.

Ben-Zion was at first reluctant to admit that, saying, 'Maybe I said something and he did not understand me,' but then conceded, 'I said what I thought would be good for me, that they should not murder me or send me to Siberia.'

'Mr Blustein, if that is the explanation for saying something false, then I am sure everybody will understand the reason.'

Despite that, Clegg continued to hammer away at the differences between Ben-Zion's statement then and his testimony to the court 55 years later and, losing patience, Ben-Zion's answers grew increasingly terse and angry. He suggested that the investigator might have written down different answers than he had given, and when Clegg asked why he would do that, Ben-Zion said, 'Maybe he was drunk. He might be. What do I know? I was a small Jew in front of an officer of the NKVD, just waiting to be released and leave Domachevo.'

'Is that the best explanation you can give, that the interrogating officer may have been so drunk that he did not understand what you were saying?'

'I do not know. I do not say . . . maybe. I could not care.'

'The fact of the matter is that you have signed a statement—'

'Correct.'

'—that is materially different from what you are saying today.'

'Yes.'

'Do you not think that today, nearly sixty years after these events, it is difficult to be accurate?'

'When you talk about life, families of Jews who were so close to me, I remember every day what happened to us in the ghetto. I remember what happened with my family. I live these things every day and every night and I cannot believe there exists a person who has not been through such a thing who can understand it. Many people who have been through this are ill. My luck is that I was fairly well and had sufficient spiritual strength. I managed to set up a family and I am happy that I could continue and reach this day, and I declare that every word I have said is the truth and only the truth. Before I said that I always say the truth, but at times when my life was in danger, I also had to lie.'

Once more the passion and emotion that Ben-Zion displayed was in marked contrast to Clegg's dry, forensic examination.

Ben-Zion was probably exhausted by now, his third day in the witness box, and had difficulty in keeping his temper at times. He was sure in his heart that Sawoniuk was guilty of multiple murders and was convinced that he had also killed Ben-Zion's own mother and siblings, but that was not what the court wished to hear at this moment, and there was an inevitable tension between his wish to tell his story, and the court's continuing desire to elicit only evidence that was directly relevant to the specific charge against the defendant. Certain in his knowledge of Sawoniuk's guilt, he sometimes went further than in his previous testimony, and Clegg was again quick to draw that to the jury's attention, picking over the details and exposing contradictions in statements that had sometimes been made over 50 years apart.

Time and again Ben-Zion tried to return to his narrative and he grew increasingly frustrated, emotional and angry as he was interrupted both by the judge and counsel, and dragged back to the narrow point: Sawoniuk's guilt or innocence on the specific charge of killing Mir Barlas.

When Clegg pointed out that once Barlas had passed out of Ben-Zion's sight, there was no way of knowing what had happened to him next, and he might have been killed or taken to Brest-Litovsk as a prisoner, he snapped back, 'How could I know? Did I go after them? Did they take me there?'

Clegg then turned to what Andrusha had said to Ben-Zion later and here, increasingly tired, irritable and anxious for the ordeal to be over, he was tempted into embellishing his earlier statements in a way that must have been obvious to the jurors. He had previously admitted that he had not seen Sawoniuk kill Barlas, but had only heard him talk about his death afterwards, in ways that might or might not have meant that Sawoniuk himself had killed him, and certainly did not amount to an explicit confession.

Now Clegg asked if Ben-Zion had actually witnessed

Sawoniuk killing Barlas or even heard him directly admit to it? The truthful answer to both questions would have been 'No', but under pressure from the defence counsel, and perhaps fearing that his tormentor across the courtroom would somehow escape justice, Ben-Zion found himself going further than he had ever done before.

'Did Andrusha say to you that he had killed Mir Barlas?' Clegg asked.

'Yes. He said.'

'Not that Mir Barlas had been killed by somebody?'

'No, he did not say that.'

'He said, "I, Andrusha killed him"?'

'He did not say it like that. He said, "He was very courageous before I killed him. We will see each other in the world to come."'

'"He was very courageous before I killed him"?'

'"Before I liquidated him."'

Clegg pounced. 'I suggest you said to the magistrate the exact opposite of what you have told the jury.'

'Even if he did not say to me, "I liquidated him",' Ben-Zion said, 'this was the biggest proof that he did it and I want you to understand we are talking about the life of a Jew, which was worth less than the life of a dog.'

'You said to Mr Nutting, "He did not say I have killed him."'

Ben-Zion was on the hook, and could only say, 'For me, what I said here is true. Maybe from the excitement I did not understand what they said to me. What I am saying now, this is the truth and only the truth.'

Clegg was not going to let that pass. 'You do not, Mr Blustein, do you, need to be a legal expert to understand the difference between "I have killed him" and "He did not say I have killed him"?'

'If your learned sir was in my place, with all the thoughts that are in my mind with which I will come here and what is going through me and what went through me then, you could have understood me better, and could understand that such a small thing for me couldn't change my opinion and that is what I testify.'

Satisfied with his morning's work, Clegg offered it to the judge as a convenient moment to adjourn for lunch, leaving the jury with an hour to mull over the latest, and potentially most damaging contradiction he had exposed in Ben-Zion's testimony.

After lunch Clegg immediately returned to the attack. Why had the death of Barlas and Andrusha's self-confessed role in it not been mentioned during Ben-Zion's interrogation by Soviet investigators at the end of the war, nor when he was first questioned by British police in Israel, nor in his lengthy, tape-recorded testimony at the Yad Vashem archive in Jerusalem?

'I do not remember. It was not so important. Besides Mir Barlas there were hundreds of thousands who were killed.'

When Clegg persisted, Ben-Zion was again dismissive. 'At that moment, to talk about an individual that I knew – and I told them about tens and hundreds that he had killed – for me it had no special meaning. I talked about tens of prisoners of war who had been killed, tens of Jews from the ghetto, about girls he had killed whom he had wanted to rape.'

Clegg, relentlessly probing, kept pressing him about his failure to mention Barlas to Scotland Yard detectives when they travelled to Israel to interview him.

Ben-Zion once more brushed it off. 'When I talked about hundreds of people who had been killed, it was not so important to me to talk about an individual Jew, and when I had completed what, in my opinion, was the more important evidence – and once again they asked whether I had anything else to talk about – then I talked about Barlas as well.'

'Mr Blustein,' Clegg said, 'I suggest that is not true. In your statement you mention a number of individual incidents that you have talked about in your evidence: Shaya Idel, Rachel Schneider are examples. There were two more. You had there the opportunity to tell the police about Mir Barlas.'

'What I want to say, after all this evidence, even today, I have names of Jews who he killed and I have not mentioned them to this day, and names that I remember.'

Still Clegg pursued it. The transcript of their interview showed that the detectives had asked Ben-Zion, 'Do you remember anything further about Andrusha?' 'You must,' Clegg said, 'if what you are telling us is right, have noticed that there was no mention of Mir Barlas in any of your answers. Did you notice that?'

'Maybe I should ask your forgiveness,' Ben-Zion said, not hiding his sarcasm. 'You can ask me the same question ten times, and ten times I will give you the same answer. My evidence is one hundred per cent correct, and for me it does not matter when I gave this evidence about Mir Barlas. The fact is that it happened.'

Clegg continued to hammer away at the point until Mr Justice Potts intervened. 'Mr Clegg, there is a limit as to how far this can go. In fairness to the witness, in relation to the questions you are asking, much depends on the questions that he was asked at the time . . . You put it to him, "You had three opportunities to tell the police about Mir Barlas, and you were not telling them." And he gave his answer, the gist of which was that there were so many killed he did not think it important to mention Mir Barlas. I think that is where we come back to.'

Knowing that the judge's patience was almost exhausted with his line of questioning, Clegg returned to the attack one last time. 'Mr Blustein, I suggest why there was no mention of any confession by Andrusha to the murder of Mir Barlas in 1995 was because no confession by him was ever made in 1942.'

'So you will have to accuse me of lying,' Ben-Zion said. 'What can I say?'

In pre-trial meetings that was exactly the tactic that, instructed by Sawoniuk, the defence solicitors had agreed with Clegg. As the only surviving Jewish witness to the events in Domachevo, Ben-Zion's testimony was obviously going to be crucial. They knew that his account of events had changed, particularly including references to Sawoniuk that had not been mentioned in earlier statements, and the solicitors wanted Clegg to call Ben-Zion a liar in court.

They had also even discussed trying to discredit his testimony by accusing him of being a Nazi collaborator. An argument could have been constructed using the facts that he had survived the war when so many others had died, and had worked for the Germans, first installing and maintaining telephone lines after the invasion, and later tending the horses at the cavalry base after the massacre.

Sawoniuk was unsurprisingly eager for them to pursue that approach, but Clegg was profoundly uncomfortable with the idea of branding a Holocaust survivor as a liar and collaborator. He knew it would trigger a storm of protest and outrage, and might well even rebound on the defence, winning sympathy for Ben-Zion rather than disbelief, and making the jury more, not less likely, to convict. In cross-examination he therefore stepped back from the brink, avoiding any suggestion that Ben-Zion had been a collaborator and also stopping short of calling him a liar, though it was certainly implicit in the questions he put to him.

When Sawoniuk, sitting alongside Steve Law as usual, realised Clegg was not going to pursue the agreed strategy, he elbowed Law in the ribs and pointed at Clegg with a furious expression on his face. Nonetheless, when Clegg sat down soon afterwards, he had succeeded in exposing the contradictions and omissions in Ben-Zion's various statements and must have done some damage to his credibility as a witness.

For his part, despite the attempts of the judge and counsel to hold him to the specific points of evidence, Ben-Zion had managed to give voice to something of the suffering of his family and community, and his emotional accounts of events in Domachevo had visibly resonated with at least some of the jurors.

The judge adjourned at that point, but Ben-Zion's ordeal was not yet quite over, for he would have to return to the witness box the following morning so that Nutting could re-examine him, with the aim of defusing some of the impact of Clegg's cross-examination.

After three days in the witness box, and under punishing interrogation for two of them, Ben-Zion seemed to have visibly aged. His eyes were more sunken and his gait a little more unsteady, and he must have had a sinking feeling as he left the courtroom. The sympathetic looks that some of the jurors gave him would not necessarily translate into votes for a guilty verdict when the time came and, had he glanced at Sawoniuk, he would not have been reassured, for he did not have the air of a man who was in trouble. As Ben-Zion passed close to him on his way out, Andrusha was trying to conceal a smirk.

CHAPTER 20

Day 8 of the trial, Friday 26 February, began with Johnny Nutting attempting to 'clarify . . . seven matters' with Ben-Zion. As Judge Potts sardonically noted to himself on his copy of the transcript, 'Nutting tries to refill the holes BZ dug for himself during cross-examination.'

He dealt first with the atmosphere in Domachevo immediately before and after the German invasion, and the impact of the killing of the Rabbi of Lubartov and his followers. 'Did the Germans make any secret of the fact?' he asked.

'On the contrary, they wanted everyone to know about it.'

The implicit message Nutting no doubt intended to convey to the jury was that even if Ben-Zion had not witnessed such killings, there was no disputing that they had occurred.

The second query was over whether the auxiliary police were volunteers, or conscripts, as Clegg had tried to suggest. 'Generally,' Ben-Zion said, 'when you want to conscript somebody, people accept a command, an order, to present oneself in accordance with the laws. As far as I know, there was no such order; these people volunteered alone to go to the police.'

Nutting then asked if Ben-Zion had detected any reluctance on Andrusha's part to 'carry out his duties as a policeman under Nazi occupation'.

'In my opinion, he did it with a will to do the work and to

be outstanding – and to get respect for the work that he was carrying out.'

Those points had been made in rapid fashion and Nutting then turned to the question of whether Andrusha had been present when the policeman called Vashka was searching the house while singing a Russian song. Clegg had spent some time pointing to apparent contradictions in Ben-Zion's statements, but Nutting drew his, and therefore the jury's attention to Ben-Zion's answer to one question: 'I am not certain, but I think I heard Andrusha's name. I do not want to give the impression that I was trying to incriminate Andrusha.'

Nutting pointed out that in his interview with the Scotland Yard detectives, Ben-Zion had mentioned Andrusha's name twice before they revealed their interest in him. 'It was not until you had mentioned and volunteered the name yourself that they asked, "What can you tell us about this man?"'

'Correct.'

Nutting moved on to the account of Ben-Zion's life that had been written by Margalit Shlain and based on the long interviews she had done with him for the Yad Vashem archive. 'She had editorial freedom, is that right?' Nutting said.

'Yes. I told her the story and she wrote.'

'Was it in the form of dictation?'

'No. It was a story about my life. As far as I understand, there are places where someone who writes wants to embellish. It was not transcription. It was not word for word what I told her.'

'Was it in your mind that the book would form any basis for the prosecution in a court of law of any individual?'

'No. I wrote the book to leave a memorial for the town of Domachevo. I distributed it free of charge to schools, to libraries. These are the thoughts I could do to leave a memorial about my town and about my family.'

Having cast sufficient doubt on the significance of any contradictions in Ben-Zion's statements and the contents of his book, Nutting moved on to Ben-Zion's interview just after the Red Army had liberated Domachevo, and what the attitude of people was to the NKVD.

'They always lived in fear,' Ben-Zion said. 'It was sufficient for someone to inform on someone else, to speak or make some remark against the authorities. There were no interrogations. This person was immediately sent to prison or Siberia. I remember them saying that in Russia three types of people live: people who have been in prison, people who are sitting in prison and people who will be in prison.'

When Nutting asked what Ben-Zion's thoughts were as he sat down for that interview, he said, 'My thoughts were that whatever he wants me to say, I will say, and whatever he asks me to sign, I will sign, and the moment he asks me questions about myself, I was very careful not to say things that he will not find favour with.'

That exchange alone had effectively disarmed any points Clegg had succeeded in making about the NKVD document in his cross-examination, and it was a little surprising that Nutting continued to labour the point for another 20 minutes. He then turned to Mir Barlas and sought to establish that Ben-Zion's accounts of Andrusha's statements to him in the stables after the killing were intended to give the sense of what he had said, rather than the exact words. He was not assisted in this endeavour at first by Ben-Zion's affirmative answer to the question, 'Do you claim to be able to remember literally word for word fifty-seven years later the precise conversation that you had?'

When Nutting attempted to follow up by saying, 'Or did you mean——' Clegg was straight on his feet, objecting that Nutting was asking a leading question. However, he then found another way, asking Ben-Zion, 'Did you supply us with the sense of the answer?'

Nutting then confronted the most damaging part of Clegg's

cross-examination. 'It has been suggested that this conversation is invented, and I want to understand and I want the jury to understand, the circumstances in which this matter arose.' Nutting then went through the successive statements that Ben-Zion had made, beginning with the interview by the regional head of the NKVD, Tokachev, focusing on their pursuit of a war criminal called Kharkhuta.

'Was it clear to you that Mr Tokachev wanted to know what you knew about Anton Kharkhuta?'

'Yes.'

'Was the name of the defendant [Sawoniuk] mentioned at all by either of you in that two-page statement?'

'No.'

Nutting then moved on to the Yad Vashem testimony, establishing that the interview had dealt with the generality of life under the Nazis but had gone into specifics only on Ben-Zion's personal story.

The first interview with the Metropolitan Police in May 1995 came next, and Nutting established that Ben-Zion had told them about violent acts by Andrusha that he had witnessed but, when talking about the killings of Russian PoWs, he made it clear that he had not witnessed the actual killings but only heard shots, ending with the chilling words, 'None of the Jews who were eyewitnesses to these killings survived the war.'

The detectives themselves had then changed the subject, moving on to the topic of uniforms. When they returned to record another interview with Ben-Zion in October 1996, they made it clear from the start that the interview was about Andrusha, and the ten-page statement they took showed that Ben-Zion had referred to the killing of Mir Barlas. The following March they returned for a third time and, among the questions, they asked why he had not mentioned three incidents involving Andrusha, including the death of Mir Barlas, during their first interview in May 1995.

Nutting read Ben-Zion's reply to the court: "'During the German occupation of Domachevo, there were many terrible events committed against the Jews. In my previous statements to the English police, I referred to specific events, having been specifically asked about them. For instance, in my statement of May 1995, I did not mention the executions of . . .'" Nutting paused, 'Then three names, including Mir Barlas, right?'

'Because I was not asked about them.'

'One final question, please. In reaction to these events, you said to Mr Clegg: "There are things that I wanted to forget that I do not remember, but there are also things that are so important to me that I will never forget." Into which category, please, does the Mir Barlas incident fall?'

'The one I cannot forget.'

'Thank you very much. I am very grateful to you. That is all the questions, Mr Blustein.'

His ordeal was at last over and Nutting's re-examination must have undone some of the damage done by Clegg's cross-examination.

The jurors were probably almost as exhausted as Ben-Zion by the gruelling testimony they had heard that week and must have been relieved to be sent home for the weekend straight after Ben-Zion had left the witness box, but Mr Justice Potts and the two counsel remained in the courtroom to deal with a point of law, as Clegg sought to persuade the judge to rule as inadmissible the evidence of two witnesses, Ivan Baglay (older brother of Alexandre) and Evgeny Melaniuk. Their testimony was about the deaths of two entire families that the witnesses had seen being led towards the forest by Sawoniuk. Although they had not seen him actually kill them, the implications were plain. No charges had been brought in relation to these allegations and Clegg argued that the testimony did not 'legitimately advance the prosecution's case' and 'the prejudice is going to be so great that the jury could not conceivably put that out of their mind'.

Nutting disputed that, drawing attention to Clegg's attempt to paint some of Ben-Zion's testimony as 'invention' and saying it 'underpins the desirability of the jury having before them all the evidence which demonstrates this defendant was involved in the search-and-kill operation'. Nutting also pointed out that Clegg had weakened his own argument by raising no objection to the inclusion of Ben-Zion's testimony about Shaya Idel, the old Jew who had been bayoneted and kicked and had his beard and side-locks set alight. That incident was not the subject of any charges but had still been admissible as evidence to show Sawoniuk's involvement in search-and-kill operations.

Clegg tried once more. 'This is not a case where he disputes the fact that he was a policeman. We do not dispute that the police were clearly involved in the search-and-kill operation. No one can dispute that. It is not an issue for the jury to resolve as to whether the defendant was part of the search-and-kill operation. The issue for the jury to resolve is whether, in relation to the individual victims identified in the four counts, the Crown can prove that he participated in their actual murder, not anyone else's.'

In his ruling, Mr Justice Potts acknowledged that neither witness was giving evidence in relation to a specific count on the indictment. 'I have Mr Clegg's forceful argument in that connection very much in mind. I am satisfied, however, that it would be right to allow this evidence to go before the jury. It is of particular relevance, in my judgement, to the issues raised by the charges of the extent of the defendant's involvement in the search-and-kill operation. It is also relevant, I am particularly satisfied, after hearing cross-examination of Mr Blustein, to the issue of invention on his part of a conversation which he asserted took place between him and the defendant in relation to Mir Barlas.'

Clegg can not have departed for the weekend in a happy frame of mind. What had seemed his most telling argument 24 hours previously — that Ben-Zion had invented the Mir Barlas story — had been turned back against him by the judge to justify the inclusion of testimony from two other witnesses that might prove terminally damaging to his client's case.

CHAPTER 21

The trial resumed on Tuesday 2 March and Ben-Zion was again in court, but this time as a spectator rather than a witness, flanked by Clara, Shalom and his old friend from Domachevo, Meir Bronstein, one of the handful of other Jews from the town to have survived the Holocaust. He had been one of 11 children, nine of whom were killed in the Holocaust, along with their parents. He had never fully recovered from the trauma of those dark times and was a heavy vodka drinker.

The remaining prosecution witnesses were all Belarusians, either from Domachevo itself or the small hamlets, like Borisy, that surrounded it. They were almost all in their seventies and, before coming to London for the committal hearing and then the trial, the majority of them had never left their country in their entire lives. Even those who had, like Fedor Zan, had done so only once when conscripted into the Red Army in 1944 to pursue the fleeing Germans to Berlin.

None of the witnesses had ever been on an aircraft before and one old lady had never even travelled on a train. A trip in a car would have been an adventure but a flight in an aircraft, a stay in a hotel with fitted carpets, central heating and limitless hot water, and the sight of a city of nine million people after spending your life in a hamlet of a few dozen or a town of a couple of thousand, must have been an unforgettable, but also rather frightening, experience.

'When the witnesses first came over for the committal proceedings it was like stepping onto a different planet,' WCU detective Charlie Moore says. 'We put them up in a hotel, which must have seemed ultra-luxurious, when back home they did not have toilets, let alone showers. We had to demonstrate how they worked.'

Jill Murray had been given the job of looking after them in London and making them feel as secure and comfortable as possible. 'They knew they were going to be giving harrowing evidence,' she says, 'and showed great courage in coming over. They were nervous, but I felt they were doing what they wanted to do, by coming here to tell their story, and that overrode everything else.' As one of the old ladies told her, 'We've waited fifty years to tell this story.'

Murray's husband had initially questioned whether the war crimes investigation and the trial were really worth the millions being spent on them. Having been introduced to some of the witnesses one evening, as they drove home, he said, 'You were absolutely right, it's well worth doing,' and for Murray herself, the case was 'life-changing'. There is an often-quoted remark first attributed to Stalin: 'The death of one person is a tragedy, but the death of a million is just a statistic.' Jill Murray's experience seems to bear this out, as she said that 'people don't associate the Holocaust with real human beings', but meeting those individual survivors and witnesses had really brought the human impact home to her.

Murray met them at Heathrow, steered them through immigration and drove them in a minibus to their hotel. They ate all their meals in the hotel and the variety and quantity of food delighted them. Every morning they piled their plates high from the buffet breakfast, and one of them filled his pockets with pastries and fruit before setting off to court.

At the weekend she drove them around, showing them some of the sights, like the Tower of London and Buckingham

Palace, and they even marvelled at things Londoners take for granted, like red double-decker buses and black cabs. Although they were given a small living allowance, for these elderly and desperately poor people there was no realistic possibility of other tourist excursions or shopping trips. Some, frightened by the noise, traffic and crowds of a city that was almost unimaginably different from the place where they had spent their lives, only left the hotel to travel to court. Others, a little braver or more robust, wandered the streets of the West End, but even they didn't go far and could only peer through the shop windows at luxuries they could never afford. The price of vodka in the hotel bar must also have been a terrible shock, with a single measure costing more than a bottle back in Belarus.

The first of them to testify at the Old Bailey was Galina Puchkina, the old schoolfriend that Ben-Zion had met again on his trip back to Domachevo. Bespectacled, small and stooped, she had lived there all her life and her lined face displayed the hard times she had endured, but there was no sign of frailty in her voice or her gait and, offered the opportunity to sit down, she said she would prefer to stand.

In the course of their evidence, Puchkina and the succession of other humble Belarusian witnesses often sat bemused as judge and counsel exchanged Latin terms and arcane points, couched in language that would not have been out of place in an eighteenth-century courtroom. At times, it brought to mind a famous exchange between a pompous judge and the legendary QC Marshall Hall, whose client was an Irish labourer.

'Is your client not familiar with the maxim *res ipsa loquitur*? [literally: the thing speaks for itself]' the judge said, barely masking his irritation.

'My Lord,' Marshall Hall said, 'on the remote hillside in Donegal where my client comes from, they talk of little else.'

Johnny Nutting's flowery opening question to Galina Puchkina – 'Mrs Puchkina, may I be so ungallant as to ask when you were born?' – bordered on self-parody. Having learned her age and the area of Domachevo in which she lived, Nutting spent some time in establishing when the *Schutzmannschaft* had been formed and where the police station had been. Only then did he ask her about Sawoniuk. She said that he had joined the police 'right from the outset and, judging from how he behaved afterwards, I believe he joined voluntarily'.

Puchkina had been a girl of 11 at the time of the Yom Kippur massacre of the Jews. It was a Sunday morning and, with her nine-year-old sister, she had gone to Mass, walking across the fields to the Catholic church, on a low hill overlooking the ghetto. As they approached the church, they heard the sound of cries and shouts from the ghetto and saw 'absolutely lots, around two thousand' Jews.

'Were you able to tell what was making them cry and shout out?' Nutting said.

'Of course I do. They were all being taken to their death by the local police and the Germans.'

Soon after they entered the church, a German official appeared with an interpreter and ordered the whole congregation out. They were made to stand at the side of the church and watch what was occurring below them. 'We immediately saw that a large group of people,' she said, 'one hundred, one hundred and fifty, two hundred, I cannot say – being taken away. Both sexes, all sorts of ages from the very old to the very young.'

'How could you tell they were Jews?' Nutting said.

'All the Jewish population had yellow sewn-on badges at the front and behind.'

'What happened?'

'They were undressed before us. They were all naked . . . The German soldiers and the local police were then beating them along towards the forest . . . After they took the first group away, I heard the sound of machine-gun fire.'

She saw three similar-sized groups led away and then the German official told them to go home. 'My sister took fright immediately,' Puchkina said, and they fled.

Several of the jurors looked surprised that the Nazis would have wanted an audience for the massacre of the Jews, but the show of force served several aims: instilling fear, encouraging anti-Semites and making the townsfolk feel complicit.

Clegg rose to begin his cross-examination. The witnesses had already testified at the committal hearing, and they were not given much additional preparation before the trial itself. A few days beforehand, they were handed copies of the witness statements they had signed to refresh their memories, but they were not told what to expect, other than that the first person to ask them questions would be on behalf of the state, and the second for the defence. So the bruising cross-examination they were all about to endure may well have come as an unpleasant surprise to them, because defence lawyers in Soviet and Belarusian courts were very rarely as vocal against the evidence presented by the state.

Puchkina was the first one to feel the force of Bill Clegg's questioning. He wasted no time in querying her claim that Andrusha had volunteered to join the auxiliary police. 'So far as Andrusha is concerned, you cannot say what were the circumstances in which he joined the police?'

'I do not know exactly but it is widely known that he went as a volunteer.'

'That is the gossip?'

'Yes. There was a general impression on the part of everybody that that was the case on account of his behaviour.'

Clegg then moved on to events following the massacre. 'It is right, is it not, that you yourself never saw any Jew in Domachevo after the day of the main massacre?'

'That is correct.'

'So you cannot tell us from anything that you saw whether any Jew was ever shot after the main massacre?'

Puchkina acknowledged that, while insisting that others had seen it, and she admitted that she had never seen Sawoniuk kill anyone. Clegg contented himself with establishing those points and Puchkina was released from the witness box.

The next witness was another woman, Fedora Yakimuk. She was 73, an illiterate subsistence farmer with a face as brown and wrinkled as a walnut, and gnarled, arthritic hands that spoke of a lifetime's labour in the fields. She had lived in the tiny, Russian Orthodox hamlet of Borisy all her life, and had known Andrusha well because his first wife, Anna, was godmother to her sister's baby son.

Although, like Puchkina, much of what Yakimuk knew about the killing of Jews was based on what others had told her, the one account of what she had actually seen with her own eyes was a chilling one. A week after the massacre in Domachevo, she had been reaping wheat on her family's smallholding. When she put a sheaf on her shoulder, the sickle she had been using fell out and gashed her arm. Her mother bound the cut with a rag and, when they got home, she put iodine on the wound and bandaged it up. However, the iodine seeped through the bandage, making a yellowish stain on the fabric. When she encountered Andrusha with some Germans, they saw the stain, took it for the yellow patch that Jews were compelled to wear on their clothing, and began shouting '*Jude! Jude!*'

'They grabbed me,' she said, 'and started dragging me away to be shot. And I was crying and begging them, exclaiming to them, "I'm not a Jew! I'm not a Jew!" and Andrusha knew me very well and did not protect me. I was actually down on my knees, crying and kissing the German on his feet,' when the officer tore off the bandage, saw the wound and the iodine and told her, 'Go home.' Andrusha had remained silent throughout.

As Bill Clegg rose to begin his cross-examination, Yakimuk eyed him rather as she might have regarded a wolf blocking her path in the forest at home, and from the start he adopted a hectoring tone that must have felt a lot like bullying to this illiterate and very nervous old lady. His first question set the tone. 'You never saw Andrusha Sawoniuk commit any act of violence against any person, Jew or Gentile, did you?'

She gave a nervous look around the courtroom before her hesitant reply. 'He ... his behaviour towards everybody was bad.'

'Yes or no, please. Did you ever see him commit any act of violence against any Jew?'

'Yes, I saw him beat people.'

'Yes or no, did you ever see him commit any acts of violence against any Gentile?'

'Yes, that is also true, but we were not allowed to see this.'

'So it would be quite untrue to say, "I never personally witnessed any acts of violence during the German occupation"?'

'We were frightened to go there. We never went there.'

Clegg laboured the point by repeating it and then quoted the statement she had made to Scotland Yard detectives in 1997. 'Today you have told us that you saw Sawoniuk beat people. That, I suggest, is something that you never said to Scotland Yard; that is true, is it not?'

'But I did see – I did see him herd people towards the sandpits.'

'You are, I suggest, changing your evidence to fit in with the stories other people are telling.'

'I am telling you what I saw, what I know.'

Clegg went on to suggest that she had talked about the case with the other witnesses from Belarus as they travelled to London; that people in Domachevo were talking about the case and the newspapers and television were reporting it. 'Everybody is saying what Andrusha did in the war, but the truth is you never saw him do anything.'

As he kept firing questions at her, she grew increasingly flustered and confused. 'Please,' she said at one point. 'I only did two classes of elementary school in Poland. I am not as literate as you think.'

Clegg did not relent and, having got her to contradict what she had said to Scotland Yard two years earlier, she then reversed what she had said in the courtroom only minutes before: 'I saw people being led away but I did not see them being beaten. I heard shots.'

Clegg went in for the kill. 'You have just been caught out, have you not, saying something that you never saw? What I suggest you are doing in your evidence is repeating a lot of gossip. There is not a word in your statement about anyone, let alone Andrusha, being seen by you herding anyone anywhere.'

'But I did see him herd people away.'

'There is not a word in your statement about seeing anybody beaten by anybody.'

'I did see him.'

'The truth is that you are just saying things that other people have told you about, is it not? Could I make it quite clear to you? I suggest that you never saw Andrusha herd anybody towards the sandpits?'

'I did, I did,' Yakimuk said, by now close to tears.

It was brutal, but as Potts noted to himself on his copy of the transcript, it was also 'rather effective', adding the politically incorrect observation, 'Fedora obviously none too bright.'

The one moment of relief for her came when Clegg asked, 'Do you remember coming to England last year and giving evidence in the magistrates' court, when Mr Nutting asked you some questions?'

Yakimuk looked blank. 'No, no, I cannot remember, you

can kill me, I still will not remember.' Clegg then pointed at Nutting and she flushed and said, 'I am sorry, they are all the same. I cannot recognise them.'

'I am the same as Mr Clegg?' Nutting said, drawing a laugh from around the court because it was hard to imagine two more different men than the tall and angular Nutting and the short and rather rotund Clegg. She broke into a smile, perhaps as much of relief at the temporary respite as of amusement, and even joined in the joke. 'You could be brothers!'

It was a brief reprieve, for Clegg returned to the attack, bringing her up short with a harsh reminder. 'Mrs Yakimuk, we have all been amused by your answers but you know that Andrusha Sawoniuk is on trial for murder, and you will appreciate that he regards the proceedings as very serious. When you were asked questions by Mr Nutting at the magistrates' court, you were given every opportunity to say what you wanted to say and what you could remember. Why didn't you say you'd seen Andrusha herd any people to their death?'

'Well, I think I answered all the questions that were put to me.'

Concluding his cross-examination, Clegg perhaps miscalculated by trying to undermine Yakimuk's account of the wound and the iodine stain, claiming, 'Andrusha was never present when any German inspected your wound from the sickle.'

She insisted it was true. 'Andrusha did not protect me. He simply said, "Jew" and dragged me away. I was very, very frightened.'

Clegg sat down, having torn parts of her story apart and, despite her denials, he had made a convincing case that her testimony against Sawoniuk came not from personal knowledge but village gossip. Yet, curiously, this may not have damaged her credibility in the eyes of the jurors as much as he must have thought. As sociologist Dr David Hirsh remarked in his commentary on the trial, Clegg had 'made her look ridiculous in cross-examination primarily because she was uneducated, unintelligent, in a wholly foreign country and setting, but not necessarily because she was a liar'.

Johnny Nutting was keenly aware of how potentially damaging the cross-examination had been and he again exercised his right to re-examine. Her last comment to Clegg had been about how frightened she was and Nutting referred back to her original statement to the Scotland Yard detectives. 'On the subject of fear, is what you told the police in 1997 true? "The population was scared of this local police unit and if they were seen to come towards our village, I and others would run away and hide." You go on, "I saw Andrusha wearing a police uniform. We were frightened when we saw a policeman uniform and we ran."'

She nodded. 'Whenever you saw him, you literally began to shake and want to get away.' Her gaze briefly alighted on Sawoniuk at the back of the courtroom but she quickly looked away again.

'What was it that caused you to be so frightened?'

'People were being caught and beaten.'

'And were they being taken anywhere?'

'Yes, everybody was taken to the sand-hills.'

Yakimuk's heart must have sunk as she saw Bill Clegg rise again to exercise his own right to a further cross-examination. 'My Lord,' he said, 'may I just put one further part of the deposition to the witness? I think in the light of what Mr Nutting has put, it perhaps, in fairness, ought to be put. Mrs Yakimuk, did you say in the magistrates' court, "I saw Andrusha a couple of times between 1941 and 1944," and was that true?'

'Yes.'

Clegg sat down again but Nutting sprang back to his feet. 'And does the next sentence explain that one of those occasions was when you cut yourself with a sickle, i.e. the incident that you have related to us today? And does the next sentence indicate that there was a further occasion, but that you couldn't remember when?'

'That is correct.'

As Nutting resumed his seat, she cast a fearful glance at Clegg, probably expecting him to rise to his feet again, but this time he remained seated and she was allowed to leave the witness box without any further interrogation.

CHAPTER 22

The first witness to be called on Day 10 of the trial, Wednesday 3 March 1999, was Ivan Baglay. He was in his early seventies and, like Fedora Yakimuk, came from Borisy. He made a patchy living by doing odd jobs like digging graves or chopping firewood, and was a heavy vodka drinker.

His younger brother Alexandre was also a witness for the prosecution. Their father, Jakov, had been a carpenter in Domachevo, specialising in building the wooden houses with shutters and ornate carved gables that were typical of the region. He was the craftsman who, after the massacre, had been employed by Sawoniuk to take down a Jewish-owned building in the ghetto and re-erect it in Sverdlov Street. When he asked for payment, Sawoniuk had refused, brandishing his rifle at him and threatening to shoot him if he ever came back.

Ivan Baglay had worked at the *bania* next door to the police station throughout the German occupation. Questioned by Johnny Nutting, he confirmed that Andrusha's brother Nikolai had joined the *Schutzmannschaft* at the same time but 'was not in the police for long at all, actually. He soon discovered what the whole racket smelt of and left.'

Baglay was 14 years old at the time of the Yom Kippur massacre and described coming into the town that morning and seeing that 'the gates to the ghetto had been opened and there was nobody about, although I did hear shootings coming from the direction of the sand-hills. The sound of gunfire was almost like that of a full-blown war. I ran home and told my mother that they had started killing the Jews.' When he later went to the sand-hills, he said, 'I saw blood seeping through the sand and lots of flies.'

Two or three days after the massacre, he was in Domachevo and 'saw Andrusha coming along the bridge, from the lake' with a Jewish woman and a little girl about six years old. Sawoniuk had his carbine slung over one shoulder and a birch pole in the other hand and, as Baglay watched, he took the pole in both hands and swung it down with such force on the woman's shoulder that she fell to the ground.

'He gave the woman such a beating that he must have broken a bone,' Baglay said. 'The little girl was screaming in a hoarse voice. Andrusha put the pole back on his shoulder. He then grabbed the woman and started dragging her, shouting, "*Schnell! Schnell! Schnell!*" When she got back to her feet, that shoulder was noticeably lower than the other one and her hand was immobile. So she took the girl instead by her left hand.'

By now Baglay was so frightened that he ran away and did not see what happened after that. 'I saw this animal behaviour and went home.' The following day he saw Sawoniuk again, this time having captured a Jewish cobbler called Biumen and his wife and two young daughters. Baglay knew them well because he had often had his boots repaired by him. Andrusha knew them too, Baglay said, because his mother used to work for the family. He saw Biumen 'constantly turning to Andrusha and imploring that he save the life of his family', but Sawoniuk just ignored him and forced them to keep moving towards the sand-hills.

'Did you ever see Mr Biumen or any of his family again?' Nutting asked.

'No.'

Baglay then described the headlong retreat of the Germans and their collaborators, including Andrusha, as the Red Army approached Domachevo in July 1944. The Germans set fire to the school, dumped their excess weapons in the well and then commandeered every horse and cart to transport their goods. Baglay, Fedor Zan and another man had been forced to drive them across the Bug River but had then escaped the Germans and fled back to their homes.

Bill Clegg's brief cross-examination focused on Baglay's claim about the Biumen family. In earlier statements he had only described them being marched towards the police station, and Clegg suggested he had now mentioned the sand-hills to bring his account into line with the other witnesses.

'Can I make it perfectly clear,' he said, 'that I do not accept that your account of either the story about the Jewish lady and the child, or the account of the Biumen family is either accurate or reliable?'

Baglay rejected that and Clegg closed by saying, 'My Lord, the jury appreciate of course, there are no charges laid as a result of either of these incidents.'

Once more, Nutting used his right to re-examine the witness to reinforce Baglay's testimony about the Biumens. 'What was it about the sight of them that day that caused you to feel sorry for them?'

'Because I saw that they were going on their last journey.'

'What caused you to believe that this was their last journey?'

'Because there was an order at the time that if anybody was found, they would be taken away and shot.'

'Is there a possibility that the policeman was not Andrusha?'

'It was Andrusha. I saw him very well.'

'In both incidents?'

'Yes.'

*

Evgeny Melaniuk was next on the stand. He had been the same age as Baglay, 14, in 1942 and came from Borisy, though he now lived in Domachevo. Other than his white hair, he showed little sign of his age, standing straight-backed and barrel-chested, with a brisk, no-nonsense air. He recounted seeing Andrusha and three other *Schutzmänner* ten days after the main massacre 'herding along' a group of eight 'Jewish people for execution'.

He had known Andrusha, he said, 'from childhood. I got to know him as a schoolboy but all the more so when he joined the police force, where he excelled himself by his keenness.'

'Was there any difference between him and the other policemen?'

'Regarding the others, very little is known,' Melaniuk said. 'They certainly were not talked about as much as Andrusha.' He said he had been 'fearful that I might also be forced to join this convoy', but when Nutting asked why, Clegg was at once on his feet to object. 'That question cannot possibly have any relevance for the jury's deliberation of the issues in this case.'

The judge upheld the objection and then adjourned the trial for the day.

Evgeny Melaniuk returned to the stand the next morning, Thursday 4 March, Day 11 of the trial, but Johnny Nutting had only one further point to establish, asking what the road to the sand-hills had been called by local people.

'It was called the Road of Death.'

In his cross-examination, Bill Clegg once more tried to highlight inconsistencies in statements made at different times, but his main focus was on the amount of discussion about the trial that had taken place in Domachevo and in the hotel where the witnesses were staying. He was again hoping to be able to claim that, consciously or subconsciously, the witnesses' accounts had been influenced by listening to each other talking about Sawoniuk, but in that he was to be disappointed. Melaniuk insisted that although he had travelled to London with the Baglay brothers and stayed in the same hotel, he had had no interaction with them. 'They are in different rooms, we have not socialised and communicated.'

'But you eat together?'

'Separately, at different tables. I have one interpreter, they have another.'

'Are you saying that since you got off the aeroplane, you have not spoken to the other witnesses staying in the same hotel as you?'

'No, we are not in contact with them.'

Once more, Clegg closed by suggesting that the witness had made up the allegation, and once more Nutting rose to re-examine. 'What is suggested is that you have invented your evidence against Mr Sawoniuk.'

'Do you think I am sick in the head?' Melaniuk said. 'I have allowed nothing to influence my evidence.'

'You have told us that there is a lot of talking in Domachevo about this trial.'

'Yes, it is their business. I have not bothered asking them questions.'

'Have you changed the evidence that you have given as a result of hearing that talk?'

'What can I think other than what I have seen?' Melaniuk said. His evidence was 'truth on the highest level. What I have seen with my own eyes could not have been influenced by other tongues.'

'Would you have made this allegation against Sawoniuk if it wasn't true?'

'No, because then I would have been cursed by God above.'

If Fedora Yakimuk's credibility had successfully been called into question by Clegg's cross-examination, Melaniuk had proved a much tougher nut to crack, and his robust rejection of any suggestion that his testimony had been invented, rehearsed, or influenced by the accounts of others, must have left a strong impression on the jurors.

Day 12 of the trial, Friday 5 March, began with yet another lengthy legal argument – 'Much more Nutting/Clegg wrangling', as Potts described it in his notes – between the two counsel about the admissibility of a photograph from KGB files of a group of ten *Schutzmänner*. They were allegedly from Domachevo and one of them appeared to be Sawoniuk. When shown the photograph in an early interview with Scotland Yard detectives, Andrusha denied it was him and claimed, 'I'm not Belarusian, and I've never been in a Belarusian uniform. I am a Polish man. I've nothing to do with Belarus.'

After an hour's discussion it was eventually agreed that the next witness could be shown the photograph but only to confirm that the uniforms shown were of the type worn by auxiliary police in Domachevo, without any suggestion that they were from the town or that one of them was Andrusha.

The jurors were then brought into court and Alexandre Baglay, a powerfully built grave-digger and tree-cutter with a weather-beaten face, took the stand. The younger brother of Ivan, he had been a few days short of his 13th birthday when he heard the massacre. A couple of days later, with his friend Valodia Melaniuk, who was three years older and also lived in Borisy, he had sneaked into the deserted ghetto, looking for clothes or shoes they could steal, but they were caught by *Schutzmänner* and taken to the police station.

Andrusha then handed them shovels and marched them towards the sand-hills at gunpoint. They were paralysed with fear, 'Crying, thinking that we would be shot as well,' but when they reached the edge of the forest, they saw two other auxiliaries there, standing guard over two men and a young woman, all with yellow patches on their clothing, next to a freshly dug hole. When Sawoniuk ordered them to undress, the men complied but the woman was too embarrassed to remove her underwear until he threatened her with a beating with a wooden club.

At this crucial moment in Baglay's testimony, the LiveNote simultaneous transcription on which Sawoniuk was following the trial, ceased to operate and Bill Clegg immediately requested a pause in proceedings until it had been rectified. The judge called a brief adjournment but, a few minutes later, Clegg asked for the judge to come back into court and the jury to retire. It transpired that Sawoniuk had gone to the Gents during the recess and there had been an incident, though Clegg was not clear what had occurred. 'I was given a message,' he said, 'and it may have been completely muddled, that he had collapsed outside. That is why I asked for the jury to retire and my Lord to come in, and I asked the matron to come, but it seems to be wholly inconsistent with what I have just observed.'

Sawoniuk was back in court a few moments later, red-faced and scowling more than usual, but otherwise in no worse apparent state than when he had left the courtroom. No further explanation was offered and the jurors were not informed about it when they filed back in soon afterwards.

Johnny Nutting could have explained Sawoniuk's ill temper, because he witnessed the immediate aftermath of the incident that had caused it, but he preferred to remain silent. At the start of the trial, Ben-Zion had asked if his friend and fellow survivor from Domachevo, Meir Bronstein, who had accompanied him to London, could sit with him at the back of the court. The defence had raised no objections, so Bronstein was allowed to join Clara and Shalom while Ben-Zion was giving his evidence, and continued to do so during the remainder of the trial.

During one of the intervals, Bronstein had gone to the Gents. While he was there, he heard a flush and Sawoniuk emerged from one of the cubicles. Since he was on bail, he had no escort, and the two men were alone. As soon as they caught sight of each other, a furious altercation erupted, with Bronstein calling him 'liar' and 'murderer', and Sawoniuk responding with 'Jew boy' and threats to kill him. Alarmed by the noise, court officials burst in and separated the two septuagenarians before they could actually exchange blows.

Had Bronstein been in the public gallery, as would normally have been the case, he wouldn't have had access to the same lavatories as the defendant, and as soon as Johnny Nutting was told about the incident, he sought out Sawoniuk's solicitor to apologise. Having asked for Bronstein to be seated in the well of the court, he had inadvertently facilitated the incident.

While Nutting was still talking to Lee, Sawoniuk stormed up to them. Either failing to register that the prosecution counsel was standing there, or simply choosing to ignore him, he then launched into a furious tirade at his solicitor. 'If that Jew boy says anything to me again,' he spat, 'I'll kill him.'

With Sawoniuk back in court, albeit still glowering, Johnny Nutting took up the questioning of Alexandre Baglay. He repeated how the young woman had been forced to strip and, after she too was naked, Sawoniuk forced the three Jews to kneel in a row next to the pit. He then stood behind them, drew his pistol and shot each of them in the back of the head at point-blank range. He pushed their lifeless bodies into the pit with his knees, then ordered the boys to fill it in.

Andrusha and the other policemen 'searched the clothing to see if there was any gold hidden in it,' Baglay said, and then he told the boys, 'You can take the clothing for yourselves once you have buried these people,' but they were too frightened to do so. After they had filled in the grave, Andrusha told them, 'If we catch you again, you'll be here as well.' So they ran away very quickly.

As Mr Justice Potts noted on his copy of the trial transcript, when Bill Clegg rose to cross-examine, 'Clegg as usual tries to discredit the witness.' He pointed out that Baglay had made no mention of witnessing the murders when questioned by the Soviet NKVD at the end of the war, and the first time he had ever done so was when questioned by Scotland Yard in 1996. However, Baglay would already have seen countless collaborators being rounded up by the NKVD and may well have feared that any perceived involvement in German war crimes, no matter how tangential, might have led to his death or exile to Siberia. In those circumstances, silence was the wisest choice.

Clegg also tried to imply that Baglay's memory was unreliable, pointing out how many years had passed and then making great play of his uncertainty about how long it had been since his friend Valodia Melaniuk had drowned. 'Do we not have here, Mr Baglay, an example of your memory playing you false?'

Baglay was not buying that. 'I lived one hundred kilometres away. People merely told me that he had drowned. The dates I did not know. It did not interest me.'

Clegg then spent some time getting him to confirm that most of the prosecution witnesses came from or had connections to Borisy — a now-familiar theme to which he would return in his summing-up. He ended by again trying to demonstrate that Baglay's recall of the events of 57 years before was prone to error, questioning him about the two other local police auxiliaries he had seen with Andrusha. 'Can you help us please? Who were these other two policemen? What were their names?'

'How could I know? How can I remember?'

Clegg must have felt like a footballer facing an open goal. 'It is far too long ago, is it, to remember?'

'Yes, that is one aspect of it, but the second point, I did not know their surnames.'

'So is the position that at the time you knew their first names, but have now forgotten them? That is explained of course by the enormous period of time between the event that you are describing and today. I make it clear. I am not suggesting that this incident did not take place, but I am suggesting that the policeman known as Andrusha was not present; do you think you may have made a mistake or you might be wrong?'

'No, people who I knew well all my life, I would remember.'

'You may, for a variety of reasons, believe Andrusha was present, but I am suggesting you cannot—'

Baglay interrupted him. 'I do not believe. I saw it with my own eyes.'

'I am suggesting you cannot possibly remember all those years ago.'

Baglay shook his head. 'I remember beautifully.'

At that point, Clegg gave up and sat down.

With Johnny Nutting absent from court that day, his junior, John Kelsey-Fry, rose to re-examine Baglay, his terse and direct style of questioning in marked contrast to Nutting's more urbane approach.

'The other two police officers at that execution,' Kelsey began. 'Did you know them as well as you knew Andrusha?'

'I knew them by sight because I would know everybody by sight – everybody went to the *bania* – but I do not know their surnames.'

'And of the police officers present, who was it gave the orders at that execution?'

'Andrusha gave the order.'

'And of those police officers, which of them shot the Jews?'

'Andrusha.'

'And which of them ordered you and Valodia to fill in the grave?'

'Andrusha.'

'Finally, which of them had marched you from the police station up to the site?'

'Andrusha.'

'Again, do you think you may have made a mistake about Andrusha's involvement?'

'No.'

Kelsey-Fry resumed his seat, having undone in five minutes Clegg's work over the previous two hours.

CHAPTER 23

The trial did not resume until two in the afternoon of Day 13, Monday 8 March 1999, when the succession of elderly witnesses from Belarus continued with Ivan Stepaniuk. He was 75 years old, gap-toothed and wrinkled, and was originally from the village of Chersk, eight kilometres from Domachevo. Prior to the Nazi invasion, he had worked on the family farm, but in order to avoid being taken for forced labour in Germany he found work in Domachevo, first as a tailor and then, after the massacre of the Jews, at the forge.

Shortly after he began testifying, there was an unscheduled adjournment for half an hour while an usher of the court was despatched to the hotel where Stepaniuk was staying to fetch his spectacles, without which he could not see the photographs of the forge that he was being asked to identify.

Once more the exchanges between Johnny Nutting and Mr Justice Potts verged on self-parody. 'My Lord, I am very sorry,' Nutting said. 'I did specifically state that any witness who needed spectacles was to be sure to bring them from Domachevo, but I did not cover the distance between the hotel and your Lordship's court.'

'Well, Mr Nutting, I would be the last person, I think, to criticise anybody for forgetting his glasses.'

'My Lord, same here, if I may so.'

It wasn't exactly Oscar Wilde, but it was at least a little light relief from the grim recital of beatings and killings.

Stepaniuk's testimony centred on his sighting of a Jew called Shlemko – a man he knew well, having worked for him as a labourer on a construction site during the Soviet occupation. Stepaniuk was walking back towards the smithy one day when he saw Shlemko being driven along by two auxiliary policemen. One of them was Andrusha, who was carrying a spade and a carbine.

'Was he doing anything with the spade?' Nutting said.

'He was beating Shlemko on the back. After he had been beaten, he fell to the ground.'

'Once or more than once?'

'Well, he was picked up and they carried on going, then he was beaten and fell down again.'

'How many times, approximately, did Shlemko fall to the ground, be picked up, and fall to the ground again?'

'Four.'

'And during that time, did you see the face of Andrusha?'

'Yes. Every time he would pick up the Jew, Shlemko, he would turn round, so I had the opportunity to see his face.'

Stepaniuk lost sight of them after they passed the forge, heading towards the forest. A few minutes later he heard gunfire echoing through the forest. Sawoniuk and the other auxiliary then returned alone and he never saw Shlemko again.

Stepaniuk said he was too frightened to go anywhere near the police station after that, and the next time he saw Andrusha was 'when our own people were being driven from our village to be shot'.

This brought Clegg to his feet, objecting that this allegation, about a massacre in Chersk, did not relate to the count on the indictment and the defence did not accept that it had anything to do with Andrusha.

Mr Justice Potts merely observed mildly, 'There is obviously going to be an issue about this, as I dare say about the other matter,' but allowed Stepaniuk's testimony to continue.

He said that he had seen Andrusha, this time with about four other auxiliaries and a couple of Germans, dragging 11 Chersk men towards the forest. They were roped together and Andrusha was holding one end of the rope. They were never seen again.

'Did you know Andrusha in the sense that you just recognised him or was he a friend of yours?' Nutting said.

'He was no friend of mine.'

'Can you remember when you learned that his name was Andrusha?'

'His brother told us that.'

'Apart from those two occasions, did you ever lay eyes on Andrusha again?'

'I saw people being taken away to their execution on more occasions, but as to who was escorting them, I cannot tell you whether Andrusha was there.'

Mr Justice Potts noted on the trial transcript that 'after a bit of wrangling with Nutting on leading questions', Clegg's cross-examination consisted of 'the usual hole-picking'.

He was able to establish that when Stepaniuk saw Shlemko being taken to his death, he didn't know Andrusha and only learned his identity a couple of days later, from his brother, Nikolai. Clegg also quoted from a statement recorded by Scotland Yard detectives in November 1995, when Stepaniuk had described Sawoniuk as having 'a thin, long face, dark-brown hair and was of medium build'. That did not sound at all like Andrusha's round-faced, fair-haired and stocky figure, but Stepaniuk merely said, 'Well, the dark-brown hair, I never told that to anybody. The rest is true.'

The court had adjourned for the day at the end of Clegg's cross-examination, but the next morning, Nutting again exercised his right to re-examine the witness. 'You told Mr Clegg yesterday that at the time when you saw the man you describe as Andrusha escorting Shlemko, you did not know that man's name. Is that correct?'

'No, it is not correct,' Stepaniuk said. 'I knew him earlier when I used to work with the Jews.'

'How did you know his name?'

'The Jews described him as the worst policeman.'

That brought Clegg to his feet again to object that the answer was hearsay. Nutting conceded that point, contenting himself with establishing that Sawoniuk had been known by everyone as Andrusha. He then referred to the phrase 'dark-brown hair' in the description Stepaniuk had given to Scotland Yard, and tried to establish that it was a mistranslation from the Russian by getting him to point to someone in court who had hair the colour he had meant. Stepaniuk did so, indicating someone with fair hair.

Stepaniuk was then allowed to leave the witness box without any further examination by Clegg, and his place was taken by Czeslaw Hamziuk, a 76-year-old from a village four kilometres from Domachevo. He had been an auxiliary policeman, although a conscript in 1943 rather than a volunteer straight after the German invasion, as he said Andrusha and his brother had been. He had fled with the Germans as the Red Army approached in the summer of 1944, crossing the Bug River on a horse and cart.

'I had to be together with the Germans. If I did not, I would probably be shot, together with the rest of my family,' he said, but he had escaped after 20 or 30 kilometres and returned to his home. From the Crown's point of view, the principal point of his brief testimony was to establish that Andrusha had fled with the Germans at the same time.

In cross-examination, Clegg seemed principally interested in establishing that the *Schutzmänner* were poorly equipped and badly paid, if at all. Yet again Nutting used his right to re-examine at least partly to counter that suggestion by escorting Hamziuk through a list of clothing and equipment that had been issued to them.

The court adjourned early that day, and the following morning, Wednesday 10 March, Day 15 of the trial, began with the penultimate prosecution witness, Detective Sergeant Michael 'Mickey' Griffiths. He was currently attached to SO13 – the Anti-Terrorist Branch at New Scotland Yard – but, as a member of the War Crimes Unit, had been one of the four-man police team who had gone to Sawoniuk's Bermondsey address on 21 March 1996, armed with a search warrant. Andrusha lived there alone and so answered the door himself. Sawoniuk was taken aback, Griffiths said, but that was not an unusual reaction to policemen on the doorstep, and after they had explained the purpose of their visit and shown him the search warrant, he invited them in. One of them then sat with him in his lounge, while the others searched the flat.

The search revealed two wartime documents in a drawer: a travel permit and a photograph of Sawoniuk in his Polish II Corps army uniform. Before leaving, Griffiths read Sawoniuk a formal notice, telling him that the police were investigating charges of murder and manslaughter in the German occupied territories between 1939 and 1945. He was required to present himself for interview at Southwark Police Station at 2.30pm on 1 April 1996, and was advised to obtain the services of a lawyer.

Nutting then turned to the subject of that first formal interview with Sawoniuk, conducted by Griffiths and Detective Constable Moore in the presence of Martin Lee and another solicitor, and recorded on audio. Nutting wanted the transcript entered into the court record but he also wanted the jurors to hear it read aloud, undoubtedly feeling it would have more impact than if it was merely handed to them as a document.

He must also have doubted whether Sawoniuk would take the stand. Had Nutting been representing him, he would certainly have argued against it, and there was no reason to believe that Clegg would be any less diligent in his client's interests. If so, this would be the only opportunity for the jurors to hear Sawoniuk's own testimony in relation to the charges.

As a result, Nutting and Griffiths then took part in a bizarre piece of amateur dramatics. Reading from the transcript, Griffiths reprised his role as lead interrogator and, since the defence was hardly likely to make Sawoniuk available to read his part, Nutting substituted for the defendant. Griffiths read his questions in a slow, deliberate and very 'policeman-like' way, while Sawoniuk's responses, originally spoken in his odd hybrid of Cockney and Belarusian-accented English, were now delivered in Nutting's plummy tones. The effect was ludicrous – as if William Rees-Mogg was addressing the House of Commons in Cockney rhyming slang – and it was another surreal touch in a trial that had not been short of them.

The interview first covered Sawoniuk's personal history and his various occupations and addresses since coming to Britain. Griffiths then began to question him about the content of documents gathered during the investigation, including his Polish Army record, his application for registration as a British citizen compiled by the Polish Resettlement Corps and a medical report dating from 1947. Copies had been handed to the jurors and Nutting asked them to pay particular attention to the signature on each one, which Sawoniuk had confirmed was his. Nutting also highlighted the response to the question 'Are you married?' to which Sawoniuk had replied with the Polish word for widower.

Nutting's only further point was to refer the jurors to a document known as an 'Admission' – a set of facts agreed by the defendant. Sawoniuk had admitted, Nutting said, that through-out the period of the German occupation, 'the defendant served as a police officer in Domachevo. At one time he was regarded as the senior local police officer stationed in the town.'

The dual performance by Nutting and Griffiths was then paused, since the remainder of Sawoniuk's police interview dealt with his reaction to evidence from Fedor Zan, who would be the last prosecution witness, and Nutting wanted the jury to hear that testimony before Sawoniuk's response to it.

Clegg's cross-examination of Griffiths was routine except that, in seeking to establish Sawoniuk's service with the Allies as a member of Polish II Corps in the latter stages of the war, Clegg referred to his army record. If Sawoniuk took the stand, that had opened the door to Nutting using the same record to ask questions about other, less savoury aspects of Andrusha's wartime military service, and was arguably another own goal by Clegg. His only other intervention was to point out to the judge that Sawoniuk's current address had been read aloud in open court during the reconstruction of the police inter-view. 'So can I just, through my Lord, urge the press to show restraint in publishing the actual address of the defendant because of the obvious dangers with people who may wish to make direct contact, which would only be counter to the interests of justice?'

Sawoniuk was already running a nightly gauntlet of abuse from local teenagers and there was an understandable fear that vigilantes might decide to take direct action against him.

Mr Justice Potts concurred, urging the press not to report the address 'for reasons that I think must be obvious to any responsible journalist'.

CHAPTER 24

The trial should have resumed the next morning, but overnight one of the four women jurors had fallen ill and been taken to hospital. Mr Justice Potts accordingly adjourned until the following Monday, 15 March 1999.

It was a beautiful warm and sunny spring morning when the court reconvened, but the continued absence of the juror cast a cloud over the proceedings. There was still no certainty about when, or indeed if, she would be fit to resume her duties, the consultant treating her having informed the court that his patient would be in hospital 'for at least another week'.

Potts had to decide whether to pause the trial until she recovered, discharge the jury and order a retrial, or proceed with a jury of 11, which, under UK law, he had the discretion to do. 'It seems to me,' Potts said, 'that in this case, perhaps more than any, a delay of a week – and that may well be the minimum period – would be highly undesirable and should be avoided at all costs.'

As a result, with the acquiescence of both counsel, the judge ordered the juror to be discharged and the trial to continue with the reduced jury of 11. Should any of the remaining jurors have fallen ill, the proceedings would have had to come to a halt, for the judge had no power under the law to reduce the numbers any further.

The final Crown witness was Fedor Zan, who was still in recovery from prostate surgery, and he made his way uncomfortably to the witness box. He had been sworn in before his walk with the jury in Domachevo and was now simply reminded of that once he had taken the stand.

Like several of the other witnesses, Zan hailed from Borisy, and had lived there for all of his 76 years. Nutting established that he had known Andrusha from childhood; they had been to the same school and worshipped in the same Russian Orthodox church. He testified that Sawoniuk had joined the *Schutzmannschaft* 'about ten or twelve days' after the invasion and had been married twice, first in the winter of 1941–42 to 'a midwife from the east' – Anna Maslova – and later to a woman called Nina, the point of which would only become apparent to the jurors later in the trial.

Nutting then questioned Zan about the arrest of his uncle, aunt and two cousins, accused of aiding the partisans. He and his mother were walking to the police station in Domachevo, bringing food, when they saw them being herded along by Andrusha and another policeman. 'They had been tied up,' Zan said, 'and were being led through the ghetto towards the sands to be executed. They were tied in a row, one after another. My uncle was in the front, my aunt was in the middle, and the two cousins were at the back.' It was the sort of telling detail that might well carry weight with the jurors.

'Was Andrusha carrying anything?' Nutting said.

'He was carrying a sub-machine gun.'

'Did you ever see them again?'

'No, no. That was it. Once they had passed through the gates of the ghetto, I did not see them again.'

'What was the season of the year?'

'This was the spring.'

'Now, we have established the German invasion was in June of 1941,' Nutting said. 'The first spring after that was 1942,

225

and the second spring after that was 1943 and the third spring was 1943—'

'1944,' Clegg interrupted, adding rather testily, 'If he is going to lead [the witness], perhaps he would get the year right.'

Zan confirmed that it was the spring of 1943. That was not consistent with his earlier claim that they had been killed ten or twelve days after the massacre of the Jews, which had taken place the previous September, and Clegg permitted himself a brief smile and a raised eyebrow — as much of a reaction as was permissible to draw the jury's attention.

Zan spoke of another incident in which he had seen a Jewish woman with a baby being marched by Andrusha towards the sand-hills. Nutting then turned to the walk through the forest that had been replicated for the jury on that bitter February day. He had been working in Brest-Litovsk at the time, and after work one September afternoon, caught his usual train back to Domachevo but got off at Kobelka station at 6.15 or 6.20 to call at his sister's house with some cloth dye she had asked him to buy. He was then heading home through the forest when he heard cries and screams. He crept through the trees and saw Sawoniuk ordering a group of about 15 Jewish women to undress. He told them to place their clothing in a pile and turn to face a freshly dug pit, then raised his sub-machine gun and shot them all.

'Did you recognise any of these women?'

'No, no one. It was far away.'

How then had he recognised Sawoniuk? Nutting asked.

'I recognised him by his size and by his face. He was famous by that time.'

'What happened to the women after they were shot?'

'I couldn't tell you,' Zan said. 'I ran away from that place.'

'That evening, tell us about the light,' Nutting said, attempting to defuse a line of cross-examination that Clegg was certain to pursue.

'The sun had not yet gone down. It was still in the sky.'

Nutting reconfirmed with Zan that Andrusha had been 'a simple policeman but after that he became the commandant of the police', and then turned to the German flight from Domachevo as the Red Army advanced on the town.

Zan had been one of ten owners of horses and carts conscripted by the Germans to speed their escape and had seen Andrusha fleeing with some of them, and his second wife, Nina, in another cart. After crossing the Bug River and travelling on for another 25 or 30 kilometres, Zan said, 'I left my horse, the cart and ran away back to Borisy.' At the time he did so, Sawoniuk was still with the Germans.

Finally, Nutting established that Zan had seen Andrusha regularly in Domachevo in 1942, 1943 and 1944, before the German retreat. His intention was clear: to undermine any attempt by the defence to claim that Sawoniuk had been absent from the town on forced labour in Germany.

Nutting sat down with the contented air of a man who felt that one of his star witnesses had done him proud. In deference to Zan's recent operation, the judge then adjourned, allowing him a night's rest before facing what was certain to be a prolonged cross-examination by the defence.

As another courtesy to Fedor Zan, the court did not sit until 12.05pm on Day 17, Tuesday 16 March, and with an hour's recess for lunch, he would probably have to face no more than two hours in the witness box that day.

He was the third of the triumvirate of key Belarusian witnesses for the prosecution and Clegg was determined to exploit any discrepancies in his statements and throw as much doubt as possible on his identification of Sawoniuk as the murderer of the 15 Jewish women. If Clegg could demonstrate that an identification from almost 130 paces in the fading light of a late September afternoon could not be relied upon, his client's chances of an acquittal would be immeasurably improved. So he began a two-pronged attack: first on Zan's credibility and then on the ability of, not just Zan, but of anyone, to make an accurate identification at such long range.

He started by stressing Zan's roots in Borisy. 'I expect you know all of the residents, do you not? Am I right that every person now living in Borisy who is older than seventy-two or seventy-three is giving evidence in this trial?'

He then moved smoothly on, sketching the outlines of the conspiracy theory on which he was relying to discredit not only Zan's testimony but that of all the other witnesses from the hamlet. In the course of 30 questions and answers, he established that Borisy had suffered badly from reprisals for suspected collaboration with the partisans, and that the *Schutzmänner* had been involved in fighting the partisans. However, when he suggested that 'the Germans used the local police to protect the villagers from partisan attack,' Zan was quick to deny it. 'The police did not protect the villagers. To the contrary, they arrested the people.'

Clegg referred to the killing of Zan's aunt, uncle and cousins, and said, 'The reason, I suggest, why Sawoniuk is hated by the elderly people in Borisy, is because of his anti-partisan activities?'

'He fought not only against the partisans but non-partisans.'

Clegg then turned to Sawoniuk's impoverished upbringing, getting Zan to agree that people called Andrusha *baistruk* – bastard – that his family had no land, and that the only employment open to him after the German invasion was to join the local police. Zan replied that Sawoniuk 'enthusiastically joined the police. Nobody coerced him.'

Clegg then tried to persuade Zan that the German troops – described by the locals as 'the Gestapo' – who had carried out the massacre of the Jews, had remained in Domachevo for some time afterwards, and it was they, not the local police, who had carried out the subsequent searches of the ghetto.

Zan was not buying that. 'The Gestapo never searched the ghetto. They gave an order to Sawoniuk, as commander of the police, to search the ghetto.'

That was an overstatement, since Sawoniuk was not the police commander at the time.

'I suggest that you have either made up that answer,' Clegg said, 'or you are just repeating gossip.'

'No, no, this is the honest truth.'

'Did you hear anyone give Sawoniuk that order?'

'No, I did not.'

Pressed by Clegg, Zan insisted that he had not seen any of the Gestapo searching the ghetto but had seen Sawoniuk doing so.

Next came Zan's confusing statement the previous day when he had talked about seeing his uncle and aunt being taken to their execution 'ten or twelve days' after the massacre, but had also referred to it being in the spring of 1943. Clegg talked him through the answers he had given and said, 'Was that all honest and truthful evidence?'

'Yes, it was true. It was the honest truth.'

Clegg then read from the statement Zan had given to Scotland Yard detectives in 1996. '"I remember a time in April or May, I can't remember the exact date, but it was before all the Jews were shot in Domachevo, when my uncle and aunt and cousins were arrested for connections with the partisans."'

'Can you help, please,' Clegg said, 'as to why you told the police the events took place before the massacre of the Jews, and three times yesterday you told the jury it was afterwards? Why did you say to the police it was before?'

'No, they could have been mistaken,' Zan said, floundering. 'It is not my fault.' He shot a glance towards the judge but there was no help to be had from that quarter. Now increasingly flustered and confused, Zan continued to insist both that his uncle and aunt had been arrested 12 days after the massacre and that it had been in the spring of 1943.

'You are just making this up, are you not, Mr Zan?' Clegg said.

'No, no, I am not. I am not making up.'

'My Lord, is that a convenient moment . . .?' Clegg said, offering the judge the opportunity to adjourn for lunch, and sat down with a satisfied smile. He had tied Zan in knots and caught him out on a number of contradictions, and that was the impression the jurors would carry with them during the recess.

When the court resumed, Clegg began to probe Zan's account of the September evening when he claimed to have seen Sawoniuk murdering the 15 Jewish women. He first focused on the time he said his train had reached the Kobelka station – 6.15 or 6.20 – and when it arrived in Domachevo – 7.30. Since it would have been a journey of no more than ten minutes between the two stations, there was an apparent contradiction, but Zan claimed he meant the time he would have arrived at his home in Borisy. Clegg then dwelled briefly on the time it got dark there at that time of year – about seven o'clock – planting the idea in the jury's minds that the light would have been fading when Zan reached the site of the massacre.

He suggested that an observation made in failing light, under stressful conditions and over a considerable distance by a man who was anxious to remain hidden could not be relied upon. Zan disagreed. He knew Sawoniuk from school, had sat behind him in class, and although he had been some distance away, he recognised him 'by his size and by his face. He was famous by that time. He was very predatory . . . These shootings were his job. He is a real criminal. He killed more people than there are hairs on your head,' he said, repeating the words he had used to DC Charlie Moore.

Clegg then switched to the first of the two statements Zan

had made to detectives in February 1996. 'There is not a word, is there, about the events in the forest, where you said that you hid and saw the fifteen women machine-gunned by Andrusha?'

'I did tell your police,' Zan said. 'I did tell them that he shot fifteen women.'

'I accept that you did in April, when they went back to see you again, but I want to know why you did not tell them in February when you first saw them?'

Johnny Nutting then rose to object to the line Clegg was taking, though once more voicing his objection with great delicacy. 'My Lord, Mr Clegg must be a little careful about this, in view of the circumstances in which this statement ended and the way in which the subsequent one began.'

The jurors would remain unaware for the moment of those circumstances, since they were then excluded and, no doubt to his relief, Zan was also given a brief respite while the two counsel and the judge argued the point.

'I am anxious that the cross-examination should not proceed under a false assumption,' Nutting said, when the court had been cleared. 'Mr Clegg has made two assumptions: the first is that the witness did not say anything about the incident in the forest when he made his first statement in February. The second, and it flows from that, is that Mr Zan had the opportunity on that occasion of saying everything that he could say about the defendant. Now the factual position is this: the witness has asserted twice that he did tell the police on that first occasion, and the fact is that Mrs Zan appeared before the statement had been finished and insisted on her husband returning home. It is in those circumstances that the officers were compelled to break off and wait to finish the statement until the April, when they returned to Domachevo. As your Lordship will see, it is not a second statement but it is in furtherance of the statement already made.'

Clegg fought his corner, saying that there was no

documentary evidence to support the suggestion that Zan's wife had intervened, and he had asked Zan if there had been 'some pressing engagement' that had prevented him from mentioning the incident at the first interview.

Mr Justice Potts heard him out but then said, 'Mr Clegg, I can say this to you with the jury out: one has to attempt to be realistic about this. You are not cross-examining some city financier. We are dealing with a man who has spent all his life in Belarus. I obviously see the force of what you say, but "pressing engagement" is not something that would necessarily trigger a response.'

Nutting then said that a document was being faxed to the court, a note made by the detectives at the time they were interviewing Zan, that would provide the documentary proof Clegg had claimed was lacking. Whether it had been overlooked by Clegg or had not been disclosed to him before was something that both counsel would pursue overnight.

Meanwhile Zan's translator volunteered the information that the witness was tiring, adding that he had said, 'Please remember that I have just had an operation.' As a result, the judge called a halt to the day's proceedings, leaving Clegg to complete the cross-examination the next morning.

CHAPTER 25

Bill Clegg began Day 18 of the trial by conceding in front of the jury that 'Mr Zan had mentioned each incident he has given evidence about to the police on 13 February, and I was wrong to suggest that he had not mentioned the incident in the forest on that day. It was recorded in another document by the police, and a personal engagement prevented the conclusion of the statement, which was in fact concluded on 26 April of the same year.'

'My Lord,' Johnny Nutting said, once more digging deep into the sugar bowl, 'may I say that it is entirely typical of Mr Clegg to withdraw a point that he feels he cannot pursue, and I am very grateful to him.'

The document that had been faxed to the court was a statement from DC Moore, making clear the circumstances in which the interview with Zan had taken place. 'We were in the council offices in Domachevo taking statements,' Moore says. 'Fedor Zan had gone out for a loaf of bread and heard what was going on. He made it clear that he had something important to say to us. He was with us for about three hours and never stopped talking. He became our star witness, and right from the start he was adamant that Sawoniuk was responsible for those terrible atrocities.'

However, before Zan could complete that initial statement, his wife, concerned that a ten-minute trip to buy a loaf of bread

233

had taken three hours, burst in, berated him and made him go home with her at once. As a result, the police interview was paused and not concluded until their next visit to Domachevo several weeks later.

Having eaten his due slice of humble pie, Clegg returned to the attack. After asking about the number of policemen present at the other incidents Zan had witnessed and whether he knew their names, Clegg challenged him. 'Can I make it clear? I am suggesting that Sawoniuk was not present at any of these three incidents – if they took place – that you have described.'

'That is not true,' Zan said, anger reddening his face. 'That is not true at all. It is the honest truth that Sawoniuk was there.'

'You believe, do you not, with some passion, that he is responsible for the deaths of some of your own family?'

'Yes, yes, he was guilty.'

'And you have appeared on television, both in this country and in Russia, and said that you think Sawoniuk should be killed for what he did to your family?'

'That is correct. That is what I said.'

Having planted the suggestion of bias, Clegg tried to keep Zan off balance by abruptly changing to the much less heated topic of Sawoniuk's living arrangements before the war, but then argued that Sawoniuk had never married Nina – the woman with whom he had fled Domachevo as the Red Army approached. 'After his wife was killed, I suggest he did some time later have a girlfriend called Nina, but I suggest they never married.'

'He did marry Nina,' Zan said.

'Did you go to the wedding?' Clegg said, with more than a hint of sarcasm.

'No, I was not at the wedding,' Zan deadpanned.

'And when he left Domachevo, I suggest he left with a horse and cart.'

'And with his wife Nina,' Zan said, unwilling to give an inch.

'I suggest no wife and no Nina.'

'Why are you lying?' Zan shot back at him.

Once more, the reason for Clegg's perseverance over the question of Sawoniuk's marriage to Nina was not yet evident to the jurors.

Mr Justice Potts's notes to himself about Clegg's cross-examination make interesting reading: 'Usual – going over same territory and finding nits to pick while slyly implying extenuating circumstances for AS [Andrusha] – fascinating!'

Zan had been much less troubled by Clegg than the previous day but Nutting still took the opportunity to re-examine his witness, dealing first with Clegg's suggestion that Sawoniuk had not been present at any of the three incidents Zan had described.

Zan gave an emphatic shake of his head. 'That is not true. He was present. He is guilty. Without him, these events would not have taken place.'

For emphasis, Nutting ran through the three incidents individually, receiving the same answer about each one, and then said, 'It is suggested that because you blame Sawoniuk for taking your uncle and aunt to be killed, you have additionally invented allegations against him in relation to Jews.'

'No, there have been no inventions.'

'It was suggested that Sawoniuk was hated by old people in Borisy.'

Zan readily agreed. 'Nobody can stand him, not only in Borisy but in neighbouring villages.'

'And it is suggested the reason he is hated is because he fought against the partisans.'

'Because he had an animal-like attitude to people.'

'You said yesterday that he fought not only against partisans but against non-partisans,' Nutting said. 'Who were the non-partisans?'

'Farmers.'

'Finally, this: you told us that by the time you saw him in the forest, the incident involving the killing of the Jews, he was famous. In what way was he famous?'

'That he was the killer.'

Clegg's smile at the end of Zan's testimony looked considerably more forced than it had been midway through the cross-examination, when for a while he looked to have had Zan on the ropes.

DS Michael Griffiths was then recalled to the stand to complete the reading of the police interview with Sawoniuk, interrupted to allow Zan to testify before Sawoniuk's reaction was read into the record. Once more Griffiths read his own words, while Nutting deputised for Andrusha.

Griffiths had delivered the traditional caution: 'You do not have to say anything but it may harm your defence if you do not mention something when questioned that you later rely on in court. Anything you do say may be given in evidence.' He then detailed the three allegations Zan had made, beginning with the murder of the 15 Jewish women in the forest.

'That name you just mentioned,' Nutting said, speaking as Sawoniuk. 'Not only that one but all them, I never heard them, I never seen, I never even seen them and I don't know them people, don't know the name.'

'The two people you had mentioned, of course,' Nutting said, reverting to his normal voice, 'were Mr Alexandre Baglay and Mr Zan.'

Reassuming Sawoniuk's persona, he read, 'I shoot, I shot, I should know some of them names but . . .'

When Griffiths put Ben-Zion's allegations about the torture and murder of the old Jew, Idel, to him, Sawoniuk had said, 'Not true innit, at all.' To hear Sir Johnny Nutting, Bart, uttering the word 'innit', was a pleasure that the Old Bailey had never had before and was unlikely ever to have again.

In cross-examination, Bill Clegg was able to elicit from Griffiths that when detectives and lawyers from the Crown Prosecution Service interviewed any potential witnesses in Belarus, a local procurator was always present. The implication was clear: the witnesses might have felt pressure to give testimony that toed the party line in Belarus.

Clegg led Griffiths through the two documents taken from Sawoniuk's flat. Griffiths confirmed that the travel permit gave Sawoniuk's height as five foot nine and his hair blond, matching the details on his Polish II Corps record.

Clegg then sought Griffiths's agreement that Sawoniuk had arrived in this country 'via the North Africa campaign and then the Italian front', drawing a mild admonition from Mr Justice Potts. 'The North African campaign, which many people might have thought was over by the time he could have got there.'

Clegg closed by saying, 'I am right that he is a man of good character?'

'He has no previous convictions, sir,' Griffiths said, which even the most obtuse of jurors would have noted was not quite the same thing.

Nutting saw Clegg's reference to Sawoniuk's service with II Corps in North Africa and Italy as an opportunity to raise his time with the Waffen-SS in the autumn of 1944, when re-examining Griffiths.

Potts intervened. 'It might be misleading to think that the defendant suddenly left Belarus and was fighting the North Africa campaign, which is one conclusion that the jury might be entitled to draw from Mr Clegg's question, but I think they ought to know the basis of this officer's [Griffiths's] knowledge.'

Griffiths replied that it was 'a document prepared by the German military authorities, a report that relates to personnel missing, killed or taken prisoner of war'. The document, a Loss Report from the *Wehrmachtauskunftsstelle* (WAST) in Berlin, related to a Waffen-SS soldier who had gone missing in

November 1944 and, Griffiths said, gave 'the same name, date of birth and other identifying features as the defendant'.

A copy of the document was then produced and, questioned by Nutting, Griffiths answered that it had been issued by the 'Waffen Border Regiment of the SS, Number 76, First Battalion'.

'The place and time of the report – is that Schallstadt, 6 December 1944?' Nutting queried.

'It is, yes.'

Bill Clegg rose to object. 'With respect, this witness cannot possibly speak to the date of this. This is just when the report was made. It cannot possibly speak to the veracity or the accuracy of when the matter was recorded.'

It was astonishing that he had not risen sooner to object to the line of questioning, because it was undoubtedly hugely damaging to his client for the jury to know that Sawoniuk had served in the Waffen-SS. The *Schutzmänner* were purely local police auxiliaries, but the Waffen-SS were – or had been – the elite of the Nazi fighting troops.

Clegg then asked to 'raise a matter in the absence of the jury' but, after hearing legal arguments about the document from both sides, whatever Potts might now rule and whatever subsequent instructions he gave to the jury, the damage may already have been done. They had been told that Sawoniuk had served in the SS. It was naive to imagine that they would forget that, even if the judge told them to disregard it.

'My Lord,' Clegg began, 'in our submission, the contents of this document must be hearsay. The officer [Griffiths] was not alive when this was written.'

'You started it, Mr Clegg,' Potts said, 'by the question you asked in cross-examination concerning the movements and activities of this defendant after he left Belarus. The impression I got from that question and the answer you were attempting to elicit – and the jury may have drawn the same conclusion – was

that after leaving Belarus in 1944, this defendant enthusiastically adopted the cause of the Allies by campaigning in
North Africa.'

'It was actually Italy,' Clegg said, rather feebly.

'Surely the fact he was for a period of time in the Waffen-SS
is admissible, providing the evidence is there.'

'This witness cannot formally prove the document,' Clegg
said. 'To ask a witness: "What do your inquiries reveal?" is
saying to the witness, "Tell me some hearsay." That is exactly
what, in our submission, the whole of this re-examination has
been designed to do.'

The legal arguments continued for half an hour, and when
the jury returned to court, Mr Justice Potts addressed them.
'Ladies and gentlemen, hearsay is not evidence. Before you left
court, the officer gave it in evidence that his understanding
was the defendant had been conscripted into the Belarusian
Waffen-SS. The basis for that was a missing persons document
prepared by the German authorities. I have been hearing legal
arguments about all that. The short point is this – and I am
sure you can appreciate it – this officer did not prepare that
document. The maker is not here and could not be here, and
the document is, therefore, not evidence, and that is where we
leave it at the minute.'

Nutting's final questions to Griffiths were intended to
inform the jurors that, under Belarusian law, everything that
had been communicated to defence solicitors in the preparation of the case was secret and the prosecution had not been
informed about it. Having established that, Nutting signed off
with the words, 'That is the case for the Crown.'

CHAPTER 26

Before opening the case for the defence, Bill Clegg made submissions to the judge on Counts 2, 3 and 4 – the charges based on the testimony of Ivan Stepaniuk, Fedor Zan and Ben-Zion Blustein. He argued that 'there is no evidence, or no evidence upon which a jury, properly directed, could convict this defendant in relation to those three counts'.

On Count 2, Clegg argued that Stepaniuk's claim to have identified Sawoniuk as the man beating and herding the old Jew, Shlemko, to his death, boiled down to 'somebody he said was the brother of Andrusha, told him that he was Andrusha's brother, and Andrusha was the man he had seen'.

Potts added that Stepaniuk's evidence was that, although Sawoniuk was carrying the carbine and the spade, and beating Shlemko with it, another policeman was with him and, when the three of them went towards the sand-hills beyond the forge, Stepaniuk was not an eyewitness to what then occurred.

'No,' Clegg said. 'He cannot say which of them shot him.'

'My Lord,' Nutting said, 'all the Crown have to prove in relation to any count in which there is no eyewitness evidence, may be stated as, "Can the jury be satisfied that the defendant was a party to the killing?"'

Clegg argued that there was an assumption in the evidence of both Stepaniuk and Blustein that the shots they had heard 'achieved the desired result. One has seen in these cases – and my Lord has heard evidence of it from Blustein – that people have escaped in extraordinary circumstances. There is no question of any body being found in relation to any of these counts, but particularly in relation to Shlemko. There is no evidence of how many soldiers were actually there at the time. They could have been taking him to a firing squad that was already there. Anything is possible. How can the jury put all these possibilities out of their mind?'

Clegg argued that leaving a verdict to the jury on the basis of 'joint enterprise' – that it was enough for the prosecution to demonstrate that the defendant had been party to the killings, even if there was no proof that he actually pulled the trigger – was unsafe and had only been advanced by the prosecution at the last minute, by implication, when they felt their case was insufficient without it.

Coupled with the uncertainty of Stepaniuk's identification of Sawoniuk– 'the man who is telling you who it was is not present at the time that Shlemko was taken past, nor does he tell you the name when Andrusha was present' – Clegg argued that there was no evidence on which the jury could safely convict, and that Count 4, based on Ben-Zion's account of Mir Barlas being taken away and what Sawoniuk had subsequently said to him, was similarly flawed.

There was no evidence that Mir Barlas was executed that day, nor that Sawoniuk had taken him to the sand-hills, nor that he was responsible for his death, if he had been killed. 'Many did escape and many died in the forest of cold or starvation, or in the subsequent partisan battles, but the partisan army was largely made up of people who had escaped from the Germans or the local police, of which, of course, Blustein was one example. We are not suggesting there is any evidence to suggest Barlas did escape. There is no evidence either way.'

Clegg then turned to Sawoniuk's alleged confession to Ben-Zion. 'The Crown have been at pains to establish that the witness claims to remember this confession verbatim after fifty-eight [sic, it was 57] years: "I remember each word." In our submission, it just does not stand up to analysis.'

On Fedor Zan's identification of Sawoniuk, the basis of Count 3, Clegg argued that it also could not be safely left to the jury to decide. 'If the evidence of recognition is inherently weak, then the court has a duty to intervene and stop the case. We do not shrink from submitting that it was completely impossible to recognise anybody from the two positions taken up by Mr Zan in the forest in Domachevo. It was longer than the length of a First Division football pitch. One has only to reflect, standing on the end behind the goal, trying to see somebody in the crowd at the other end, with no impediment at all, a completely clear pitch, to demonstrate that this is completely and utterly impossible. From where Zan stood, there could not be any recognition at all. At best, he could see a shape in the distance that could have been the defendant.'

In reply, Johnny Nutting referred to Stepaniuk's sighting of Andrusha, with a carbine and a spade, forcing Shlemko along the Road of Death. 'It does not, if I may so,' Nutting said, 'with the greatest respect, require rocket scientist analysis to acknowledge the spade was being taken on this journey by the defendant for a specific purpose and it is perfectly clear the circumstances and the use to which that object was going to be put. My Lord, all the evidence points to the safe conclusion that Shlemko was killed and that the defendant was at least a party to the shooting.'

He advanced similar arguments about the death of Mir Barlas, about which Ben-Zion had testified, and then turned to Fedor Zan, vigorously making the case that it was by 'no means inconceivable' that Andrusha would have been recognisible to the witness over a distance the size of a football pitch, and it was only fair to let the jury decide on the matter. 'My Lord, to take a count away from the jury – and this, I think, is what Mr Clegg is really inviting you to do – on the basis that your Lordship may have formed a view yourself over that distance would be, if I may say so, usurping the jury's function.'

After hearing further arguments in rebuttal from Bill Clegg, Mr Justice Potts made his ruling. On Count 2, he said that 'it became perfectly clear that Mr Stepaniuk was only able to identify the defendant as the policeman in question as a result of something said to him days later by a man whom he, Mr Stepaniuk, identified as the defendant's brother. I am satisfied that identification of the defendant by Mr Stepaniuk depended, as Mr Clegg has submitted, on hearsay. I remind myself again that the charge is murder. I emphasise that the court is concerned with events that took place over fifty-six years ago. I have reached the firm conclusion that no jury, looking at the whole of Mr Stepaniuk's evidence, could safely convict the defendant. Therefore, I accede to the defence submission in relation to Count Two.'

That ruling cannot have been unexpected but Nutting still gave a slight grimace as Potts announced it. Clegg's expression did not change.

Turning to Count 4, Potts referred to Ben-Zion's initial testimony on what Andrusha had said to him about the death of Mir Barlas. 'Mr Blustein was asked questions about that conversation on many occasions,' Potts said. 'It is sufficient to say that during the course of his answers, he contradicted himself. On occasions he said that he had, in effect, drawn the clear inference from what the defendant had told him, that he had killed Mir Barlas; on others that the defendant had made a direct admission. It seems clear to me that the Crown's case on Count Four hinges on this evidence. If it were the case that Mr Blustein had given a clear and unambiguous account of what the defendant had said to him, I would have no hesitation in leaving this count to the jury. However, I have reached the clear conclusion that in respect of this charge, I am satisfied that were the jury to convict on the evidence presently before the court, that conviction would not be safe.'

This time Clegg did show the flicker of a smile as he cast a glance across the courtroom to see how Nutting was taking the news. This time it was Nutting who now sat impassive, awaiting the ruling on Count 3. If that were also to go against him, the Crown's case would be hanging by a thread.

'Count Three raises different issues,' Potts said. 'Fedor Zan knew the defendant well, he knew him all his life. He has told the jury that he saw the defendant shoot a number of Jewesses. He has described the position that he was in when he observed the defendant carry out the executions. He has identified the spot where the executions took place.'

Potts said that he had given 'the most careful attention' to Clegg's submissions, but 'I am satisfied that there is evidence fit to go to the jury. In my judgement, were no further evidence adduced, the jury could safely convict on the evidence of Mr Zan and the other evidence remaining. So,' he said briskly, 'Counts Two and Four go; Counts One and Three remain.'

Having already gained a 50 per cent success, Clegg at once rose to inform the judge that when the court reconvened the next morning, 'I will be applying to discharge the jury in relation to the remaining two counts, on the basis that they have heard evidence that they ought not to have heard, particularly [from] Mr Ben-Zion Blustein, that is of such a prejudicial nature that it would prejudice the fair trial on the remaining counts.'

CHAPTER 27

On the morning of Day 20, Friday 19 March, with the jurors again absent, Bill Clegg duly began his submission for them to be discharged on the remaining two counts. His contention was that the evidence relating to them that had now been dismissed was 'uniquely prejudicial in the experience of courts in this country' and 'no fair trial is possible of this defendant on the remaining two counts'.

There was some debate between Clegg and Potts about what the crucial issues actually were and what case the defence was arguing. 'The inference that I drew from your cross-examination,' Potts said, 'was that the defendant did not take part in the search-and-kill operation. It was certainly ventilated with one witness that the police's job was to protect the ghetto and fight partisans.'

Clegg replied that the defence did not dispute that Sawoniuk had searched the ghetto, but claimed he did so only to seek clothing and shoes, not to search and kill.

'That is a crucial issue in the case, is it not?' Potts said.

Clegg demurred. 'We would say it was a collateral issue. The crucial issue – there are only two issues in the case, fundamentally. One is: was he the person Zan saw in the forest shooting fifteen ladies? Was he the person Baglay saw? They are the two issues. Whether he took part in the search-and-kill operation is not in any sense determinative of those answers.'

'It is a step on the way,' Potts said. 'It is a crucial issue. If it gets that far, I will direct the jury in clear terms that he is not charged with being a policeman, he is not charged with taking part in the search operation. The issue raised by Counts One and Three is whether he shot the victims.'

Clegg then moved on to Ben-Zion Blustein's testimony, saying it 'contained enormous prejudice' due to the harrowing nature of the detail, and was 'perhaps some of the most emotive evidence that a jury has ever heard in any trial'.

Clegg was arguing that nothing the judge could say to the jury would erase the impression created in their minds by Ben-Zion's testimony. 'My Lord, despite the state that the trial is in, and despite the high profile of this case, we submit that justice demands that the jury be discharged. We submit that there can be no fair trial before this jury on the remaining counts.'

For the Crown, Johnny Nutting told Potts that he did not accept Clegg's 'nice distinction' between the search-and-kill operations and the killings. Search-and-kill was 'part and parcel of one policy: to ensure any Jew who had escaped the principal massacre would be brought to the nearest killing ground and murdered. One of the main questions is whether this man was a policeman who was involved in that search-and-kill operation, such that, as a participant, he not only searched but he also killed.'

Nutting said that Ben-Zion's testimony was entirely relevant to that issue, demonstrating that, unlike his brother who had left the police as soon as he realised what it would involve, Andrusha had been 'an enthusiastic policeman, intent on pursuing the policy of the German occupiers to seek out and murder all remaining Jews.'

He went on to remind Potts of his ruling earlier in the trial about the evidence of Ivan Baglay and Evgeny Melaniuk that was unrelated to any specific count on the indictment. 'I have Mr Clegg's forceful argument in that connection very much in mind,' Potts had said. 'I am satisfied, however, that it would be right to allow this evidence to go to the jury.'

In his rebuttal, Clegg argued that 'one cannot merely say to a jury at this stage of the proceedings: "Well, you heard Blustein give a lot of evidence about mass murder. All that is really to be put to one side. Ignore it." It places the defence in a hopeless position. A direction, "Do not pay any attention to that", cannot conceivably remove the prejudice that this defendant will inevitably face.'

Despite that impassioned plea, from the tenor of Mr Justice Potts's earlier comments, Clegg would already have sensed the tide was running against him and the judge duly ruled against him on a succession of points.

'I have heard the evidence of Mr Zan,' Potts said, 'and I have heard Mr Zan cross-examined. During the course of that cross-examination, the nature of the defendant's case emerged. I would only say that, having heard the cross-examination, I am satisfied that I correctly admitted the evidence of Ivan Baglay and Evgeny Melaniuk when I did. I reject the submission of Mr Clegg in this respect.'

Despite throwing out Count 4, the judge also argued that Ben-Zion's testimony was still relevant, saying, 'I am satisfied that the jury, properly directed, can fairly try the defendant, despite the evidence of Mr Stepaniuk. It follows that in the exercise of my discretion, this case must proceed on the remaining counts.'

When the jury at last returned to court, Mr Justice Potts addressed them, outlining the reasons why they could not safely convict on Counts 2 and 4. This necessitated an immediate formal procedure of acquittal on those counts, which required the jury to return verdicts in line with the decision.

The Clerk of the Court then instructed the Foreman of the Jury to stand. 'Mr Foreman, on your Lordship's direction, do you find the defendant in this case not guilty on Counts Two and Four?'

'Not guilty.'

'And that is the verdict of you all?'

'Yes.'

The verdict was a shattering blow to Ben-Zion, who had not been privy to the discussions between judge and counsel about his testimony and must now have felt that it had all been in vain.

Johnny Nutting had seen the chances of a guilty verdict halved, but tried to put the best gloss he could on the decision. 'If the jury throws out two charges, it goes to show that the judge is scrupulous, but he also thinks that there is a possibility of a successful prosecution for the other charges.'

When later asked how his client had felt at that moment, Bill Clegg was for once at a loss. 'I don't know what he thought. He wasn't particularly thankful that we got two charges thrown out, but he was a very undemonstrative person orally. He didn't show a great deal of emotion unless someone crossed him, in which case he just hit them!'

Steve Law, who was probably closer to Sawoniuk than any other member of the defence team, having spent so much time with him, believes that he was 'no longer hopeful of a good result. He felt all four charges should have been thrown out and his demeanour deteriorated, fearing that there would now be an inevitable progress towards a guilty verdict on the remaining charges.'

Law also felt that the judge should have declared a mistrial, since, just as Clegg had argued, there was no possibility that the jury would put out of their minds the damning testimony they had heard in relation to charges that had now been dropped, and it would inevitably colour their judgement on those remaining.

Clegg still felt that no fatal damage had been done to the defence case and was sanguine about his failure to persuade

Potts about the prejudicial nature of Ben-Zion's testimony. He believes things might have been different 'if we could have kept out all evidence of other wrongdoing, but as the jury had already heard quite a bit of evidence that wasn't reflected in any charge, I don't think it made any difference to them at all'.

However, another potential minefield for Clegg was now looming. A defendant may choose not to testify in his own defence, and juries are instructed to draw no inference of guilt from their exercise of that right. Clegg had felt that it would be disastrous for his hot-tempered client to testify, opening himself up to cross-examination, but a barrister can only advise. His client makes the final decision and, after listening to the prosecution witnesses describe his crimes day after day, Andrusha was so incandescent with rage that nothing would stop him from testifying.

His temper had not been improved by his confrontation with Meir Bronstein in the Gents earlier in the trial, but Steve Law says that Andrusha also felt 'Clegg hadn't done his job properly and was not fighting his corner. His faith in the defence team had deteriorated, his back was up and he felt the system was stacked against him.'

'This is supposed to be a free country with blind justice,' Sawoniuk had said to Law. 'I am supposed to be innocent.'

When his client insisted on taking the stand, 'My heart sank,' Clegg says. 'I felt he could only make things worse, but he had a delusion that somehow he would talk himself out of it, as opposed to doing the opposite. His character was also such that he wanted to get up and shout at all the people who'd been shouting at him.'

When it became evident that nothing he could say would persuade his client not to take the stand, Clegg gave him 'some very strong advice on how he should give his evidence: listen to the question carefully before you answer it, don't argue with counsel, keep your answers short, and don't go on to make a speech'. Whether Sawoniuk would heed that sage advice would soon be revealed.

Maintaining his outward show of confidence, Clegg now began to lay out the case for the defence. 'Ladies and gentlemen, two verdicts of "not guilty" already. Two counts remain for your consideration. You will hear in due course the evidence of the defendant who is determined, despite his physical difficulties, to give evidence before you in this trial, that he is not guilty of each of those remaining counts.

'Let us just reflect for a moment on the evidence that you have heard. Neither Zan nor Baglay told anyone about what they claim to have seen for fifty-four years. Curiously, neither lived in Domachevo. Both lived in Borisy and are neighbours of each other. Neither case is supported by any forensic evidence. In relation to each allegation there is only one witness alive. Zan said he was alone. Baglay said he was with a man called Valodia but never mentioned the killing until after Valodia had died, drowned while drunk in a lake.

'The defence approach to this is quite clear: Sawoniuk was not present at either event. We do not accept that either event occurred. There is no way we are able to make an admission that fifteen women were shot in the forest at that place we all visited last month. Because Sawoniuk was not there, he cannot confirm it; on the other hand, he cannot deny it. One thing is clear: fifteen skeletons or bodies of women have not been found on that spot. There is no evidence that it happened, independently of what Zan says. But on the other hand, if you are not physically there, as Sawoniuk was not, he cannot say that it did not happen.

'We say it is for you to decide, when you have heard all the evidence, whether you can feel sure the incident did happen and, if you are sure it did happen, whether you can then be sure that it was Sawoniuk who was there – two separate issues.

The same applies for Baglay. We do not accept the incident occurred. It may have done. It may not have done. If it did, Sawoniuk was not there.

'Now the defendant will give evidence before you. He is now an old man. He is seventy-eight. He is deaf in one ear and blind in one eye. He is lame, diabetic. He has got heart problems and his memory is not good. I am sure all of you will appreciate that this trial has placed him under an enormous strain. I ask you, on his behalf, to make allowance for that. Leaving aside his health, he is trying to cast his mind back almost sixty years and he is going to get things wrong.

'He is going to say things that you think cannot be right in relation to peripheral issues, like perhaps his house or his schooling. He is going to forget details that might have been put on his behalf, and remember things that were not put on his behalf. Things will come back to him that he had hitherto forgotten. You will hear about his life. It was not an easy life by the standards of peasants living in Belarus sixty or seventy years ago – no father, no breadwinner, mother died when he was a teenager, a man with no land or job.'

Clegg was setting out to paint a very different picture from the enthusiastic recruit to the *Schutzmannschaft* that Nutting had described. He asked the jurors to picture Sawoniuk as 'an orphaned teenager . . . You may describe him as a willing volunteer, but can we just think what other employment the teenager may have had open to him as a career under German occupation.' In Clegg's account, there was nothing voluntary about Sawoniuk's decision. The choice was to join the *Schutzmannschaft*, or risk deportation for slave labour, or go on the run, and that, Clegg implied, was really no choice at all.

'When the war first hit that part of Eastern Europe in 1939,' Clegg said, 'before it was carved up between Hitler and Stalin, he was about seventeen or eighteen years old. He joined the police when he was twenty. We have had a lot of talk about conscription and volunteering, as though it was like going down to the Job Centre in South London and filling out a card, deciding whether to take a job or go on the dole. Life in Belarus was very different from that. He was effectively placed in a position where he had no real choice but to join the police. There was nothing else for him to do. There was no work. There was no other way that he would eat.'

Short of peeling an onion or playing a lament on the world's smallest violin, Clegg could not have done much more to enlist the sympathies of the jury for his client. In contrast to Nutting's rather lofty persona, Clegg's style was very much to present himself as the voice of sound common sense from the man in the public bar. In previous cases, he had also often deployed his quick wit and sense of comic timing to good effect, and now tried to use humour to defuse the prosecution's claims about Sawoniuk and put as much distance as possible between the horrors of the Holocaust that Christopher Browning had described and the role Clegg was claiming for him as an insignificant minion in the Nazi hierarchy.

The local police – Clegg was careful to avoid the term *Schutzmannschaft* – were, he said, 'never paid money. All they were given was a bit of food. What this was – let us be realistic and sensible – was a ramshackle local defence unit, most of the time, certainly in 1943 when he became the commander, at that time engaged almost exclusively in seeking to fight and protect villages from partisan attack. Until then, just an ordinary policeman. I do not use the word "constable" because it implies an altogether too elevated and sophisticated role.'

In his efforts to paint Sawoniuk as a hapless underling, a mere pawn in the schemes of others, Clegg even invoked a classic BBC comedy. 'This man was not giving orders. He was not making decisions. There was nobody of lower rank than him. He was twenty or twenty-one years old. Through the evidence of Professor Browning, we have heard about Hitler and Himmler, and all the plans they put into effect. What has all that to do with him? Do you think Hitler has a hotline to a hut in Domachevo to discuss his policy with Sawoniuk? It is like comparing Churchill consulting Pike of *Dad's Army*.'

Clegg referred to the witness testimony about the massacre on the eve of Yom Kippur and pointed out that 'not only is Sawoniuk not charged with playing any part in the main massacre, there is no allegation he had ever done anything before that at all'. The police station clerk at the time had told detectives he had seen Andrusha among the auxiliaries leaving the police station on the morning of the massacre, but he was not called to give evidence at the trial, and none of the other living witnesses could claim to have seen him that day.

Two people had given statements to the KGB after the war, confirming Sawoniuk's presence at the massacre. One, Michal Danilovich Kozlovski, admitted to being a member of the police cordon. 'The German unit went straight to the place allocated for the shooting,' he said. 'Kornelyuk also went there, taking six or seven police officers with him. They included Andrei Sawoniuk.' That was confirmed by Pavel Vasilyevich Taradanyuk, who took a group of Jews to the execution site during the mass execution and remembered that Sawoniuk also took part. However, since those witnesses were either dead or could not be traced by the War Crimes Unit, their statements were not admissible.

'The Gestapo, as I anticipate the defendant will call them,' Clegg said, 'or the *Einsatzgruppen*, as they were described by Professor Browning, stayed in Domachevo for more than a week after the massacre. They were the killing squad, in Domachevo to root out and search for the Jews that survived the main massacre.'

He conceded that Sawoniuk had 'searched – I presume a modern term might be "looted" – the ghetto; not that there was much by way of value there, only clothes and footwear, but apart from that, he played no part in the search operation at all'.

Clegg also attempted to gloss over what he would later describe as 'one of the biggest own goals of my career' by painting the visit to Domachevo as part of the defence's strategy. 'You know,' he told the jurors, 'that it was our application on behalf of the defendant that you should visit Belarus, Domachevo and, in particular, the forest where the evidence in relation to the Zan count is so crucial. We make no apology for that at all, because whatever physical inconvenience the journey may have caused, in our submission the value to you eleven jurors of going to that town and into the forest was immeasurable. Each of you has gone and stood where Zan says he stood. Each of you have individually had the opportunity to look across the distance to the place where he says the shootings took place. We do not shrink from saying that each one of you could answer the question posed by that count on the strength of your visit to Domachevo without recourse to anything else at all. You saw with your own eyes the distance, and the opportunity to be able to recognise anyone at that length. Your conclusion, we confidently anticipate, will be that it would be completely impossible to recognise anyone at that distance.'

In a further attempt to discredit Zan and the other prosecution witnesses, Clegg returned to the conspiracy theory he had outlined in his opening statement. 'You may think that it is a very, very odd fact indeed that the tiny village of Borisy, where the defendant was never stationed, every solitary person alive today, who was alive in the war and of the necessary age, has come here to give evidence. You have not seen a solitary person from Domachevo, except Galina Puchkina, who saw nothing so far as the defendant was concerned, at all. So it is very odd.

'Finally, before I call the defendant, could I ask you to try to – I almost say "to try to do the impossible". There can be no trial in our history that has been more emotive than this. It would not be possible for anybody to have sat through this trial, be they lawyer or juror, and not to have been moved by the accounts of the Holocaust in Eastern Europe. The descriptions given clinically by Professor Browning would make anyone's blood run cold. However, difficult as it is, we urge you to put all that into its proper position in this case. It is background. It is awful. It is something that happened in the war. It is not his fault that it happened.

'You are not here trying to achieve justice for the Holocaust victims. What you are here to do is to just look at those two counts on the indictment, the only two that are left, and to say in relation to those, "Can we possibly accept Zan's evidence? We have been there, we have looked at it, you cannot see a thing. Look at Baglay. Look at the inconsistencies. Look at all the problems with his evidence. Can we possibly accept that?" If the answers to those questions are "No", then that is all you are here to do.

'There is so much prejudice in this case, so much by way of allegations that are not the subject of any charge. People say all sorts of things about him, none of which has been charged, none of which are for you to decide on, so far as guilt or innocence on this indictment, but it is bound to have an effect on your approach unless you guard very much against allowing the prejudice that you have heard to swamp the evidence on the individual counts. In our submission, if you confine yourself, as I know you will, when properly directed by my Lord, to a proper approach to the evidence in this case, then we are perfectly confident that the proper verdict will result.

'I have said the defendant is anxious to give his evidence. He has waited five weeks to do so. He will wait no more. My Lord, I call the defendant.'

Had Clegg been wearing a circus ringmaster's outfit, he could scarcely have done more to herald Sawoniuk's arrival in the witness box.

CHAPTER 28

The outcome of the trial was still very far from certain. With no physical evidence, as Clegg had reminded the jury, the two remaining counts both relied on the uncorroborated testimony of a single eyewitness, about events that had occurred more than half a century before.

Zan had witnessed a crime at such a distance that Clegg was able to argue the identification of the perpetrator was unsound. Alexandre Baglay's claim could not be similarly dismissed, for he had been only a handful of paces from Sawoniuk when he alleged that he shot three people, but he had been a boy at the time and, like Zan and Blustein, had never testified about the crime until interviewed by Scotland Yard detectives over 50 years after it had been committed. He also came from the same small hamlet as Zan and most of the other witnesses, and Clegg had firmly planted the suggestion that his testimony could have been shaped either as a deliberate conspiracy or simply by absorbing village gossip.

Despite what Steve Law had felt about Andrusha's state of mind, the man himself appeared increasingly confident that he would walk free – perhaps unaware that his chances of acquittal had been weakened by two crucial errors.

The first was that, when interviewed at Southwark police station, while refusing to answer any questions about the specific events on which he was being charged, 'either because of the advice he received at the time or his own notions,' Clegg says, 'he foolishly chose to answer a few identifying questions. The witnesses were talking about a man called A. Sawoniuk, who lived in Domachevo, used to be called "pigeon boy", took water to the Jews on the Sabbath, and whose mother was a washerwoman. Thinking that he was not doing himself any harm by it, he confirmed all those details.

'His solicitor should certainly have said to him, "Don't answer that," and it was the most extraordinary mistake, because if you're not going to answer questions about the allegations, then you shouldn't answer any questions at all, but presumably thinking that he was not doing himself any harm by it, he answered the questions that confirmed his identity.'

If he had not done so, Clegg said, the question of identity – whether, 57 years on, the man in the dock really was the Andrei 'Andrusha' Sawoniuk that the witnesses were saying had carried out those crimes in Domachevo – would have made it 'almost certain that he would not and could not have been prosecuted'.

The difficulties of identification after so long an interval had been emphasised by the shambles of a 1988 war crimes trial in Israel. Ivan Demanjuk was a Ukrainian, who had changed his first name to John when he emigrated to the US in 1952, and had been working at a car plant and living in Ohio for 25 years. In 1977, eyewitness testimony from five Holocaust survivors identified him as having been a notoriously vicious guard at the Treblinka extermination camp, known as 'Ivan the Terrible'.

After a prolonged legal battle, he was extradited to Israel to stand trial accused of war crimes and crimes against humanity under the Nazis and Nazi Collaborators (Punishment) Law of 1950. In 1988 three judges found him guilty 'unhesitatingly and with utter conviction', and sentenced him to death.

He had maintained his innocence throughout the trial, insisting he was a victim of mistaken identity, but he was actually in the condemned cell, listening to the sound of the scaffold on which he was to hang being constructed, when fresh evidence emerged, casting doubt on the validity of his conviction.

Four of the men who had originally identified him as Ivan the Terrible had died before the trial began. The testimony of another had been ruled unreliable and a sixth had appeared confused as he gave his evidence. As a result, the testimony of yet another witness, Eliyahu Rosenberg, had been crucial. Asked if he recognised the defendant, he requested that Demanjuk's glasses be removed, 'so I can see his eyes'. He moved towards him and peered into his face. 'I say it unhesitatingly, without the slightest shadow of a doubt. It is Ivan from Treblinka, from the gas chambers, the man I am looking at now. I saw his eyes. I saw those murderous eyes.'

However, during the appeal hearing, it was revealed that Rosenberg had previously testified that Ivan the Terrible had been killed during an uprising by prisoners at Treblinka in 1943. It was a body blow to the identification and it was further damaged when it was revealed that 37 former guards at Treblinka had signed written statements that Ivan the Terrible had been called Marchenko, not Demanjuk. One described him as having brown hair, hazel eyes and a long scar down his neck, whereas Demanjuk had no scar and was fair-haired, with grey-blue eyes. A photograph and a description of Ivan the Terrible taken in 1942 were also produced, and they appeared to be nothing like Demanjuk.

In 1993, the verdict was overturned by the Israeli Supreme Court, on the grounds that it was not certain beyond a reasonable doubt that he was the notorious guard at Treblinka. His release was hugely controversial in Israel, but even the famous Nazi-hunter, Simon Wiesenthal, admitted that, although he had earlier been convinced of his guilt, he would have acquitted him after seeing the new evidence.

However, Demanjuk was not a completely innocent victim of

mistaken identity. He had been conscripted into the Red Army in 1940, but was captured by the Germans in 1942 and put to work as a concentration camp guard, though at Sobibor, not Treblinka. He could still have been put on trial for his admitted role as a guard there but, fearing it would breach the double jeopardy rule, Israel declined to prosecute him. He returned to Ohio in 1993, but his US citizenship was revoked, and in 2009 he was extradited again, this time to West Germany, on 27,900 counts of accessory to murder – one for each person killed at Sobibor during his time as guard there. He was duly convicted and given a five-year prison sentence, but released pending an appeal. He died in a German nursing home in 2012 before a final judgement on his appeal could be pronounced.

Sawoniuk's solicitor, Martin Lee, now admits that identification was the key to the case and says in retrospect his 'biggest regret' was the interview at Southwark. Officers usually used their own police station for such procedures, but the WCU had been moved from Scotland Yard to a tiny office in Whitechapel, with no space or facilities, so they had to clear out a floor at Southwark. Lee describes that as 'destabilising', and says the questions relating to Sawoniuk's identification were not 'the usual way that these things were done'.

The defence made no attempt to produce witnesses to his good character. As they had discovered, there were very few who would have testified to that anyway. Even his son, who attended part of the trial as a spectator, was not called, and when approached by a journalist, told him, 'I am not speaking to anyone – not to you or anyone else – not now, not ever.' The *Southwark News* reported that the man they called 'Tony Sawoniuk Junior' – not the name he went by – had 'two young daughters of his own. Relatives say the news of his father's crimes has been very distressing to them all but there is little to add as he was never around to form a bond with his son, and his wife died five years ago.'

'We weren't in the least bit interested in finding character witnesses among Sawoniuk's neighbours and former
workmates,' Bill Clegg says, because it would have allowed
the prosecution to produce a score of them to testify to
Sawoniuk's anti-Semitism, cruelty and brutality, and his service in the Waffen-SS. So the only witness that the defence
called in person was Andrusha himself. That was entirely
against the wishes of his counsel and was his second crucial
mistake. Until then, Johnny Nutting had been doubtful about
the possibility of persuading the jury of Andrusha's guilt. 'I
only started to build confidence,' he says, 'when Sawoniuk
took the stand.'

Clutching his stick, Sawoniuk walked briskly to the witness
box, as if impatient to have his say, and swore the oath on a
Bible. Despite having lived in Britain for half a century, his
English was less than fluent. Clegg began by leading him
through the catalogue of medical problems that he had already
outlined in his opening address, with Andrusha adding the
detail that in addition to a heart bypass operation in 1994, he
had also been given a course of electric shock treatment as an
in-patient at the Maudsley Hospital in the 1950s.

'Why was that? What was the matter with you?' Clegg said.

'I do not know. Mental illness.'

Raising his voice until he was almost shouting to ensure
that Sawoniuk could hear his questions, Clegg then asked him
about his marriages and what had happened to his first wife,
Anna, during the war. 'She was killed during partisan attack
on Domachevo,' Sawoniuk said, and for the first and only time
in the trial, he showed an emotion other than anger, lowering
his head as a tear trickled down his cheek.

When he had recovered, he denied ever having been married
to his second partner Nina, describing his relationship with her
as, 'Just friendly. That is all. Nothing serious.' He then spoke of

his short-lived marriage to Christina van Gent and the slightly longer one to Anastasia that produced a son.

Clegg then backtracked to Sawoniuk's upbringing, establishing the poverty of his family and the tiny house in which he, his half-brother and his grandmother all lived after his mother died, all sleeping in the same room together. Andrusha said there had been no anti-Semitism in Domachevo before the war and relations between the Jews and the Christians had been 'Perfect. There was nothing wrong. Everybody lives there happy.' But after the Soviet occupation, he said, there was 'not no work at all'.

Turning to the aftermath of the German invasion, Clegg asked him how he had come to be a policeman. Andrusha said that the mayor's son, whom he had known since before the war, 'asked me if I could join the police. I say, "I am not very keen to join the police, you know," because I had always been on move, and my intention was never to spend my life in Domachevo. I said, "What happen if I do not join the police?" He said, "I cannot give you correct answer, but probably you will be in trouble. Probably the Germans send you to Germany for work. If I was you, as I know you, I should advise you to join the police." And that is what I did.'

'Throughout the war, were you ever paid any money by way of salary?'

'None whatsoever.'

Andrusha also insisted that the police had never been given uniforms, only an armband, that some wore and some did not. The police had instead equipped themselves with clothes taken from 'dead Russian soldiers', and the only weapons they had were 'what the Russians left behind, that is all'.

'Were you told anything about what your duties would be?'

'They said, "As you know there is many Russians run away from Domachevo and most of them went to the forest. You have to keep an eye on them in case they give you some trouble.

You have to protect people who live in Domachevo." And this is what we did.'

'Now, after the German occupation and before the massacre,' Clegg said, 'did the Jews live in an area of the town that was known as "the ghetto"?'

Sawoniuk's answer must have been as much of a surprise to Clegg as it was to everybody else in the courtroom. 'There never has been ghetto there, never.'

Clegg's attempts to steer Sawoniuk towards a more plausible answer were not noticeably successful. When he then asked him what religion the people were who lived in the area of Domachevo surrounded by a yellow line on the map he was shown – the ghetto – Andrusha, peering through a magnifying glass, replied, 'Mostly Catholic', but then, seeing Clegg's expression, said, 'Am I wrong?'

'I am afraid you cannot ask me whether you are wrong,' Clegg said. 'Put your magnifying glass away for a minute and I will ask some other questions. Was there a time in 1942 when the Jews who had lived in Domachevo were no longer there?'

Sawoniuk smiled broadly. 'In 1942, the Jews were free to go wherever they liked. There was no restriction for them. Nobody kept eye on them and they were doing whatever they wanted to do.'

The answer was so preposterous that there were a few suppressed giggles from the public gallery, but Clegg, his expression set like concrete, persevered. 'Was there a time when the Jews were not there anymore?'

'Well, after the massacre, there was not Jews anymore there, but before that—'

Clegg cut him off. 'Well, just concentrate on the massacre. Now, as best as you can remember, when was the massacre?'

'I do not remember the date. I was not there on that particular day. I was about ten miles away from home. I had been told when I came back.'

Clegg then spent several minutes, with and without maps, trying to get Sawoniuk to pinpoint the site of the police station. He eventually succeeded, but Andrusha then said that 'it was on the main road, opposite the ghetto', revealing that there had been a ghetto after all. Probably suppressing the urge to tear his remaining hair out by the roots, Clegg continued to cover ground that must have been explored many times in pre-trial discussions, but Sawoniuk continued to be full of surprises.

Having told the court that he had not been in Domachevo on the day of the massacre, it must have been surprising to everyone, not least Clegg, when he answered the question, 'Were you in Domachevo on the day that the Jews were all shot?' in the affirmative.

'Did you hear my question?' Clegg said.

'I do, yes.'

'What did you say?'

'Was I there on the day when the massacre – is it? I cannot remember now. I forget it now.'

'Take your time, Mr Sawoniuk. Were you present in Domachevo on the day of the massacre?'

This time Clegg finally got the answer he was expecting. 'I was not there, no. I left Domachevo about two, three days before the massacre began and I came back about two or three days after.'

Although it was inconceivable that, alone among all the police auxiliaries, Sawoniuk would not have been present and participating alongside his Nazi overseers, he insisted that, 'I went to a village but I cannot remember its name. It was about eight or ten miles away. I walked there. I can only remember the direction of the village was past the railway station and into the forest. I wish I could remember the name of the village but I cannot.'

His alibi was not altogether convincing since, as he admitted, not only could he not remember the name of the village, nor could he remember the names of the friends he was supposed to have been seeing. However, since no living witness could state that they had seen Sawoniuk at the massacre, no presumption of his involvement could be made.

Andrusha said that the Germans and Hungarians he claimed had carried out the killings remained in the town for another week. He had seen them searching the ghetto and 'I guess they probably was looking for Jews. I looked for clothes, shoes, and something like that. I never looked for the Jews.' He conceded that other policemen could have, but insisted, 'I never seen any killing personally, by my two eyes.'

'You know it is suggested you shot fifteen ladies in the forest, is that true?'

'It is a lie.'

'It is said that you shot three other people.'

'It is another lie.'

'Did you kill any Jews in that period following the main massacre?'

'I never did and I never had the intention to kill Jews. I never hate Jews. My Jews, they were my best friends from day I was little child. I was born next door to them. I have grown up with them. I went to school with them. I have got nothing against the Jews. I have been accused by the people who came here to this country.' He was now shouting. 'Why are you calling prisoners to give evidence that they see me killing Jews? They should be locked up in a British jail for life, them witnesses.'

'Let us just pause,' Clegg said, very aware that his client was now puce with rage.

Sawoniuk ignored him and gesticulated furiously towards the back of the court, where Ben-Zion Blustein and his old friend and fellow Domachevo survivor, Meir Bronstein, were sitting. 'Including—'

'Pause,' Clegg said sharply. 'Wait for the questions.'

'Are you all right?' Mr Justice Potts asked Sawoniuk. 'If you

264

wish to sit down, remember, please do. If you want a break, you say.' Clegg waited until Sawoniuk's anger had subsided a little before asking what his feelings were about the partisans.

'I hate them because they were killing people. Not us were killing people. That is the people who done murders, not police or Germans, or anyone else for that matter.'

'Did you kill any partisans?'

'Yes. They tried to kill me, so I kill them first.' Sawoniuk then claimed to have left Domachevo at the end of 1943.

'Did you leave alone or with Nina?'

'By myself. Nina had nothing to do with it. She was just a friend, that is all.'

'Did you leave with a horse and cart?' Clegg said.

'No, walk, trains. I went to Brest by train, I walked for about two days – I do not remember the towns and villages – then I again went on a train. Bit walking, bit riding, that is what I done.'

When Clegg moved on to the interview with the War Crimes Unit, Andrusha claimed that he had lied about never having been married when he came to Britain, on the advice of a friend who told him that if he said he was a widower, he would have to prove his previous wife was dead before being allowed to marry in Britain. 'I said, "I cannot prove it because I come from a Communist country. I cannot go down there. They will shoot me." So he said, "The best way is for you to keep your mouth shut. Do not say to nobody nothing." That is what I did. I have been married twice in this country. I never told my wife, not one of them. I never told nobody.'

He also conceded that he hadn't admitted at first that he had been in the auxiliary police in Domachevo, because 'I was frightened they probably are going to deport me back to Belarus or Russia. So I said no, I was not. This is the only reason. That is the only lies I tell them. I am not come here from Russia to this country to tell lies like some other people do.' As he said it, he once more glowered down the court-room towards Ben-Zion.

Mr Justice Potts intervened. 'They were the only two lies you told?'

'That is correct, sir.'

Clegg, who had now been shouting questions at his partially deaf client for several hours, then said to the judge, 'My Lord, it is quite tiring for me at this volume in examining the witness. I think that I have concluded my examination-in-chief. Would my Lord consider rising now and allow me to reflect over the weekend in case there is a matter I have not covered?'

Potts agreed and, as he discharged the jury for the weekend, he cautioned them that, 'You appreciate we are now at a very important stage in the case. There is a great temptation to com-pare notes among yourselves, and a great temptation, if asked, to give impressions to others who were not there. Resist all of them, please. When you go out of that door, I strongly suggest that you do your level best to put the case out of your minds until Monday morning.'

CHAPTER 29

When the trial resumed at 10.30am on the day after Sawoniuk's 78th birthday, Monday, 22 March, Bill Clegg rose to his feet merely to announce that he 'had no further questions by way of examination-in-chief'.

So Johnny Nutting's cross-examination began at once. There was an almost palpable sense of anticipation around the court as he did so. The packed public gallery was still and silent, and the press bench had discarded their cloak of cynical detachment to sit bolt upright, poised over their shorthand pads. Ben-Zion, still at the back of the court, flanked by his wife, son, and Meir Bronstein, leaned forward, intent on hearing every word, his hawk-like gaze fixed on Sawoniuk.

Nutting began in a deceptively languid fashion, asking Sawoniuk if there was anything that he wanted to change from the evidence he had already given. Having covered his admitted lies to the police about his marital status and his service with the auxiliary police, Nutting asked him, 'Was anything else that you said to the police untrue?'

'Not so forever, never.'

'Tell me this: did you ever see a Jew killed or maltreated during the war?'

'Let me make that point straightaway,' Andrusha said. 'Just put it to me and I tell the whole truth and nothing but the truth. There is no one Jews, or for that matter anybody has been killed by police or by Germans. No one.' His voice and his face were already showing his anger and the cross-examination had barely begun. 'As I said it. No one ever done – German lost a life, Jewish lost a life – because they have been killed by police or by Germans. No one kill them. There is only Jews lost a life when the Gestapo come and done – and kill them. Before that there is no one, Jew or anybody, lost a life whatsoever, and that is true.'

Nutting was starting to frame his next question when Mr Justice Potts intervened. 'Mr Nutting, the defendant has not answered your question. I think "maltreated" was the word, was it?'

Nutting bowed to the judge and then repeated that part of the question. 'Did you see any Jew being maltreated?'

'No, no. They had a very good relation with the Jewish people. They make no trouble to nobody, not the police, not to Germans. They behaved themselves proper ways and there-fore they was entitled to do what they wanted to do. That lies from the witnesses, the Euro witnesses, was all lies, nothing but lies. There has never been Jew treated as an animal or any-body else. They have been free to go anywhere and there was not ghetto whatsoever. There was no wire around Domachevo where they lived.'

It was an extraordinary claim to make: that uniquely among all the territories the Nazis had conquered, the Jews of Domachevo were not persecuted and were free to come and go and live untroubled lives, subject to no restrictions at all.

Nutting led him back, point by point, over everything he had just said. Had the laws and customs of the courts not required barristers to remain motionless, betraying neither by facial expression nor gesture any emotions or signs of approval or disapproval, Nutting would no doubt have been smiling broadly and rubbing his hands with glee. As Clegg had feared, his client was lying about almost everything and was already showing that he was likely to be of much greater help to the Crown case than his own defence.

Andrusha carried on piling up demonstrable falsehoods, insisting there had never been any anti-Semitism before the war or during it, that Jews never had to register, carry identity cards, wear yellow patches on their clothing, obey a curfew or need a permit to leave the ghetto, which he continued to claim did not exist, and which was never surrounded by barbed wire.

Nutting next turned to the incident described by Ben-Zion when the population had been forced to assemble on a field in the pouring rain, and hand over their valuables while their homes were ransacked.

'Not true innit,' Sawoniuk said. 'Not true whatsoever. Never that happened.' Once more his voice was rising, and his face growing redder as his anger mounted. 'You take notice for the people who come here and tells you lot of lies, and they say all lies, but nothing than lies, and everyone going against me or anyone else, and there is nothing true in it whatsoever. Nothing. There is nobody touched – put their hands on a Jew till the Gestapo come and they finished it off completely, their life.'

'You lived in Domachevo between 1941 and 1944?' Nutting said.

'I left Domachevo in 1943, end of 1943. I do not know nothing of what happened in 1944, or 1945 or 1946.'

'Forgive me, Mr Sawoniuk,' Nutting said. 'Do yourself justice.' It was a polite way of saying, 'Stop lying'. 'The police station was burned down on 23 November 1943, right? Vashka Trebunko was killed in that attack? You became the leader of the police after that event?'

Sawoniuk first tried to deny it. 'Not me, someone else.' But under repeated questioning, he was forced to admit it.

'You became the senior policeman?' Nutting said.

'All right, I became the—'

'Forgive me, right or wrong?'

'Right,' Sawoniuk said, shouting his answer.

'I know this is very difficult for you, Mr Sawoniuk,' Mr Justice Potts said, 'but you must not – you must just listen to the question.'

'I am,' Sawoniuk said, his fists clenched and his face purple.

'Just calm down now,' Potts said.

While admitting that he had been police commander at some point, Sawoniuk then tried to claim that someone else had taken over from Trebunko for a few months, 'six months-ish, or something like that'.

It was another open goal for Nutting. 'Well, if that person took over from Trebunko and was senior policeman for six months, that would take us well into 1944 before you became head of the police, would it not?'

'I was not in Domachevo in 1944. That is what I can tell you.'

'And that is your final answer?' Nutting said, channelling his inner quizmaster. 'So there is no question of you being in Domachevo after the end of 1943?'

Andrusha's idea was probably that if he claimed he had left Domachevo in 1943, his denials that he had fled with the Nazis in the summer of 1944 and joined the Waffen-SS would carry more weight, but he had only succeeded in tying himself in knots and damaging his credibility with the jury.

Nutting then returned to an earlier theme. 'Between June of 1941 and September of 1942, did you ever see a Jew with a yellow patch on his clothing, back and front?'

'I might did, I might didn't. I do not remembers it. It is fifty-seven years ago. How can I remember everything? I cannot remember. I lost my memory a long time ago and I cannot describe it. I tried to. I am not here to lie. I come to clear my name, not to lie to you or anybody else. I try to help you as much as I can but if I cannot remember, I cannot remember and I can tell you nothing.'

'Was there any order that came from the Germans to you policemen to ensure that Jews wore some special insignia on their clothing?'

'Never. Never,' Sawoniuk said, immediately rediscovering his memory.

'June of 1941 the Germans invaded, correct? You told the British police that after the invasion no one was shot and life got back to normal very quickly. That was a truthful answer, was it? Were you not aware that the Rabbi of Lubartov and forty of his followers were shot in the aftermath of the German invasion?'

'Never. Untrue. Lie. I said it only two occasions: there was never been nobody shot in Domachevo by police or Germans. Nobody was shooted. Please understand me and believe what I say.'

Nutting then turned to the location of the police station where Sawoniuk had been based. 'It was pure chance, was it, that the police station was opposite what we have been told was the gate of the ghetto.'

'Correct, yes sir.'

'Pure chance?'

'Yes, opposite the ghetto.'

Nutting pounced. 'I thought you said there was not a ghetto in Domachevo?'

'Well, you call them ghetto, I say not ghetto.'

'Every witness who has come to this court has spoken of the Jewish ghetto in Domachevo.'

'They have to speak that, do they not? They have been told by the Russian KGB, innit, to say that. They all tell the lies, every one of them, every one.' Once more, Sawoniuk was shouting and banging his clenched fist on the rail of the witness box.

'Let us be calm, Mr Sawoniuk,' Nutting said, his mild, courteous demeanour in pointed contrast to Sawoniuk's fury.

'Them devils come in here and tell their lies against me. Why the Scotland Yard did not bring the witnesses from Domachevo where I live, that people knows me? They could not find nobody in Domachevo, witnesses, to come and say against me. They went to Brest, fifty miles away.'

Once more, having watched Sawoniuk dig a pit for himself, Nutting was only too happy to gently tip him over the edge. 'Well, since you asked the question, your solicitors have been to Domachevo on your behalf, have they not? And are there any witnesses coming from Domachevo to speak on your behalf?'

Sawoniuk began a meandering reply but Nutting dragged him back to the point. 'I wonder whether you would do me the courtesy of answering the question. Are there any witnesses waiting outside this court to give evidence on your behalf?'

'As far as I know, no.'

Nutting then moved to Sawoniuk's service with the *Schutzmannschaft*. When he came to his time as police commander, once more he denied it – 'Rubbish. Never been' – and then contradicted himself within a few seconds.

When Nutting contrasted Sawoniuk's denials that they had a police uniform with Czeslaw Hamziuk's insistence that they had all been issued with one, Andrusha's temper flared once more. 'We never had a uniform, never had a uniform,' he yelled. 'Now why the people come here and say—'

Mr Justice Potts again intervened. 'Just calm down now, Mr Sawoniuk.' Potts then called a short adjournment to allow tempers, or one temper in particular, to cool, recording a note to himself that Sawoniuk 'obviously gets hysterical and digs himself into an even deeper hole'.

When they resumed, Nutting picked up again on Hamziuk's testimony and, as he may have expected and probably hoped, Sawoniuk's fuse was as short as ever, as he railed about the KGB and Scotland Yard conspiring to influence the Belarusian witnesses to testify against him to avoid being jailed in their home country.

'But Mr Hamziuk comes from Poland,' Nutting said.

'He might did. I do not know where he comes from.' Nutting then pointed out that Ben-Zion lived in Israel.

'I know he did,' Sawoniuk said. 'He should live there for good.'

'There is no KGB,' Nutting began, but then did a double-take as he registered what Sawoniuk had said. 'I beg your pardon?'

'He should not be coming here,' Sawoniuk said, scowling at Ben-Zion, 'telling lies against me.'

'There is no KGB in Israel, is there?'

'I do not know. Well, the Jew – there probably no KGB in Israel, I do not say there are, but he comes here, he lost his brother, he lost his sisters by Germans. Now he wants me to be behind bars, innocent man. He do not care who it is, as long as it is somebody behind bars. That is what he came here for and say that.'

'But that does not make sense, Mr Sawoniuk.'

'Well, it is sense to me. I never done a crime in my life.'

Sawoniuk's struggles with English grammar and his often wild, self-contradictory and patently false testimony, had led some people in the public gallery to start sniggering and even laughing out loud as he spoke.

As a result, Bill Clegg rose, asked for the jury to be excluded and then told the judge that he was 'very concerned about the conduct in the public gallery', and if it continued, that His Lordship should clear it.

'I hope I can be heard in the public gallery,' Potts said, peering up at the row of faces looking down into the court. 'If there is any behaviour of that sort – and I will ask the court staff to watch the public gallery – then I am afraid I will have no alternative but to clear the whole of the public gallery.'

With the jury back in place, Nutting began again. 'Now, Mr Sawoniuk, this is your opportunity,' he said brightly. 'Whether you remember Mr Blustein or not, it is clear from your evidence that no Jew living in Domachevo would have any reason

273

to testify against you, right? They would have no reason to invent lies about you, right? Mr Blustein is not subject to the influence of what you call the KGB, is he, living in Israel? Can you help the jury about any reason, please, why he should come to this court to tell lies about you?'

'I just said it,' Sawoniuk said, launching into another tirade about Ben-Zion wanting 'someone, anyone, behind bars'.

When Nutting again turned to Hamziuk's testimony, Sawoniuk shouted, 'Liar, big liar, professional liar. I never killed nobody. Nobody in my life, this one thing about it, I never did and I would not do. I would not dream to do it. I am not a monster, I am ordinary, working-class, poor man. And what can I do? I cannot stop them people tell the lies if they want to say the lies. I have got no tongue to tell them that. I was in the magistrates' court for six weeks, I did not have a chance to say nothing, not even one word. This is my first speech, what I am saying in now here, and I come here to clear myself, because myself is fed up with the lies, what the people have been saying about me. I cannot take it no more.'

As Mr Justice Potts noted to himself, Sawoniuk's testimony was 'Much more denial (of everything). AS ties himself in knots and is often borderline inarticulate.'

Sawoniuk's eyes had been rimmed with tears as he fell silent and Nutting allowed him a few moments before resuming his relentless probing at his story. He turned to the description of the auxiliary police as 'look-outs' that Andrusha had used when interviewed by Scotland Yard. 'It is a pretty inadequate description, is it not?' Nutting said. 'Why did you just call them look-outs if you risked your lives shooting partisans?'

'I have to because he is after my life,' Andrusha said, not for the first time misunderstanding the question. 'You do not expect him to kill me first, then I kill him. Then I am dead.'

'But you had the complete opportunity to describe to the police what activities they had.'

'I tell them everything true to the police. I never lie to them. If you got there, that probably is lie by police, not by me.' Andrusha then launched into another tirade, in the course of which he brought up an allegation the police had put to him: 'I have been accused of for them, that I have been SS man. Is it possible to say lies like that?'

Clegg's outward demeanour remained unaltered but once more he must have been dying inside. Having gone to considerable lengths to try to avoid Sawoniuk's alleged service with the SS being aired in court, here was his client, unprovoked, giving voice to it.

Mr Justice Potts once more intervened. 'You have to listen to Mr Nutting's questions. He is asking you about these answers that you gave to the police. Do you understand? Just let us deal with one thing at a time.'

As the forensic cross-examination continued, Andrusha continued to contradict himself, piling one lie upon another, before being trapped into damaging admissions. After a few more questions about the *Schutzmannschaft* and the police station, Nutting pointed out that, once more, Andrusha was contradicting what he had told Scotland Yard. 'I do not care what they said down there,' he said, gesticulating at the police statement Nutting was reading from. 'They could print anything. They have been printing a lot of lies about me, not only one that question.'

Potts again interrupted him. 'Now, Mr Sawoniuk, this was a tape-recorded interview. Are you saying the tape got it wrong, or are you saying that this record does not interpret the tape properly? Just take it slowly please, because this is important.'

'And do yourself justice,' Nutting added, goading him a little more. 'Are you saying that this answer has been deliberately falsified for this court?'

'Definitely,' Andrusha said.

'Is there no lie you are not prepared to tell?'

'I got no lies whatsoever. I been accused for the last five years. I come here to clear my name. My conscience is clear. I got nothing to hide and when I am dead, I am going to heaven.'

Nutting was now moving on to even more dangerous ground for Andrusha, beginning with the build-up to the Yom Kippur massacre. Having established that he suspected that the Jews were going to be murdered, Nutting then asked him whether the other policemen had, 'like you, very good relationships with the Jews?'

'I am the one who had a good relation with the Jews. Nobody else. I never killed one Jew, and my Jews was best friend. I born to them next door, I grow up with them, I played with them, and I worked for them, and most of the time I work for them for nothing. I still waiting for my pay day.' For the first time since he took the stand, the ripple of laughter around the court was with him, rather than at him.

Nutting's next question stilled the laughter. 'Did you share your suspicions about what would happen, or might happen, with any of your Jewish friends?'

'No. I got no reason to believe that. I did not know what going to happen, did I?'

'But you thought that they might all be murdered? Did you not communicate your suspicions to some of your Jewish friends?'

'I could not do that because if the Germans find me out about it, I be dead.'

The court then adjourned for lunch, giving Andrusha a brief respite.

CHAPTER 30

When Johnny Nutting resumed his relentless interrogation that afternoon, the defendant was soon tying himself in knots again, disputing for no evident reason the number of Jews who had lived in Domachevo before the mass killings. Nutting allowed him to restate that he had not been there at the time of the massacre, and then said, 'When you returned, you must have been appalled at what had happened?'

'Of course I was, because that is my good friends, Jewish.'

'And you must have learned that the local police had been forced to participate in the massacre?'

'No, that never happened.'

'Helping to round up the Jews?'

'Never that happened. Except, as I said, the SS who was killing them Jews, they come with their own twenty people.'

'You are not suggesting, are you, that twenty people would have been enough to round up all the Jews of Domachevo and take them off to be murdered?'

'Quite sure, yes. Positive.'

Nutting went on to construct his next trap, inviting Andrusha to agree that he did not want to remain in a police force that had helped the Germans to massacre Domachevo's Jews.

'Definitely not.'

'So you took steps to leave, no doubt?'

Once more Andrusha obliged. 'Correct. I just went without

anybody telling, I never had an intention to stop in Domachevo. I did not see no future for me. There was more life in a cemetery than all Belarus.'

Nutting then enquired why, if so, it had taken him a further 14 months by his own account – or two years according to the Crown's witnesses – before he actually did leave. His response was a rambling statement about him being his own man who makes his own decisions about when to leave or not leave a place. Words were now pouring out of him in such a torrent that Potts intervened to ask him to speak more slowly.

'Okay, I try,' Sawoniuk said. 'But I get a bit excited, that is all.'

He became even more excited as Nutting pointed out that people could leave the auxiliary police without fear of retaliation, just as Andrusha's brother, Nikolai, had done. 'Was it because he realised what the whole racket smelt of?' Nutting said, quoting the phrase Ivan Baglay had used.

Andrusha said his brother never told him why he left the police. 'He was not well, but whether he leave because over his health or some other reason I do not know.'

'The real reason,' Nutting said, 'was because he did not like what he had to do, was it not?'

'Yes, he one of them persons, same as myself. He did not want to do it, such things like, you know, hitting people or killing people, he would not do that. I never done it, he never done it, but he did not like it, what was going on in Domachevo with the Jewish. That is why, you know, he decided to leave police.'

Realising his mistake, Sawoniuk then tried to row back his statement about 'killing people' by repeating his claim that Nikolai never told him why he had quit. Over 20 more questions and answers, Nutting pressed him about exactly what it was that had been 'going on in Domachevo with the Jewish' that his brother did not like. The most he could extract from him in response was 'because the Jewish people never had their freedom'.

Fedor Zan, a key prosecution witness.

Fedor Zan pointing to the site from which he witnessed the
killing of 15 Jewish women.

Alexandre Baglay standing outside the Old Bakery on the Road of Death.

Ivan Baglay standing on the spot from where he saw Sawoniuk herding a Jewish woman and her child along the road and beating her with a birch pole.

Ben-Zion, Clara, Shalom and Tomer Blustein in Domachevo with Scotland Yard detectives and Israeli police.

Itinerary of the jury's visit to Domachevo.

Judge and counsel outside Sawoniuk's home in Domachevo in February 1999. From left, Sir Humphrey Potts in his 'Noddy hat' or 'Arctic-grade judicial wig'; Bill Clegg QC, 'looking like an escapee from a local asylum'; Johnny Nutting QC, 'resembling a patrician KGB officer'; junior prosecution counsel John Kelsey-Fry; and junior defence counsel Kaly Kaul.

The jurors trudging through the snow.

Local people, inured to the biting cold, watch the British invasion of Domachevo.

Andrei Sawoniuk's half-brother Nikolai outside his shack in Domachevo.
The letter that Andrusha wrote to him seven years after the war eventually
led to his discovery and arrest.

Three amigos – partisan comrades reunited many years after the war. From left, Jack Pomeranc, Ben-Zion Blustein and Meir Bronstein.

Summary of the four indictments.

Ben-Zion and Clara Blustein arriving at the Old Bailey to give evidence against his childhood friend.

Andrei Sawoniuk outside the Old Bailey.

Sawoniuk belied defence claims about his frailty by throwing a stone at a photographer outside his Bermondsey flat, then hurried to retrieve it so he could throw it again.

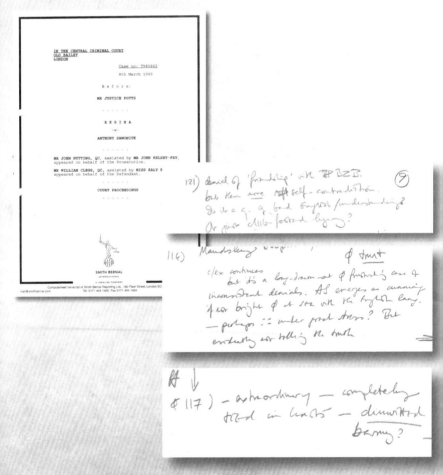

Some of Sir Humphrey Potts' waspish annotations on his copy of the court transcript.

ONE LETTER SNARED EVIL NAZI BUTCHER

Killer son of Jewish teacher

Face of fear ... Sawoniuk in uniform as a Nazi stooge

The *Sun*'s verdict on Sawoniuk, showing his use of a walking stick as a weapon when confronting a photographer.

'The best revenge would be to show the Nazis my big family, living in our own independent country, and say, "We won!"' The Blustein family, including Ben-Zion (fourth left in back row), son Shalom (second left in back row), grandsons Ben (at left in centre row) and Tomer (holding the small boy in the centre row), and Ben-Zion's wife Clara (second right in front row).

The massacre site in Domachevo. The Soviet memorial is the obelisk in the centre of the image.

Nutting then quoted his answer of a few minutes before back to him: '"He did not want to do it, such things like, you know, hitting people or killing people." What was it in the early winter of 1941 that alerted you and your brother to the possibility of Jews being killed?'

'Out the question,' Andrusha shouted. 'Lie. Absolutely lie, nothing true in it.'

'What is a lie?'

'The way you saying it.'

'But I am repeating your answer to you.'

'Yes.'

Sensing this was a key moment, Nutting kept hammering at the point. 'I will give you one more chance to answer the question,' he said, and then gave him at least a dozen, before Sawoniuk tried to close the book on it. 'He was not all that perfect health,' he said. 'That is the one reason. The second reason, yes, you just mentioned that I told you he would not kill Jew and I would not kill Jew, because we lived all our life together with the Jews. And if Germans did tell him to kill them Jews – and that is a big if – he would probably have to do it, because if he did refuse to do it, he would be dead himself. That is the answer. That is all I got to say. I got nothing else to say.'

Nutting now rammed the point home in case the jury were in any doubt. 'What you have done, I suggest, is to lift a corner of the truth by that answer. What I suggest is that all those answers this morning about how well the Jews were treated under the German occupation were lies. And what I suggest you have told us as the reason for your brother's leaving the police is lifting the corner of the truth because your brother left the police because he did not like having to ill-treat or kill Jews.'

'Correct,' Andrusha said, before immediately contradicting himself and Nutting. 'But this is not the reason why he left.'

Once more, Mr Justice Potts's private notes to himself about the exchanges were very revealing: 'Extraordinary – completely tied in knots – dim-witted? barmy?'

Nutting at last moved on, but only to cite a number of other men who had joined the police and then left. He then invited Andrusha to consider what would have happened after the massacre, had he seen 'a Jew who had survived, who had been a friend of yours'.

'If I see any Jewish after the massacre, I would do my best to help him. I did help whoever I could very secretly and they know it. I bet the Jews – I know they are dead – I bet if they come to life and tell here on the front of my face that I was good to them and helped many, many, many Jews in their life.'

He also insisted that he had never taken part in any search-and-kill operation. 'Nobody gave me instructions to go in a ghetto and looking for the Jews. I went there on a couple of occasions, not looking for the Jews but looking for clothes or a pair of shoes. And if I did find them Jews, I would hide them. I would do it my best they are safe.'

Apart from the lunch adjournment, Andrusha had now been under cross-examination for over four hours and Mr Justice Potts enquired, 'How are you feeling, Mr Sawoniuk? Can you manage another ten minutes?'

'Sure, sure, yes,' Andrusha said, a response he might soon have been regretting for, determined to finish the day on a high and leave the jurors with a vivid last impression, Nutting challenged him once more about the aftermath of the massacre. 'What we have heard is that you were a very busy policeman after 20th September.'

'You would say that.'

'Well, yes, I suppose I would,' Nutting said, 'but you see, I am only telling you and reminding you what the evidence is.' Having lit the blue touchpaper, Nutting then sat back to enjoy the show.

'Everything been saying it. Everything what has been saying it in the magistrates' court for six weeks and in this court,'

Andrusha said. 'There was no other people was involved in the murdering or killing Jews, only me. What I hear from you all the time: "Andrusha! Andrusha! Andrusha! Andrusha! Andrusha!" and "Andrusha!" again!'

Once more, he was shouting, his face suffused with rage. 'You never mentioned nobody else, only my name. There was another fifteen policemen in Domachevo. Nobody done murders, only me. The other fifteen policemen were standing behind my back and watching while I was killing people and clapped their hands. Is that right? According the witnesses, that is what it is, and that is what you are accusing me, for killing Jewish and killing Jewish. "Andrusha! Andrusha! Andrusha!" I hope you remember that name for the rest of your life.'

Bill Clegg must have been tempted to put his face in his hands, because Sawoniuk's outburst seemed much less a denial of guilt than a self-pitying complaint that he was the only one on trial for murder, while others were getting away with it. However, Clegg remained impassive, seeing his only option in reaction to his client's testimony 'to nod sagely and pretend you're happy, even if you're inwardly despairing'.

As Andrusha paused for breath, Nutting gave the pot another stir. 'But you see, Mr Sawoniuk, just help us: the reason why you say these people from Borisy and Domachevo have told lies about you is because they resent the fact that you were a very effective policeman with the partisans? If they resent the fact that you were so effective killing partisans, why should they invent stories that you killed Jews?'

'Because they are professional liars. They are criminals. Some of them witnesses, they done twenty-five years in a Russian jail. Alcoholic.' As he saw Nutting about to ask another question, Andrusha said, 'Excuse me, sir, I have not finished. I want to finish. I have had it long enough on my chest.'

Nutting was only too happy to allow him more rope, merely saying, 'Please. Direct your answers to the jury.'

'All witnesses: I had a machine-gun on my left shoulder, a rifle on my right shoulder, the shovel in my left hand and a hammer on my right arm, and that is what I have been doing, killing and hitting, with the shovel, with the hammers and everything. Nobody else done it, only me. And these everyone witnesses saying the same story. So anybody could believe them people, what they are saying, that I could hit people, children and a woman, hit them with a shovel and a hammer. Is there anybody in this court – I do not think that nobody believed that, but you probably believe that,' he said, turning back to Nutting. 'That is your job to believe the lies, not me.'

'The one person they would invent lies about killing Jews is you, who had the best relationship with the Jews before and during the war?'

'And after and still am. I was the best friend of Jews. Why you saying that I killing Jews? Why you saying that?'

Mr Justice Potts intervened for the final time that day to say, 'Now, I think we have been here once before, Mr Sawoniuk.'

Potts then dismissed the jury for the day, but with the counsel and the defendant still in the courtroom, he raised an issue which he had already noted to himself: 'Case over-running time', citing the reason as 'AS's garrulous answers to questions'. 'Mr Clegg,' he began, 'I hardly know how to say this, but I think I ought to. I am reluctant to interfere with the defendant's answers. He is obviously under great emotion. And the last thing that one wants, is for him to be stopped by the judge. I am just wondering if there is any way in which we can convey to him that it is perhaps not necessary for him to go into the sort of detail that he has gone when answering Mr Nutting's questions. I hope I make myself clear?'

'My Lord does,' Clegg said. 'And indeed, it will probably come as no surprise to my Lord or Mr Nutting to know that I strongly urged the defendant to keep his answers short in cross-examination. I say that again now in his hearing,' he said, giving

Andrusha a meaningful look, 'so that he can reflect on that advice again overnight.'

Potts's further notes to himself, penned that evening, ruminated on whether Andrusha's 'greater and more histrionic denials' and his penchant for self-contradiction were 'a question of bad English/understanding, or just club-footed lying?' It was a question that the jurors were no doubt also asking themselves.

In a title fight, either Sawoniuk's corner would have thrown in the towel by now or the referee would have stepped in and stopped it to save him from further punishment. As the combat was a battle of words taking place in Court 12 of the Old Bailey, there was to be no relief for him just yet, and his ordeal would resume in the morning.

Although Nutting's cross-examination so far had been something of a disaster for Andrusha, it was still possible that no terminal damage had been inflicted. True, he had frequently lost his temper and shouted at Nutting as he questioned him, but that could as easily have been the fury of an innocent, inarticulate man, wrongly accused, as the lashing out of someone trying to hide their guilt. He had also frequently contradicted himself and said things that were demonstrably false, sometimes risibly so, but Clegg had prepared the ground well, drawing attention to Andrusha's ill health and the potential for memory lapses about events that had occurred so long ago. Whether the jurors would take his lies and contradictions as proof of guilt or just the understandable confusion of an ill, stressed and elderly man, was as yet unclear.

Nutting now insists that he wasn't trying to make Andrusha lose his temper. 'It wasn't a prosecution tactic,' he says. 'You can't provoke someone into giving evidence, but if the evidence you're calling is such that he feels it's going to go wrong for him, that's what makes him take the stand. He was just so furious that he wanted to go in there and have his say, despite what his counsel was advising.'

Clegg also accepts there was no need for the prosecution to try to provoke Sawoniuk because 'just asking him a perfectly civil question was enough to send him off the deep end'. As well as his near-brawl with Meir Bronstein, a series of other ugly incidents outside the court had demonstrated that he was not a difficult man to provoke. Lord Greville Janner of Braunstone, QC, was a former MP who after the war had worked for 18 months as a war crimes investigator with the British Army of the Rhine and had piloted the War Crimes Act through Parliament in 1991. 'Watching Sawoniuk at his trial,' he said, 'I thought of the Nazi murderers I had arrested. My most frightening memory: how ordinary they were, simple workers, farmers or tradesmen, often surrounded by wives and family. Then I would look out my documents and see that they had destroyed innocent lives, without mercy.'

When he saw Sawoniuk in the lobby outside the courtroom, Janner, with his trademark carnation in his lapel, was unable to contain his anger. He walked straight up to him and said, 'How can you sleep at night after what you have done, you bloody murderer?'

According to one account, he responded by punching Janner on the nose, though Steve Law disputes that, saying that he stepped in front of Janner and told him, 'You may be a QC, but you have no place in this trial and you should not be making accusations against a man who should be presumed innocent until proven guilty.'

'On that occasion it was the witness who went for Sawoniuk,' Bill Clegg admits, 'but he was not someone who would ever step away from confrontation.'

Sawoniuk's short fuse was further demonstrated when he threw a stone at a photographer taking pictures outside his block of flats, and then ran after him to try and throw another one, and when Jon Silverman, the BBC Home Affairs Correspondent at the time, was filming a report from the street outside the flats, well before the trial, the next thing he knew was that Andrusha was advancing on him brandishing a metal bar.

Silverman claims it was his report on this incident that persuaded the Attorney-General, John (later, Lord) Morris, to authorise charges. 'Morris told me that he was being urged by Sawoniuk's legal team to drop the case,' Silverman said, 'because he was suffering from a range of medical complaints. However, when the news report showed an apparently robust Sawoniuk lurching towards me with a threatening iron bar, the decision to charge suddenly became less contentious.' If he was fit enough to attack Silverman, he was certainly fit enough to stand trial. However, that version of events is contradicted by Clegg: 'I'm quite certain that had no influence at all on the decision to prosecute.'

CHAPTER 31

The trial resumed at 10.30 the next morning, Tuesday 23 March 1999. It was Day 22 and yet there was still no end in sight, though both counsel had expressed the belief – or perhaps it was the hope – that they would have completed their closing statements before the court adjourned for the weekend.

When Johnny Nutting resumed his cross-examination, the jurors could have been forgiven for getting a strong sense of *déjà vu*, because he was covering what was already pretty familiar ground. He again rehearsed Andrusha's claim that the *Schutzmannschaft* had never received any instructions about the Jews, and that, in his words, 'nobody ever seen them Jews after the massacre'.

'It follows then,' Nutting said, 'that anyone who says that they saw you in company with a Jew after the massacre is lying?'

Having prepared the ground, he then worked his way through every allegation that had been voiced against Sawoniuk, pausing each time to ask him, 'True or untrue?'

'Ivan Baglay – a woman and child whom you were beating?'
'It is lies.'

'The Biumen family who were begging for their lives?'
'Untrue.'

'Alexandre Baglay – you forced him and his young friend to bury three Jews whom you shot?'

'Untrue. Absolute lie.'

'Mr Zan said he saw you escorting a woman and a baby into the police station?'

'Untrue. He would say that, wouldn't he?'

'And that woman was subsequently taken in the direction of the sand-hills?'

'Untrue.'

'Mrs Yakimuk – instead of protecting her from the allegation that she was a Jew, you did nothing.'

'Untrue.'

'After the massacre you were heard with Vashka searching in the ghetto?'

'Untrue.'

'On the same day you and other policemen were seen to kill children?'

'Absolutely lies. I never killed a child – the children are my life and I never put a finger on children.'

'You were seen by Evgeny Melaniuk to escort a group of eight Jews towards the sand-hills?'

'Absolutely dirty lies.'

'Mr Zan saw you machine-gunning sixteen [sic, the allegation was 15] Jewish women in the forest?'

'Absolutely dirty lies.'

'Ben-Zion Blustein saw a man he knew brought into the cavalry base by a number of Christians in order to obtain flour or salt or some other reward?'

'Lies.'

'And the last time he saw him was when he was put into your custody and taken away?'

'Untrue.'

'Mr Blustein saw you given the custody of a man called Mir Barlas and you took him away and he never saw him again.'

'Untrue.'

'Did you ever boast about what happened to Mir Barlas?'

'No, I am not interested. I do not keep a record of whatever happened to people.'

'You said to Mr Blustein that he better not suppose that he, a Jew, would survive if the Germans left, because he too would be murdered?'

'I never said that to nobody.'

'Rachel Ipsun Schneider – you found potatoes on her and you and another policeman savagely beat her?'

'Untrue.'

Despite Andrusha's denials, as Nutting no doubt intended, the sheer weight of allegations against him must have made some impression on the jurors.

In the course of further questioning, Andrusha kept referring to the ghetto. 'That is the third time you have used the word "ghetto" this morning,' Nutting said. 'I thought your case was that the ghetto did not exist.'

'Well, you keep using ghetto, saying ghetto and ghetto, so I repeat after you.'

The denials continued as Andrusha insisted that he had never had a house removed from the ghetto and rebuilt, and even claimed that there had never been a *bania* – a public bath – in Domachevo. As Mr Justice Potts noted to himself, 'AS ties himself in more knots (Clegg must have been having kittens).'

When Nutting turned to Fedor Zan's testimony, Andrusha reverted to his conspiracy theory. Witnesses like Zan were 'told to do that by KBG [sic] Russian police, and most of them from Scotland Yard as well. They could not find them proper witnesses who come here and tell the true story about me. That is why they been looking all over Belarus to find them witnesses which is all lies and lies and lies, and nothing else.'

Andrusha admitted that he and other auxiliary policemen had found some partisans in the cellar of a house in the village where Zan's uncle lived but denied taking him and his wife and children away to be executed.

'Untrue. When we killed – when we found them partisans in a bunker – there was nobody round that area. You could not see nobody because everybody was frightened, because there was shooting going on, and if you did try to see somebody in that area, you could not find them. Nobody was there. Absolutely nobody.' Once again, this sounded less like a denial of murder than an assertion that no one could have been there to witness it.

Nutting now reached the point where Sawoniuk had fled Domachevo – at the end of 1943 in his version, or July 1944, according to several witnesses. 'Anybody who says you left by horse and cart in July 1944 is lying? And anyone who says that you left with Nina is lying?'

'I only knew her as a friend, nothing serious. I did not need nobody to escort me nowhere. I am by myself.'

'And there was no question of any marriage to Nina? No question of Nina coming with you or ever being with you later in the war?'

'Out of the question, no. Definitely not.'

Under Nutting's questioning, Andrusha then embarked on a rambling and contradictory account of how, mostly on foot, but occasionally by train, he had travelled from Domachevo to Krakow, and then to the German border, where he had been 'catched down, caught by police and then we have to work on a farm'. Having heard that the Free Polish Army had formed in France, he then escaped from the farm, travelled right across Germany without any papers or documents, crossed into France and joined the Polish Army. He claimed to have had 'nothing to eat, just rotten apples from the forest and the odd cabbage', as he made his marathon walk across Germany and France.

The only problem with this account, as Nutting gleefully pointed out, was that Sawoniuk was claiming to have heard of the Polish Army's formation in France and to have travelled to join them at a time when the country was still under German occupation. 'How could the Poles have been organising the recruitment of anybody in France before D-Day? You are lying again, are you not?'

'I am not,' Andrusha shouted, shaking his fist at Nutting.

'Mr Sawoniuk, Mr Sawoniuk, Mr Sawoniuk . . .' Potts said.

'I do not like it they call me liar.'

Nutting then tossed another hand grenade at him. 'Did you ever serve in the German Army? Did you ever tell anybody that you had served in the German Army?'

'How could I say to anybody, tell these lies, when I never did serve the German Army?'

Nutting then invited him to look at 'a document, which is your Polish Army file'.

Before he could do so, Clegg objected to the file being cited. Documents can be forged and therefore are only admissible if the person who produced them testifies to their authenticity. Neither Sawoniuk's Polish II Corps file nor the record of his membership of the Waffen-SS were therefore admissible, since those who compiled them could not be brought to court to testify that they were true.

Potts then pointed out that Clegg was on shaky ground since he had made use of the Polish Army file himself when question-ing Detective Sergeant Griffiths. When Clegg then claimed it was only the description of Sawoniuk's blond hair that he had been referencing, Potts lost patience with him, saying, 'Well, you cannot pick and choose bits of the document.'

He eventually ruled that Nutting could question Sawoniuk about the army record but if he denied the contents or that it was his signature at the bottom of it, Nutting could go no fur-ther with it. However, the file would be admissible if Sawoniuk could be enticed into authenticating it himself, and Nutting therefore approached the subject with great care. He first got him to agree that his name – Andrei Sawoniuk – was written on the cover, replacing another name. 'One is scratched out,' Nutting said.

Sawoniuk shrugged. 'Why?'

'I was hoping you were going to tell us.'

'No.'

Sawoniuk then agreed that, as the document showed, he had joined the Polish 10th Hussars in December 1944, that the date and place of birth recorded were his, that his mother's name was Pelagia, though he denied that he had listed his brother as his next of kin, saying, 'We never had a good relation, so it do not matter to me. When I am die, I am dead.'

Nutting then reached the crucial point, asking him to translate the Polish phrase *Sluzba w army obcej,* referring to the period between 1 August 1944 and the date that Andrusha joined the 10th Hussars, 27 December of that year.

Andrusha hesitated and then said, 'It means, you know, I joined that army, as a Polish Army, that is all. Nothing much.'

Nutting was not buying that. 'Let me suggest a translation: "Service in a foreign army."'

'No, it does not say foreign army.'

Nutting led him through it word by word, ending, 'And what does the last word *obcej* mean?'

'*Obcej* means somebody else,' Andrusha said.

'Foreign?'

'Yes.'

'What were you doing after 1st August 1944? Nutting said.

Sawoniuk floundered. 'Must be France or Italy. As I told you many occasion, it happened fifty-seven years ago. It is impossible to answer you. I am sorry to that, but I tried to help you as much as I can, but if I do not know or do not remember, I cannot answer.'

'Were you serving in the German Army?'

'You asked me same question again and again and again, and I give you answer again and again and again: I never ever joined the German Army. Never.'

Nutting held up the document. 'We have had that manuscript

writing translated. What it says is "1.8 to 11.11.1944. German Army according to his own statement".'

Incandescent once more, Andrusha shouted, 'I ask you question: prove it to me in black and white. Prove it. Rubbish. You lying here in front of jury and in front of everybody. You try to put me behind bars. I hope this jury does not believe you.'

Nutting switched to another document. 'Did you ever join the Waffen Border Regiment of the SS, Number 76, 1st Battalion?'

Now shaking with rage, Andrusha snapped back, 'You call me liar twice. I call you liar.'

'Did you go missing from that regiment on 20th November in Altkirch-Wittersdorf in the Upper Alsace?'

'Do not talk to me about German Army. I will not answer you no more questions about German Army. That is, sir, my lot.'

Nutting continued as if Andrusha had not spoken. 'Just look at that document, please.'

'I do not have to look at that.'

'Mr Sawoniuk,' Mr Justice Potts said, once more pouring oil on the troubled waters. 'Are you prepared to look at that document or not?'

'I will do, yes, with your permission.'

Once more, Nutting led him through the personal information it contained: name, place and date of birth. 'Does it say "Rank/Position: Korporal of the Schuma"? Were you Corporal of the *Schutzmannschaft* when you left?'

'Never. What you mean when I left? I never been in German Army. I cannot stand that lies. I have been listening to lies for three months and I am not going to listen no more. Do not mention to me about German Army. I am going,' he said, shouting even louder and starting to leave the witness box.

Bill Clegg intervened. 'I was wondering if it would be a good idea to have a very short break for the defendant, just to collect his composure?'

'He is clearly excited,' Potts said, 'but at the same time, Mr Clegg, Mr Nutting must not be prevented from putting what, up until now, have seemed to be material and fair questions.'

Potts offered Andrusha a break, which he declined, and the judge then said in his sternest voice, 'Mr Sawoniuk, will you please understand that if you are asked an improper question, I will stop Mr Nutting? So far, you have not been asked an improper question. Now, are you prepared to listen to Mr Nutting's questions and answer them?'

'My Lord, I am not preparing to listen on the German Army. I am sorry.'

'I see,' Potts said, but before he could continue, Nutting said, 'Mr Sawoniuk, bear with me. I only have two more questions for you.'

The usher tried to hand him back the document but Sawoniuk again refused to look at it until Potts stepped in once more. 'Will you take it back if I ask you?'

'I do anything you want me to do.'

'Yes, well, I am asking you to take the document back.'

Sawoniuk did so and Nutting questioned him about the German words for 'married to' followed by 'Nina S'. The jurors were about to discover why Nutting had spent so long trying to establish that Sawoniuk had been married to Nina, and that they had left Domachevo together. 'What was Nina's last name?' Nutting said.

'I do not know her name. She was a Russian girl. I never bothered to ask her. It not interested me.'

'Would "Nina S" on that document refer to Nina Sawoniuk, by any chance?' Nutting asked innocently.

'Never.'

'How is it that a German Waffen-SS document should contain your name, your date of birth, your place of birth and the word "Nina S" on it?'

Sawoniuk erupted once more. 'That is everybody down there print that,' he shouted, pointing at DS Griffiths. 'That is his idea.'

'This is a Scotland Yard conspiracy? All part of the KGB conspiracy?'

'They working together, don't they?'

Under the rules of evidence, as Bill Clegg had been at pains to point out in legal argument, documents unsupported by eyewitness testimony are not admissible. Despite this, Nutting had found a way to mention Sawoniuk's membership of the Waffen-SS during his cross-examination. As John Kelsey-Fry admits, 'The record was not in my view admissible at all, but that didn't stop Johnny Nutting from exploiting it and then letting the balloon go up when it was too late to do anything about it!'

Nutting was using Sawoniuk's claim to have walked from Poland to France in a timescale which was clearly impossible, to justify raising it, because the date on the Waffen-SS card proved this. Steve Law has a grudging admiration for Nutting's sleight of hand, but feels the SS record was 'hugely damaging and must have been in the jurors' minds despite Mr Justice Potts's instructions to disregard it'.

As the jurist Otto Kirchheimer once remarked, arguments about the admissibility of evidence and attempts by judges to get the jurors to put it out of their minds, only tend to make 'the forbidden fruit' more tempting and, despite his furious denials, the jurors' knowledge of Sawoniuk's SS involvement can only have hardened their view of his character.

Potts now once more offered Andrusha the chance of a few minutes' break. 'Are you tired, Mr Sawoniuk?' Nutting asked, with at least the appearance of solicitude. 'I have one more topic to ask you about, but I do not want to ask you about anything if you are too tired to answer the questions.'

'I am tired enough of you and everybody else here, them

sitting down there. In the British history, nobody criminal waiting five years like I just did wait, and I am going to tell you everything, whatever I got it inside me.'

At that point Potts insisted on a break. Fifteen minutes later Sawoniuk was back in the witness box, with Nutting producing another document, this time an admission form from the Maudsley Hospital, compiled in 1956. It soon became clear that Nutting's purpose was not to dwell on Andrusha's history of shock treatment – electroconvulsive therapy – but to establish that he had entered his marital history on the form as: 'First wife dead. Second wife divorced.'

When Scotland Yard detectives had interviewed him, he claimed never to have been married before coming to England. The reason for that, Nutting suggested, was because Andrusha knew that, under the Nazi occupation, married men were exempt from conscription for forced labour. 'Is the truth that you did not and could not admit to police that you were married to Anna because if you had done so, it would have shaken the faith in your story that you were sent to Germany for forced labour?'

'I do not think so,' Andrusha said. 'Please, listen to me for just a minute. I want to express my view, what I got inside.'

'No, Mr Sawoniuk,' Potts said. 'Would you just answer the question, and then you can comment?'

'In April 1996,' Nutting said, 'when you were interviewed by the British police, the account you gave them was that you never served in the police and were sent to Germany as forced labour.'

'No, no, no, no, no! I did not say that. The reason why I said to Scotland Yard that I was not in the German police, because I was scared I would probably be deported back to Belarus. I got a very, very shock and I still got it inside me. I cannot forget, myself, when I see the four policemen outside my door. This is only one reason and this is probably only one lie what I give of that evidence in this court, that I told them that I never been police.'

'The truth is that you had decided to lie, or try to lie your way out of this allegation of murder. What you pretended was that you had been deported by the time of the massacre in order to give yourself an alibi for the Jews you murdered?'

'Once again you say that Jew murders. I am not Englishman but I spent fifty-three years in this country and I know little law. Before you accuse anything for the murder, you have to prove it, black and white. You do not want to listen to me that tells truth. You like listen lies, therefore you call me murderer.'

When Andrusha denied again that he had ever told Scotland Yard that he had been a forced labourer, Nutting and Potts, in tandem, eventually prevailed on him to read aloud the relevant section of the interview transcript: 'In September 1942, I was in Germany working the farms.' Having done so, he said, 'I told you once before, what you got down there and who has printed that? Scotland Yard.'

'Have I to understand that you did not say that?' Potts said.

'My Lord, as honest to God, I never say that.'

Under repeated questioning, he then shifted his ground again, saying it had been a mistake and he had actually meant to say 1943, not 1942.

Nutting's last question was, 'May I just finally say this to you, so that there is no doubt between us about the allegation that I am putting to you? What I say to you, Mr Sawoniuk, is that you are prepared to tell any lie, to make any allegation and to invent any story in order to evade your responsibilities for murdering Jews in the autumn of 1942 in Domachevo.'

Andrusha swung round to face the jury. 'I swear it once in this box and I can swear it again, I never, never, ever killed a Jew, or anybody for that matter, and I ask you, jury, to believe me.'

Nutting sat down, probably well satisfied with his two days' work. Mr Justice Potts noted to himself that Sawoniuk's testimony under cross-examination had been 'a long drawn-out and frustrating case of inconsistent denials. AS emerges as cunning, if not bright, and at sea with the English language, perhaps because under great stress? But evidently not telling the truth.' He added a final summary of Sawoniuk's performance, emphasising it in block capitals: 'BASICALLY UNDOES HIMSELF – DID CLEGG TRY TO DISSUADE HIM FROM TAKING THE STAND?' Had he asked him, the answer would have been an emphatic 'Yes!'

A less determined, or possibly less optimistic barrister than Clegg might have been tempted to sit on his hands at this point but he was still determined to do his best for his client, despite that client's efforts to make the task far from straightforward. So he chose to re-examine Sawoniuk, hoping to leave a less damaging impression in the jurors' minds than the one painted by Nutting. However, since, as he submitted to Potts, 'My Lord, it has been a very long day for the witness,' he was able to delay it until the following morning.

Before adjourning, with the jury absent, Potts heard submissions from both counsel about some photographs that Clegg proposed to put before them. In an attempt to discredit Fedor Zan's testimony of what he had seen in the forest from 127 paces, he had commissioned a photographer to take a series of pictures of a dummy with a picture of Tony Blair's face on it, at increasing distances – 25, 50, 100 and 125 yards – with the aim of demonstrating that it would have been impossible for Zan to have identified Sawoniuk at the distance he claimed.

Mr Justice Potts did a double-take as he looked at the pictures. 'I am sorry, I do not understand this,' he said. 'These are not photographs of Domachevo?'

'No,' Clegg said, 'they have been taken in London.' He went on to claim that they had been taken in 'probably somewhat better conditions so far as light and visibility, and in our submission they are clearly of some potential assistance to the jury in assessing the reliability of Mr Zan's evidence.'

Nutting objected vigorously. 'They are misleading in the sense that they substitute the camera for the human eye. They furthermore are taken in town rather than in the country, at a different time of day. The jury have seen the scene. It is for the jury, using their own understanding of the view itself and their own knowledge of the distance of 127 paces, to make up their own minds what the human eye is capable of at that distance.'

After hearing further arguments, Potts pointed out that, 'on the application of the defence' – how Clegg must have winced at that reminder – the jury had visited the crime scene, and stood in the place from where Zan said he had seen the killings. What might or might not be visible in images taken in London, on a February day in 1999, could not be legitimately compared to what could be seen with the naked eye in a forest clearing in Domachevo in September 1942. 'I am satisfied that, were these photographs adduced, they could only mislead the jury. These photographs, in my judgment, are simply not like with like, and I rule against the application.'

They then turned to the timetable for the remainder of the trial, and whether Clegg's re-examination of Sawoniuk, videotaped evidence by two defence witnesses who were unable to travel to London from Domachevo, and the closing speeches by both counsel could be completed in the next two days, leaving the judge to begin his summing up the following Monday.

'I am very anxious not to have speeches broken by the weekend. Mr Nutting promises to be brief,' Clegg said with a smile. 'I do not know whether to trust him.'

'Well, you are always brief, Mr Clegg,' Potts said. 'We will just have to do our best.'

CHAPTER 32

The following morning, Wednesday 24 March, Day 23, as usual, Steve Law collected Andrusha from his flat in a London black taxi, running the by-now customary gauntlet of shouting yobs. When he entered the witness box just after ten o'clock, Clegg began his attempt to repair some of the damage from his client's disastrous cross-examination.

He tried to enlist the jurors' sympathy by getting Andrusha to remind them that his memory was 'not all that good – most of them damage done when I was in the Maudsley Hospital. On top of that I had an operation on my knees,' he said, adding somewhat surprisingly that it had 'damaged my brains and the nerves'.

Clegg then asked him if he had tried to remember what happened during the war in the half century since it ended. 'Not really,' Andrusha said. 'It is a bad memory for me. I tried to forget it, not to remember.'

Unsurprisingly, Clegg covered Andrusha's travel from Belarus to France and service with the Polish Free Army without any reference to the German Army. He then asked him about his professed hatred for both the Germans and the Russians.

'I said it that I hate them two nations,' Andrusha said, 'and I got reason to hate them. The Russians killed them 16,000 Polish soldiers in one bunker,' he said, referring to the notorious Katyn massacre, 'and many, many thousands more been killed in Siberia, and the same goes to the Germans, and that is why I hate them two nations.'

Probably with his heart in his mouth, Clegg then reminded him of the two allegations against him, beginning with Fedor Zan. 'This man is not human being,' Andrusha said, his temper visibly rising again. 'Because if he was, he would not come to this country and tell this sort of lie, even if he was forced by KGB and Scotland Yard to say that. He never seen me, but he been told my name and what I been doing, and therefore he tells a pack of lies about me.'

Clegg finished his re-examination a few moments later, but before Sawoniuk was released from the witness box, Mr Justice Potts had a further question for him, querying his claim that he had never known or met Fedor Zan, even though Zan said they had been at school together.

'I never met him, never in my life,' Andrusha insisted.

He was then at last allowed to step down.

Clegg next addressed the jury on the video evidence they were about to see from two witnesses, Jozef Boguszewski, whose wife was too ill to be left, and Mrs Choraza, who was too frail herself to leave Domachevo. 'The jury may be slightly alarmed to see a cat disappear up the chimney in her kitchen during the course of my examination-in-chief,' Clegg said, eyes twinkling. 'It was a distraction to me but I can assure the jury, in case they are alarmed, it emerged later, completely unharmed.'

Clegg established that Mrs Choraza had known Sawoniuk by sight but not personally, and that 'throughout the whole of the occupation, she had never seen him ill-treat any of the Jewish people who lived in Domachevo'. The benefit to the defence case was rather mitigated by the fact that, when asked about the partisans and who had defended Domachevo against them, she responded, 'Nobody defended. The partisans did what they wanted to do and they went away.'

Nutting's cross-examination, recorded on the same videotape, established that Andrusha had been one of the first policemen to volunteer, that he had become the commander of the police and had fled from Domachevo with the Germans. Re-examined by Clegg, she then said she could not really be certain that Andrusha was a volunteer. 'If someone was poor, it was a very hard time and people were trying to survive somehow.'

'And was Sawoniuk's family rich or poor?'

'They were very, very poor.'

As a result, the defence had probably had slightly the better of the exchanges.

Jozef Boguszewski's videotape came next. He said that after the German occupation, he had been approached 'very often' about becoming a policeman, and on one occasion had been taken to the police station but had run away.

Asked by Clegg why he had run away rather than just saying he didn't want to join them, Boguszewski said 'there was no excuse' for not joining. On a second occasion when he was taken to the station and given the declaration to sign that committed him to joining the police, he said that, because he was young, he would need to consult with his parents before signing. He managed to avoid joining the police at all, though many others weren't so lucky. 'They were afraid. They had to obey. Those who did not, were punished.'

Clegg asked him about Andrusha and, like Mrs Choraza, Boguszewski said he 'never saw him using violence, acting violently against anybody'. Cross-examining, Nutting established that he was 23 at the time he'd said he had to ask his parents' permission, and he admitted that he was never punished for refusing. He confirmed that Andrusha had joined 'right after the invasion', that 'people were afraid of him, even his colleagues', and that he had become police commander and fled with the Germans.

*

With the video evidence completed, after a brief adjournment, the jury returned to hear Johnny Nutting begin his closing speech for the prosecution. He started by referring back to Bill Clegg's opening remarks about the jurors needing to 'try to do the impossible' by setting aside their personal feelings in reaction to the testimony they would hear, and reminded them 'you are not trying to achieve justice for the Holocaust victims'.

However, while urging them to concentrate on the two specific counts, he added, 'That of course is not to say that you need to confine your consideration of the evidence to those two witnesses and the testimony that they gave.' The other evidence they had heard, he said, would enable them to 'set the allegations in the two counts into a fair and proper context. The Crown can prove, if you accept the evidence, that he [Sawoniuk] was diligent in seeking out Jews after the massacre – the *Schmutzarbeit*, or dirty work, to which Professor Browning referred. That is the context in which you should judge the two counts.'

He then dealt briefly with the other counts on which the judge had directed the jury to return formal not guilty verdicts. Stepaniuk was dismissed in a few words. 'Forget Mr Stepaniuk and all the evidence he gave. I do not propose to refer to his name again, but very different considerations apply to the evidence of Mr Ben-Zion Blustein.'

Having conceded that the judge had ruled it was unsafe to rely on Ben-Zion's recollection of a conversation about Mir Barlas's death from 57 years before, Nutting said, 'that does not mean you ignore Mr Ben-Zion Blustein's evidence in relation to other matters. Do not suppose for one moment that the direction to acquit in relation to that count means that you must treat Mr Blustein as a liar. Far from it.

'On the essentials, the question for you is: have the witnesses told the truth? Are the events that they relate so indelibly printed on their minds because of the sheer horror of what they saw, that their description, even over this period of time, can be safely and satisfactorily relied upon? And judge the defendant by exactly the same standard. Ask yourselves, was he at least making an attempt to tell the truth, or was he a witness to whom, on occasions, the oath seemed almost an irrelevance?'

Nutting was even able to make a show of offering sympathy for Sawoniuk, though it did not altogether hide his barbs. 'Make allowance for the strain on him of giving evidence over the period of time that he was in the witness box. Do not hold his outbursts against him. Do not judge him on the basis of wild allegations flung across the court in temper – mainly, it has to be said, against the police in this case. An accusation hurled across this courtroom in temper is a very different thing from a calculated lie designed to deceive you. If you find that the defendant has lied, then you must ask why has he done so? Is it because he cannot face the truth? Is there a sensible possibility that he has lied for any reason other than to conceal his guilt on these charges?'

He then began running through the multitude of lies that Andrusha had told, asking why he had claimed not to have been married. 'Was he worried that a record of his marriage might exist and would therefore reveal that he was in fact in Domachevo after the massacre – the one event and its aftermath for which he was so anxious to produce an alibi? The Crown say that he had a very real motive for lying to the British police and it was a deliberate lie.'

Nutting pointed out that Sawoniuk could not conceal or deny his name, date and place of birth – there was too much documentary evidence. His only hope of concealing his guilt was to tell the British police that he had never been a local policeman and had left Domachevo early in the war, before the Yom Kippur massacre. 'He knew – because he knows perfectly well what the police got up to during the war – that any admission that he was in the police might prove extremely difficult for him.' However, Nutting said, when Andrusha saw 20 witnesses at the committal hearing at the magistrates' court testifying that he had been in the police, he realised his previous lie could not stand and changed his story.

Nutting then turned to Clegg's comment that the prosecution was attempting to 'elevate Sawoniuk's importance'. He quoted Clegg's sarcastic comment about Hitler's 'hotline to a hut in Domachevo to discuss his policy with Sawoniuk', and his claim that it was like comparing 'Churchill consulting Pike of *Dad's Army*', but then threw the comparison back in Clegg's face. He detailed Andrusha's ludicrous claims about the Domachevo Jews: 'No ghetto, no restrictions on freedom, no yellow patches, no forced labour, no guards. You have heard the eyewitness descriptions of the ghetto and in particular the detail given by Ben-Zion Blustein – the fear, deprivation, the restrictions, the confiscations, the collapsing morale as a whole community faced the prospect of collective death.' He let the silence build for a few moments and then thundered, 'Members of the jury, this defendant was no Pike! And the police unit in Domachevo was no *Dad's Army*!'

The evidence the jurors had heard, Nutting said, proved that Andrusha had 'played an effective part in searching out and killing Jews in the weeks after 20 September 1942. To carry out his policy of the mass murder of Jews in Eastern Europe, Hitler and the Nazis needed willing executioners. The Crown's case was, and remains, that this defendant, albeit in the one town, and albeit in relation to a limited number of Jews, played a part, however small, in carrying out this policy.'

Nutting was very happy to leave the jury with that as their take home message for the day, and successfully suggested to Mr Justice Potts that it would be a convenient moment to adjourn.

CHAPTER 33

In an attempt to complete the closing speeches of Crown and
defence that day, the court began sitting for Day 24, Thursday
25 March, at 9.30am but, before the jurors came in, Potts,
Nutting and Clegg dealt with the question of arrangements
for Sawoniuk over the weekend. The court was not sitting on
the Friday, meaning it would be three days before the trial
resumed, and Potts was concerned about Andrusha's physical
and mental health if he was allowed to remain alone, brooding
on the possible outcome. He had been bailed and allowed to
return home to his Bermondsey flat at the end of each previous
day, but Potts now felt that closer supervision was required to
avoid the risk of him either absconding, or committing suicide.
However, he was anxious that Andrusha should not see this as
'the result of any conclusion that I have reached about the state
of the evidence or the charges that he faces. My anxiety is for
his well-being.'

Clegg argued that his client's well-being would best be
assured by him remaining on bail. So far, he had attended court
punctually every day he had been required to do so. Although
Potts did not feel there was a substantial risk that Sawoniuk
might fail to surrender to custody after the weekend, he
remained concerned about his physical and mental state.

'I have been advised that were bail withdrawn, the defendant
would be held in the hospital wing of Belmarsh Prison, that a

number of rooms would be available there for his use, that he would be segregated from other prisoners, that medical attention would be available, and that he would have what has been described as a carer, who would be in a position to see to his welfare at all times. My advice is that the carer would accompany him to court in a vehicle containing no other prisoners, and return with him to Belmarsh at the end of the day. I have come to the conclusion,' Potts said, 'that against the whole background of this case, and bearing in mind particularly the manner in which the defendant gave his evidence over the last two or three days, that bail should be withdrawn for his own protection.'

Although Potts's motives and the steps he had taken to ensure Sawoniuk's safety were not in question, Belmarsh Prison's reputation was enough to strike fear in the heart of any potential inmate. A super-secure Category A prison on the site of the old Woolwich Arsenal, it was used to house terrorist suspects and long-term, violent criminals, and some of its staff had a not entirely undeserved reputation for the excessive use of force. It was unlikely that Andrusha would see the revocation of his bail and his transfer to Belmarsh as anything other than confirmation that the judge thought a guilty verdict was on the way.

Having informed the counsel of that change of arrangements, but concerned that the jurors should not hear about it and draw any inference from it, Potts added that he was 'extremely anxious' that the case should proceed exactly as it had up to that point 'so that there can be no inkling given to any observer that the position of the defendant is any different'. Clegg raised no further objection and left his junior, Kaly Kaul, to explain the decision to Andrusha.

When the jurors had been admitted, Nutting resumed his closing speech. He reminded them that he had been talking about the Nazis needing 'willing executioners. The question we have to ask is whether the defendant was one of those.' He dismissed Andrusha's claims that he had joined the *Schutzmannschaft* to avoid forced labour, or been compelled to join because there were no other jobs, since many others, including Fedor Zan, the Baglay brothers and even Ben-Zion – a Jew – had found work. Nor was it impossible to resign from the auxiliary police; Andrusha's own brother was one of several who had done so.

Nutting again contrasted Andrusha's risible claims about the tranquillity and contentment of Domachevo's Jews with Ben-Zion's evidence. He dismissed the 'wild allegation' of a conspiracy between the KGB and Scotland Yard, or the residents of Borisy, and pointed out that Ben-Zion and Evgeny Melaniuk had both rejected opportunities to implicate Sawoniuk. Ben-Zion had said, 'I do not want to give the impression that I am saying things to incriminate Andrusha,' and Melaniuk had testified that he had seen policemen leading people to the sand-hills, but could not say for certain if Andrusha Sawoniuk was among those policemen.

Nutting cited the evidence of a number of witnesses about Sawoniuk's actions in the aftermath of the massacre, 'in complete contradiction to the evidence he gave about his own activities'. He went through the litany of incidents of brutality and referred to Ben-Zion's comment that after Sawoniuk became a policeman: 'He became a man of power, a master, and I was a Jew. He used to behave cruelly whenever he wanted and with whomsoever he wanted.'

Mr Justice Potts noted to himself at this point that so much of the Crown's evidence was 'based on the reliability of circumstantial evidence, based on 50-year-old recollection. Real question is how much do individual <u>independent</u> memories corroborate each other?'

Having painted the background, Nutting then turned to the two specific counts. He reprised Alexandre Baglay's testimony about the three killings he had witnessed and reminded the jurors that when Clegg had put it to Baglay that he might have been mistaken in claiming that Andrusha was there, he had replied, 'No. People whom I knew all my life I would remember . . . I do not believe. I saw it with my own eyes.' When Clegg persisted, saying Baglay could not possibly remember after all those years, he answered, 'I remember beautifully.'

Nutting told the jury that defence counsel, 'like every barrister in the land, only appears in court on the basis of instructions given by the defendant. I am bound to say to you that the defendant proved himself to be a fluent liar in the witness box, who on various occasions gave an account inconsistent with what had been put on his behalf by his counsel.' In other words, Sawoniuk had repeatedly changed his story, even from what he had told his own counsel before the trial began.

Nutting went through a list of points where Alexandre Baglay's testimony contradicted Sawoniuk's and, referring to questions of whether a boy so young would have an accurate memory of those events 57 years later, he said, 'Age distorts the ability to remember time spans, as you will no doubt know from your experience of your parents or your grandparents; but age preserves, like an engraving on the mind, the events of childhood and adolescence, particularly if those events have been frightening or in some other way memorable.'

He then invited the jurors to put themselves in young Baglay's shoes and talked them through the whole incident one more time, ending with the rhetorical questions: 'A forgettable incident or an incident that becomes engraved on the mind? An incident in which you forget the identity of the principal participant, a man whom you knew well, or the identity forever engraved on your mind?'

Finally, Nutting turned to Count 3. Once more he detailed the contradictions between Fedor Zan's testimony and that of Andrusha about other matters, particularly whether the two knew each other and when Sawoniuk left Domachevo. Andrusha's story only covered a handful of weeks between late 1943 and 27 December 1944; 'months and months and months of that year are missing'. Zan's account, Nutting said, was more plausible and was also supported by several other witnesses.

Once more, he found ways to remind the jury that the Polish Army file and the Waffen-SS document were not admissible as evidence, and then referred to their contents. 'You will appreciate that the reason why that question was not explored,' he told the jurors, 'was not because it would have been discreditable for the defendant to have served in the Waffen-SS; after all, he admits serving the Nazis in Domachevo in the police force. The reason why it assumed an importance was because if he had served in the German Army, that would tend to confirm that he had retreated from Domachevo with the Germans, as those seven witnesses told you, and would be in conflict with the account that he gave himself.'

He then described the two other incidents involving Sawoniuk that Zan had witnessed before coming to the murders in the forest. Nutting knew Zan's long-range identification of Sawoniuk was crucial, and he turned again to Clegg's football pitch analogy. 'Supposing one of a group of football players of a particular team, a man you had known for years, was standing around in the goalmouth at one end of a football pitch, as you in the other goalmouth at the other end watched him over a period of five minutes as he moved around. Can it really be suggested that it would be completely impossible for you to recognise him? Of course it would not. On all the evidence,' Nutting said, 'I suggest that Mr Zan could and indeed did correctly identify and recognise the defendant. Would not the events of that evening be almost as indelibly imprinted on his mind as the events of Count One would have been imprinted on the mind of Alexandre Baglay?

'If you think on a consideration of this case that the defendant's account to you is true, or that there is a sensible possibility that it is true, then you will take an early opportunity of acquitting him of the grave crimes that he faces. If, however, on consideration of the whole of the evidence, and following the whole of that evidence to its ultimate and logical conclusion, you take the view that the defendant is guilty, then that must be your verdict, from which, however heavy the responsibility, you should not, and I know will not, shrink. You represent the public. You must do justice between this defendant and the public. The oath that you took was to bring in a true verdict according to the evidence. If that true verdict according to the evidence is not guilty, then say so without further ado or unnecessary delay, but if that verdict according to the evidence is guilty, on either or both of these charges, then that is the verdict which you are bound by your oath to return. On behalf of the Crown, I leave the evidence and the verdict safely in your hands.'

Mr Justice Potts now called the lunchtime adjournment, but before the jury could leave the courtroom, the junior counsel for the defence, Kaly Kaul, stood up. 'My Lord, may I please apologise on behalf of Mr Sawoniuk for his prolonged absence during Mr Nutting's speech this morning?' Upset and angry that his bail was being revoked, Andrusha had not been in court, though he had followed the speech on the LiveNote transcript.

Anxious to ensure, as he had already indicated to counsel, that the jurors would not draw any inference from the withdrawal of bail, Potts at once tried to silence her. 'That was all understood before the jury—'

However, determined to have her say on behalf of the distressed client with whom she was in daily contact, and for whom she clearly felt a great deal of sympathy, Kaul ploughed on. 'Yes, my Lord, but he instructs me that he wishes the jury to know that he was very distraught as a result of your Lordship having withdrawn his bail and he has been sent to prison today.'

There was immediate uproar. Potts, absolutely furious, asked the jury to leave and then said to Clegg, 'I cannot believe that I heard what was said. Did I hear aright?'

'My Lord, yes,' Clegg said.

'Well, you had better think about it. I am absolutely amazed. You, I take it, had no inkling that your junior was going to get up and say what she did. Did she—'

'Well, I think it is better if I say nothing,' Clegg said, not wanting to antagonise the judge, nor hang his junior out to dry without speaking to her first.

'Well, I want some explanation at some stage.'

'My Lord, I was not by that indicating I am never going to say anything,' Clegg said hastily.

Potts scowled at him. 'The upshot is that I am not going to keep the jury out longer than is necessary. We will have to sit earlier for an explanation. I would like a full explanation. At the moment I can only say that I am amazed.'

They resumed early after lunch, in the absence of the jury. 'My Lord,' Clegg said, 'the position is that I was sent a note in the course of the morning, indicating that I was instructed to inform the jury of the effect of the early decision, and merely wrote, in the briefest form, on the note that that would not be happening. That is really all I can say to assist. Miss Kaul is willing to explain what she did to the court.'

Potts was in no mood to be pacified just yet. 'I am not going to take up time at this point having an explanation from her. It is something that should never have been done. If defence had instructions to raise the matter in front of the jury, it seems to me as plain as anything might be that the matter should have been canvassed in the absence of the jury first, in view of the — obviously – implications of doing otherwise.'

One of those implications was that by potentially prejudicing the jury against the defendant, the incident might be used as grounds for appeal if he was convicted. After some discussion of the best way to inform the jury, Potts told Clegg, 'I am going to insist on the defence stating what the position is. I am determined that the defendant should have a fair trial.'

Kaly Kaul's attempts to explain her actions were brusquely cut off by the judge. 'I have heard enough for the moment. I am not going to keep the jury waiting.'

When the jury had filed back into court, Clegg rose to address them. 'Ladies and gentlemen, before I begin, could I just say a word or two about what was said immediately before you rose for the luncheon adjournment? You will understand, I am sure, that what was said cannot possibly have any relevance to your task as jurors in deciding the true verdict in this case. What was said ought not to have been said, and it would be much better had it not been said. We are confident that you will put it completely out of your minds as a wholly irrelevant factor in this case. You will obviously not allow it to prejudice or influence you in any direction at all. Let us forget it was ever said.'

Clegg then began his own closing speech, trying to present a persuasive argument for acquittal, despite the rambling, evasive, incoherent and self-contradictory testimony of his client. He adopted a very different tone from Nutting's solemn, magisterial pronouncements, with a rather whimsical approach at first. He invited the jurors to picture themselves back in Borisy in 1942, eavesdropping on village gossip between Fedora Yakimuk, Evgeny Melaniuk, Fedor Zan and the Baglay brothers. They were comparing notes on the 'extraordinary coincidence', in Clegg's words, that they had all just happened to go into Domachevo and there chanced upon 'that wicked policeman, you know the one, Andrusha, herding people towards the sand-hills.'

Mr Justice Potts's private note to himself on this passage of Clegg's speech makes very revealing reading. Clegg, he noted, 'rubbishes Fedora Yakimuk's (admittedly inchoate) testimony – easily done – and Melaniuk's, Zan's, but Clegg's argument is already <u>specious</u>. Clegg tries to make all prosecution testimony seem as circumstantial as possible, but tenor of his speech is that of a <u>flailing barrister</u>!'

Having spent some time involving almost all the key prosecution witnesses in his imagined wartime conversations in Borisy, Clegg at once discarded Andrusha's wild theory that the KGB and Scotland Yard were hand in glove. 'It is not necessary,' Clegg told the jurors, 'in order to return a true verdict, for you to resolve that allegation which you may think is unsupported by any evidence. What he was saying then – not the only time, you may think, when put under pressure in cross-examination – was another way of saying, "It is just not true and I do not believe it."' It was as elegant a way as possible of both addressing and then disposing of it.

'What is the defence approach?' Clegg said. 'Can I make it clear? All the defendant can tell us, his lawyers, by way of instructions is, "I was not there. I never saw it. Not me." Now, there are two possibilities. Either it did happen, but he was not there, or it did not happen, but the defence cannot know which of those is, in fact, the true position.' There was of course another possibility: that it did happen and the defendant was guilty, but it was not Clegg's job to point that out.

He again drew attention to the lack of any forensic evidence, such as recovered bullets, that would have established the type of weapon that had been used, and the fact that no bodies or human remains had been found that would have confirmed the alleged victims had been shot, before returning to what he was now labelling 'the Borisy coincidence'. 'It is there. It is staring everyone in the face. You must ask yourselves: do we accept that those five people each stumbled across the incidents they describe by pure luck? Five times, they just happened to be in the right spot at the right time, some of them repeating their luck more than once?'

He reminded the jury that none of the incidents with which Sawoniuk was charged had been reported to Scotland Yard's War Crimes Unit during initial investigations. All had only been alleged after the witnesses learned the identity of the suspect, and with the exception of Ben-Zion Blustein, whose testimony, he said, was now irrelevant since the charge based on it had been dismissed, all the witnesses came from Borisy.

That hamlet of 30 households had been a focus of partisan activity and *Schutzmannschaft* reprisals during the war. This was no coincidence, Clegg suggested, arguing the testimony of the witnesses from Borisy was revenge for Sawoniuk's admitted involvement in killing partisans – some of them their relatives. They alone claimed to have seen him committing murders, whereas no witness from Domachevo could point to any crime by him that they had actually witnessed. The rest was all hearsay and village gossip.

If it was not a deliberate conspiracy, Clegg argued, their testimony could also have arisen from the communal memory of the war that must have been discussed, refined and probably embellished innumerable times in the retelling among themselves. There had also been considerable recent publicity about the events leading up to the trial, heightened by the British judicial and media circus that had descended on Domachevo. All that must have increased the possibility that, in the eyes of the Borisy villagers, Sawoniuk's guilt was already a given when they came to testify.

In a later interview, Clegg said he was at this point 'trying to minimise Sawoniuk's culpability in the eyes of the jury'. Although the Nuremberg trials had shown that 'I was only following orders' was not a defence against a charge of war crimes, he wanted the jurors to believe that Sawoniuk was in a kill-or-be-killed situation, facing his own death if he did not follow Nazi orders. 'It wasn't a defence,' Clegg said after the trial, 'but might have made him seem more sympathetic.'

In attempting to portray the Germans as the killers, while the auxiliary police merely carried out standard police duties and fought the partisans, Clegg hoped to paint Sawoniuk as 'just a pawn in a much bigger scheme of others', but as he now admits, that strategy had one serious drawback. 'The trouble was, he was an <u>enthusiastic</u> pawn.'

Clegg did his best to challenge Alexandre Baglay's testimony, reminding the jurors that he was only 12 at the time. 'Without his evidence there is no case. The verdict must be not guilty.' He also made a renewed attempt to cast doubt on Fedor Zan's account, pointing out that at that time of year, 'One: it gets dark in Domachevo at 7.00pm. Two: the case advanced by the prosecution is that the train from Brest gets to Kobelka at 6.20. Three: you have seen how far it is yourself from the Kobelka halt to where the incident is alleged to have taken place, without bothering with the stop at the house, to realise that it must have been dusk before anybody could have got there. So forget about high summers, forget about good daylight, it is autumn and it is dusk. It is 127 paces.

'When you cast your mind back to that scene and ask yourselves, "Could we recognise anyone at that distance?" then we do not shrink from submitting that the conclusion you will be driven to, having been taken there and shown it, you will say, individually and collectively, "It is ridiculous."'

He then turned to the vexed issues of Sawoniuk's innumerable lies and the accounts of what he had or had not done in 1943 and 1944, offering the jurors what he must have hoped would be a tempting way to cut through the morass of conflicting evidence. 'We invite you to concentrate on the evidence around 1942, September to Christmas, and to focus your attention in particular on the evidence of the Borisy residents and the four people from Domachevo, and ask yourselves the question: "Do we, the jury, think it is necessary to resolve what happened a couple of years later? Do we, the jury, think that is going to help us arrive at a verdict?" If the answer to that is "No", you can forget all about it. It is your right. It is more than your right. It is your duty, if you do not think it is going to help you. You may think there is quite a lot in this case by way of evidence that is not actually going to help you very much, if at all, in arriving at the true verdict.'

Clegg then turned to Sawoniuk's behaviour in the witness box, offering, as Potts noted to himself, an 'apologia for Sawoniuk's conduct as a witness and his inconsistencies and lies. Attempt to iron this out.'

'It would be idle to pretend,' Clegg said, 'that in giving evidence in the way that he did, he necessarily advanced his own case. He clearly lost his temper at times and said things that perhaps he ought not to have said. That will obviously go against him in your eyes. It is inevitable. We have had to face up to the fact that he lied to the police. We acknowledge it. We advance a reason why he lied and we ask you to accept that.'

Clegg said that Andrusha had acknowledged that he was an active participant in the war against partisans, but 'the prosecution do not suggest that the killing of people by the defendant in partisan actions is a crime; nor, we would argue, against the relevant conventions.' Secondly, Clegg said, the mere fact of being a policeman in occupied Germany could be viewed as an offence. 'The defendant, you may think, is not a particularly sophisticated man, nor perhaps a particularly deep thinker. He portrays, does he not, in everything about him, a man of comparatively limited education, but we would invite you to accept that in his mind he had reasons to fear telling the police the truth connected with his part in the partisan war.'

Clegg next dealt with the Yom Kippur massacre and Andrusha's claim that he had not even been in Domachevo.

'Now, there has been much incredulity cast on that evidence by the prosecution. Can we just try to be fair to the defendant? What is the evidence? If somebody has never been accused of taking part in a massacre, and not one of the witnesses says he is even present, how fair do you think it is to put into evidence against him, all the terribly emotive accounts that we heard of what happened that day? You have heard it, every heartrending moment of that evidence that we have had to live through. He is not even charged with it. Remember that, please.'

He then moved on to the testimony of Ben-Zion, still sitting at the back of the court, as he had through every minute of the trial, since completing his own evidence. Having reminded the jurors that the charge based on that evidence had already been dismissed, Clegg talked of Ben-Zion's physical and mental condition after eight days in a bunker without food and water, and how that must have impacted on any account he gave. He referred to him being the only Jewish survivor of Domachevo to testify, and added, 'No one could criticise him for feeling strongly about somebody who served in the police. It does not mean that his evidence is reliable.'

Clegg pointed out the discrepancies in the various statements Ben-Zion had made to the Soviet NKVD, to the Yad Vashem archive, in interviews with detectives and in evidence in the trial. 'We invite you to say that his evidence is not going to assist you. If anything, it provides a little bit of background as to what happened in the ghetto and so on. We invite you to say that you ought to put it to one side when looking at the Zan and Baglay incidents.'

For Ben-Zion to hear his testimony, his anguished outpourings on behalf of himself, his lost family and his vanished community described as 'a little bit of background as to what happened in the ghetto and so on', must have been like a knife through his heart.

It was now too late for Clegg to conclude his closing statement that day, and with the promise that he would be finished well inside 60 minutes on Monday morning, the court adjourned for the weekend. Before doing so, Potts cautioned the jurors that, having now heard the submissions from both sides, 'there may be a temptation among yourselves to talk about the case and reach conclusions. You have not, however, heard my summing-up. The appropriate time to talk among yourselves about the case is when the summing-up is concluded, in the privacy of your room. Please, therefore, no discussion with anybody about this case, once you leave the court this afternoon.'

After the jury left, there was a brief flurry of activity about Andrusha's weekend arrangements. As instructed, he had brought an overnight bag with him that morning, but had brought only his medicines and had forgotten a change of clothes. Arrangements were eventually made for the vehicle taking him to prison to detour via his flat to pick some up.

Clegg also voiced some concern about whether Andrusha would be returned by the time the court resumed on Monday morning. 'It is a brave judge in this building,' he said, 'that will ever guarantee the arrival of anybody from Belmarsh Prison, anywhere. Bitter experience has led one to know that the system is fallible, but because he is coming by secure ambulance, I would sincerely hope.'

The principals then dispersed for their long weekend. Johnny Nutting had already left at lunchtime that day, leaving John Kelsey-Fry to listen to Bill Clegg's closing speech, and only two people in the court were probably not looking forward to their break. Kaly Kaul would no doubt be spending her time wondering what the consequences for her career would be after her well-meaning but very ill-considered intervention on behalf of her client. Andrusha himself, having arrived at court that morning hoping to be back at his flat that night, was now on his way to one of Britain's most infamous prisons, where he would spend a long weekend locked up alone but for a 'carer', who was actually a prison warden.

CHAPTER 34

When the court reconvened on the Monday morning, 29 March, Day 25, Bill Clegg's whimsical approach was once more in evidence. He first invited the jurors to imagine they were in the year 2056, examining the case of a British soldier facing charges relating to a crime committed in 1999, when he was 21 years old, and then talked about a hypothetical British pilot dropping bombs on a civilian target in Germany in 1942. 'Could you imagine, if that matter were brought to trial now in 1999, the difficulties that that young man would face in trying to answer the charges?'

He quoted Andrusha's response to a question about whether he could remember an event: 'Remember? I have spent fifty-seven years trying to forget the war,' and then cited a celebrated jurist's opinion that 'justice delayed is justice denied'.

'There are, in our submission,' Clegg said, 'unique problems in putting old men on trial for acts done while they were teenagers or young men.' It was not Sawoniuk's fault that it was 49 years after the alleged crimes before the UK passed the War Crimes Act and a further eight before he was put on trial. He cited the region's troubled history, and said that, 'Just as Poland was caught in the middle of two evil powers, so you may think its citizens, Sawoniuk included, were very much caught in the middle.'

He ended by restating three points relating to 'the Borisy

coincidence': 'One. Both of the counts turn solely on witnesses from the hamlet of Borisy. Two. Borisy suffered during
the partisan actions and the defendant was the most prom-
inent fighter of the partisans in Domachevo, promoted to
commander in 1943. Three. The partisans, after 1944, were
regarded as heroes of the Soviet Union, and those who fought
them enemies of the Union and liable for execution.' All the
Borisy people who claimed to have witnessed Andrusha's
crimes had done so, Clegg said, 'by chance, luck, fluke. None
of them normally on the street of Domachevo, just going to
the town for a particular purpose at the very moment there
was something to see.

'We say, on behalf of this defendant, that on the evidence
you have heard, the true verdict in this case must be one of not
guilty, and I leave the defendant in your charge.'

On the narrow grounds of the two specimen charges of
murder, Clegg had at least constructed an argument that
Sawoniuk's guilt had not been established beyond a reasonable
doubt, but the cumulative impact of allegations about his conduct throughout the war could already have made an indelible
impression on the jurors' minds. They might even have come
close to deciding their verdict before Clegg began his closing
address the previous Thursday, since for the first time in the
trial, the jurors had been spotted that lunchtime in apparently
relaxed mood, having a couple of drinks in the pub across the
road from the Old Bailey.

Mr Justice Potts gave the jurors a short break. In their absence,
as his own notes put it, talking about himself in the third
person, he returned to the subject of 'Kaly Kaul's indiscretion
on Thursday. Bail withdrawn only in AS's interest – alone, ill,
room in Belmarsh hospital – but Potts's decision open to mis-
interpretation by jury on account of KK's wording.' He ended
his note to himself with a rhetorical question in block capitals:

'WAS KK'S INTERVENTION A PROFESSIONAL FOUL?'
intended to sway the jury in Andrusha's favour.

Asked by Potts to express his opinion, Clegg felt that any further mention of it in front of the jury could only make things worse. 'My instincts are the least said now, the better. I cannot see how anything that my Lord says will not, to some extent, dig a deeper hole.'

When Nutting was in turn invited to comment, he responded with relish, suggesting that Kaul's words may have led the jurors to believe that 'this elderly defendant, not in the best of health, should be confined to a prison cell and brought here with other prisoners, in what is conventionally known as a "paddy-wagon"'. Nutting was just as anxious that the jury should not think Andrusha has been taken to hospital through some illness. 'That equally would be a false picture, but to prevent the wholly false impression that this defendant is being confined in the way that normal prisoners are confined, would rectify one, at least, of the woeful mischiefs which have been created by the outburst from Miss Kaul.'

Clegg then said that the conditions in which Andrusha had been held over the weekend were 'far removed from what my Lord hoped' and went on to explain that he had been kept on a wing with a lot of other prisoners and had a very distressing weekend. He asked if Andrusha could be excused from attending the judge's summing-up, so he could get some rest.

'He can be released from any part of my summing-up,' Potts said, waspishly, 'providing your junior will give an undertaking not to make some outburst as to the reasons he is not here.'

When the jury returned to the courtroom, Potts first referred to Kaly Kaul's indiscretion. He outlined the arrangements made for Andrusha over the weekend and said, 'It would be quite wrong for you to have drawn the conclusion that, to use the vernacular, he has been banged up in a cell with others on remand since Thursday. I emphasise again that it is essential that your minds, particularly at this stage, should not be troubled by irrelevancies.'

Having dealt with that, Potts began his summing-up. 'The stark issue in this case,' he said, 'is one of fact. The Crown's case is that the defendant was a willing executioner of Nazi policy, that he shot the Jews referred to in Count One and Count Three. The defendant's case is one of complete denial of either of these charges. He admits to being a policeman, but he says: "At all times I was a friend of the Jews." The witnesses, he says, who gave evidence against him are liars in league with the KGB and Scotland Yard. There is the issue, and it is for you to resolve it.

'The burden of proving the defendant's guilt,' Potts continued, 'rests on the Crown. Before you can convict him on either charge, the Crown must make you sure of his guilt on that charge. Nothing less than this will do. There are two counts on the indictment. Consider them separately. They do not stand or fall together.'

He told the jurors that the identification evidence was crucial and pointed out the differences between the two charges. Alexandre Baglay knew Sawoniuk and was standing next to him when he said he saw him shoot three Jews. Fedor Zan was 127 paces away from him, and while Zan said he knew Andrusha and had been to school with him, Sawoniuk said he was a liar and that he had never met him.

Potts then turned to Sawoniuk's lies. He had admitted to lying twice, but for innocent reasons, whereas the Crown claimed he had lied repeatedly. The jury, Potts said, first had to decide if he had lied, and if so, what his motive had been. If there was some innocent explanation, then they should ignore the lies, but if not, they pointed towards his guilt. Potts also drew their attention to the dispute about when Andrusha left Domachevo. 'Mr Clegg, in his final submission to you said, "It did not matter tuppence whether he left in 1943 or 1944." Can this be right? I would suggest to you not.'

He reminded the jurors that the Polish Army and Waffen-SS documents were inadmissible as evidence, but by summarising their contents yet again, it was possible that he might have left another, more lasting impression in their minds. He told them to approach their task dispassionately, neither believing that 'someone must pay for what happened to the Domachevo Jews', nor that 'an old man of seventy-eight should not be prosecuted for crimes alleged to have been committed long ago and in a faraway country. Put such thoughts out of your minds. We live, members of the jury, in a democracy. The War Crimes Act was passed by Parliament. It is our duty, yours and mine, to obey the law, to follow the Act loyally.'

Potts told them that Sawoniuk was not charged with devising Nazi policy, being a member of the local police, nor being a collaborator of the Nazis. The charges were that he was a willing and enthusiastic executioner of Nazi policy and of the unknown Jews. He drew their attention to Professor Browning's description of the duties of *Schutzmänner*: 'Tasks which the Germans might find unpleasant,' Potts said, quoting Browning, 'including "killing of Jews, *Schmutzarbeit* – dirty work", were left to the local police.'

Turning to Andrusha's own testimony, Potts contrasted his descriptions of untroubled Jewish life with Ben-Zion's evidence of maltreatment, brutality and killings, and quoted his comment that Andrusha 'became a man of power, a master, a lord'. Potts also mentioned Ivan Baglay's comment about Andrusha's brother, who joined the *Schutzmannschaft* but 'smelt what a racket it was' and left.

In relation to Bill Clegg's 'Borisy coincidence', Potts pointed out that Ben-Zion 'was not a Borisy man, he has never lived in Borisy and he has been in Israel for the last fifty-odd years.' He added that the fact that no witness had claimed Andrusha had been in Domachevo at the time of the Yom Kippur massacre might be 'another nail in the coffin of the alleged Borisy conspiracy'. Had there really been a conspiracy, Potts said, 'it would have been the simplest thing in the world to orchestrate things to put him in the front rank of the local police on 20th September. The evidence does not do that.'

Potts then adjourned until the next morning and, after the jury had left, Bill Clegg reapplied for bail, citing two changes of circumstances. One was that 'the long period when the defendant would be without support has now passed and he would only be there overnight. The second is the conditions in which he is being kept are so much at variance with what you had been advised, that it amounts to a change of circumstance.'

Far from being held in a suite of rooms, Clegg said, Andrusha had been placed in a small isolation cell and then held in 'the equivalent of a psychiatric ward, with people who are mentally disturbed. He has been subject to a considerable amount of personal abuse during the course of the weekend. He has had to be taken handcuffed from this building and is handcuffed when in prison. He has been subject to a number of strip searches. All his clothes have been removed and he has become deeply distressed and, indeed, was very distressed this morning when I saw him in the cells.' The medication that Andrusha needed for his heart condition had also been hidden by the other inmates who further amused themselves by goose-stepping around his bed, performing Nazi salutes. As a result, Sawoniuk hardly got a wink of sleep.

Potts then agreed to Sawoniuk being bailed and returned to his flat, but warned Clegg, 'Having said that, I put you on notice that we might have to review the position tomorrow. There will be a further change of circumstances when the jury is out.'

CHAPTER 35

Mr Justice Potts resumed his summing-up the next morning, Tuesday 30 March 1999, the 26th day of the trial. He began by quoting Andrusha's comments about his relationships with the Jews: 'I am the one who had good relation with the Jews, nobody else. I never killed one Jew, and my Jews was best friend.' He then moved on to the search-and-kill operation, contrasting Andrusha's denials of having taken part with the testimony of Ben-Zion and the other witnesses.

Having painted the background, Potts came to the evidence on which the two counts of murder hinged. He detailed Bill Clegg's attempts to shake Alexandre Baglay's certainty of what he had witnessed and his reply that he 'remembered beautifully'. He reminded the jurors that Baglay was testifying about events that had occurred 57 years before, when he was a boy, and even if he believed he was telling the truth, 'as the years pass, impressions harden and take form in the mind as reality, and people do, after a time, speak forcefully of having seen things when close enquiry shows that their recollection must be wrong.' However, he added a powerful postscript to that – 'But the real question for you is this, is it not: is the incident that he purports to describe one that a thirteen-year-old boy would ever, could ever forget?' (*Sic*, he was twelve.)

Finally, Potts reminded them of Fedor Zan's testimony. 'Even if you are satisfied that Mr Zan came here intending to speak the truth, if you reject the defendant's assertions that he is a professional liar, you would still have to consider whether the identification of the defendant as the gunman shooting down these fifteen Jewish women is one that you can rely on to be sure of guilt.'

Potts ended in very low-key fashion, merely saying, 'Members of the jury, that is all I am going to say about the evidence. You may have heard of something called majority verdicts. When you retire, I require from you a unanimous verdict upon which all eleven of you are agreed. If the time comes when I can accept a majority verdict, then you will get a direction from me to that effect, but until you get that direction, please, unanimous verdict.'

The jury retired to consider its verdict at 2.22 that afternoon, 30 March 1999. Over the 48 days since the trial opened, they had sat through opening and closing statements from the prosecution and defence counsel, 26 days of witness testimony and cross-examination, and the judge's lengthy summing-up. They had also travelled to Belarus to see for themselves the crime scenes where the murders had happened. Somehow they now had to set aside any human emotion, whether it was sympathy for the frail old man before them, or revulsion at the terrible crimes he was alleged to have committed, and distil from that mass of often confusing and contradictory evidence, a true and fair verdict.

After the jury had been deliberating for two hours, with no sign of a verdict, Potts and the two counsel agreed that the jurors should spend the night sequestered in a hotel. Knowing that there would be widespread media coverage of the day's events, there was some discussion about whether they should be allowed to watch TV. 'I would have respectfully suggested that the appropriate course,' Nutting said, 'is for your Lordship to ensure in some way that they watch programmes other than news.'

'I suspect it is a question of watching all programmes or nothing,' Potts said.

'What sometimes happens is two or three rooms are set aside and they can choose which television programmes they want to watch, and those programmes are supervised by ushers,' Nutting said, evidently blissfully unaware that there was scarcely a hotel in the country that did not have a TV in every room.

'I think they are individual sets, Mr Nutting,' Potts said, with evident pleasure. 'Times have moved on.' He noted to himself that it was 'quite amusing that Nutting didn't realise they'd have access to TV!'

'I am always behind the times,' Nutting said.

'I agree with Mr Nutting,' Clegg said, with a smile. 'He is always behind the times.'

Potts then asked the clerk in charge of the jury arrangements to 'take the necessary steps'.

'Yes, my Lord. It is all or nothing. In this case it will be nothing. By the time we have had dinner and one thing or another, it will be time to go to bed anyway, I hope,' the clerk said, perhaps wearying of his task after weeks of nurse-maiding the jurors.

Discussion then turned to the overnight arrangements for Andrusha, and Potts asked Clegg what had happened the previous night.

'He was able to have a proper meal at home, to relax, have a bath and get an early night,' Clegg said, 'and he was in good spirits this morning when those instructing me collected him and brought him to court. They phoned a couple of times during the course of the evening to make sure all was well. Exactly the same arrangements exist for tonight.'

Potts then granted bail under the same conditions and the court adjourned.

*

The jurors resumed their discussions the following morning, 31 March, Day 27. After several hours, the foreman sent a note to the judge, asking for clarification of exactly what Alexandre Baglay said he had seen. That led to further wrangling between Clegg and Nutting about how much of the evidence-in-chief and cross-examination should be repeated in answer to the question, but just after four o'clock, Potts summoned the jury back and for 20 minutes he read them the relevant portion of the transcript. He then sent them back to the hotel for a second night.

CHAPTER 36

Day 28 of the trial – 1 April 1999 – was three years to the day since Sawoniuk's first interview with Scotland Yard's War Crimes Unit. It was also April Fools' Day, but whether that was an omen, only time would tell.

Before the jury was admitted, Potts reviewed 'the arrangements in relation to the defendant if and when the jury return'. Unlike a normal trial, Sawoniuk had not been sitting in the dock at any point, and Potts was now concerned about his possible reaction if a guilty verdict was returned. A defendant sitting in the dock could swiftly be hustled down the steps to the cells if he became aggressive and abusive on hearing the verdict. Removing Sawoniuk from the well of the court would be a much more lengthy and disruptive process, if he reacted badly. Given his repeated outbursts from the witness box, that was a strong possibility.

'What I do not want,' Potts said, 'is an embarrassing scene, or the defendant to be more upset than necessary. The suggestion has been made, Mr Clegg, if there were a guilty verdict, then I would adjourn so the defendant could be moved into the dock before I sentence him. I have to say that my own inclination and, indeed, desire, would be to have this whole matter dealt with as quickly as possible.'

'There is no legal requirement for him to be sitting in the dock before sentence is passed,' Clegg said, and urged Potts to leave Andrusha sitting in the place he had occupied throughout the trial. Once sentence had been pronounced, Potts could adjourn, 'and then arrangement can be made for him to be moved as comfortably as possible.'

At 11.45 that morning, a fresh note from the Foreman of the Jury asked how they should present their verdicts. Potts found the note 'v. abstruse, quite hard to follow, tho' I think it's related to relative unanimity on counts/verdicts. Count 1 seems to have been decided on, Count 3 still under discussion.'

Judge and counsel then had a brief discussion on whether the jury should return and pronounce that verdict before resuming their deliberations or continue until they had resolved the verdict on the other count.

Nutting had no doubts. 'The Crown is firmly of the view your Lordship ought to accept the verdict that has been reached in relation to the count on which the jury have indicated agreement. I can see advantages in that course and no disadvantages.'

For once Clegg was not minded to take issue with him. 'I would not suggest, for one moment, one should not accept the verdict. It is a question of whether it is piecemeal or together. I leave it in the hands of my Lord.'

After 14 hours and 20 minutes of deliberations spread over the course of three days, the remaining 11 members of the jury filed back into Court 12 at 11.57 that morning, to announce their unanimous verdict on Count 1: the murder of two Jewish men and a young woman witnessed by Alexandre Baglay. All were solemn-faced, and those looking for omens would have noted that the three women jurors and a couple of the men shot anxious glances towards Andrusha as they took their seats.

The Clerk of the Court asked the foreman to stand. 'Members of the jury, have you reached a verdict in respect of Count One on this indictment, upon which you are all agreed?'

'Yes.'

'Mr Foreman, please answer me only guilty or not guilty.

Members of the jury, do you find the defendant, Anthony Sawoniuk, guilty or not guilty of murder as charged on Count One of this indictment?'

'Guilty.'

'You find him guilty as charged on Count One and that is the verdict of you all?'

'That is.'

Those in search of symbolism were quick to note that the verdict had been pronounced on the day of the Jewish festival of Passover.

When the verdict was announced, pandemonium in the courtroom might have been expected with people in the public gallery shouting, applauding or booing, but in the event, although the reporters scrambled for the exits to alert their news desks, and there was a burst of chatter from the gallery, the reaction was relatively subdued.

However, whether through a fault in the technology or because the stenographer had become distracted by the drama, the LiveNote screen had stopped working. As Andrusha was sufficiently deaf to have been reliant on it, he did not know at first what the verdict had been. As Steve Law explained it to him, two prison officers moved into the court to sit at either side of him. Whatever the verdict on the second charge, he was now a convicted murderer.

'Mr Foreman,' Potts said. 'Your note concluded: "We are still discussing Count 3." Is that the position at this moment? Would you therefore please return to your room and continue your deliberations?'

At 11.59, just two minutes after entering the court, they were on their way back to the jury room. In their absence, Potts and Clegg discussed the ongoing arrangements for Andrusha. Potts did not think there was any risk of him absconding but added, 'it would probably be inappropriate if he was now in the public area'.

Despite their earlier conversations about it, no arrangements had been made, but within a few minutes Clegg was able to tell the judge that a private room within the building had been found, with a prison officer and a carer to supervise him.

Some time later, a fresh note was delivered from the jury, asking for clarification about whether Fedor Zan had been standing on the site of the shooting when the jurors pushed their way through the bushes to view the crime scene or if he had moved to the site after that.

As he was pondering that question, a thought struck Mr Justice Potts and he pencilled a note to himself, its capital letters perhaps suggesting the importance he attached to it: 'INTERESTING NO BODIES/REMAINS FOUND AT SITE OF EXECUTION OF 15 J. [JEWISH] WOMEN. Any remains ever found at site of execution of 2 J. men and woman?' After a few more moments' thought, he added a postscript: 'Propositions never used by Clegg, I think.'

On the face of it, it was a surprising, even extraordinary omission by Clegg. He had referred to the lack of forensic evidence but had not gone on to reinforce to the jury the fact that no human remains had ever been discovered at the site of either alleged murder, which could have been a powerful point for the defence. There was obviously no incentive for them to request an exhumation that might turn up remains pointing to Andrusha's guilt, and if the prosecution had ever considered it, the idea was soon abandoned. All the death- and grave-sites were regarded by Belarusians and Jews alike as sacred ground, and any attempt to dig them up would have met with fierce and quite possibly violent opposition.

With the agreement of the two counsel, Potts had a note prepared answering the jurors' question and he then read it out to them when they returned to court at 2.17 that afternoon. They then retired again at 2.21, but an hour later a further note was sent. In the light of its contents, Potts sought agreement from

Clegg and Nutting that a majority verdict – ten of the eleven jurors – would now be acceptable. The jury was then brought back to the courtroom at 3.49, and the Clerk of the Court asked the foreman, 'Members of the jury, have you reached a verdict in respect of Count Three of this indictment upon which you are all agreed?'

'No.'

'Members of the jury,' Potts said, 'at the conclusion of my summing-up, I directed you that I required from you a unanimous verdict. I also indicated that if the time came, then I could give you a direction as to a majority verdict. I give you that direction now, I say simply this: would you retire again and continue to try to reach a unanimous verdict? But if you are satisfied that you cannot do this, I will accept from you on this Count a majority verdict, that is a verdict with which at least ten of you are agreed.'

There was nothing improper about that. Since 1967, English law had allowed juries in criminal cases to return majority verdicts with no more than two jurors dissenting, providing they had deliberated for at least two hours before deciding that a unanimous verdict was impossible. However, since one of the original jurors had already been lost to ill-health, in this case, no more than one of the remaining 11 could dissent if they were to return a true verdict.

They retired again at 3.51 and, in consultation with the two counsel, Potts decided to allow them a further hour before calling a halt for the day. In the event, while they were still discussing that, a further note was delivered from the jury and they were back in court for the last time at 4.01 that afternoon.

'Members of the jury,' the Clerk of the Court said. 'Have at least ten of you agreed on a verdict in respect of Count Three of this indictment?'

'Yes.'

'Members of the jury, do you find the defendant, Anthony

Sawoniuk, guilty or not guilty of murder as charged on Count Three of this indictment?'

'Guilty.'

'Is that the verdict of you all or by a majority?'

'A majority.'

'How many agreed to that verdict and how many dissented?'

'Ten agreed, one did not.'

'You find this defendant guilty of murder as charged on Count Three of this indictment by a majority of ten to one of you?'

'That is correct.'

Both counsel declined the opportunity to say anything before sentencing. There was no point; the sentence for convicted murderers had been set by statute as life imprisonment and judges had no discretion about imposing it.

'The defendant, I take it, has been advised of the inevitable consequences of this verdict?' Potts said.

'He has.'

Once more the LiveNote screen had malfunctioned, either for technical reasons or because the stenographer had again become so caught up in the drama that she had stopped typing and, once more, Sawoniuk had not understood the verdict. Mr Justice Potts declared a short adjournment while order was restored and Andrusha transferred to the dock. Potts then asked him to stand up to receive sentence, but he remained seated.

'Mr Clegg, I wonder, can the defendant hear?' Potts said, looking doubtfully at Andrusha, still flanked by Steve Law and two prison officers.

'No,' Clegg said. 'He knows now what will inevitably follow and we will make sure he fully understands it after my Lord has risen.'

That assurance did not satisfy Potts, so he then asked Law to bring Andrusha closer to him. Law, more sympathetic to his client's distress than the judge's request, refused. 'I am not his jailer.' Potts remained silent but his expression spoke volumes.

The two prison officers then picked up Sawoniuk's chair while he was still seated in it and carried it to the front of the court.

'If he could position himself so his good ear is opposite me,' Potts said, 'then there may be some prospect, but I think it is important he should hear.'

'I think he is probably in the best position,' Clegg said.

'Do sit down, Mr Sawoniuk, please,' Potts said as Andrusha struggled to his feet. 'Can you hear me now, Mr Sawoniuk?'

'Yes.'

As he prepared to pronounce the mandatory sentence, Potts told Sawoniuk: 'I want to say this to you. No words of mine can add anything of value to those words already written and spoken about the events in which you played a part. I only say this: that although you held a lowly rank in the hierarchy of those involved in the liquidation of Jews in Eastern Europe, to the Jews of Domachevo, it must have seemed otherwise. Mr Ben-Zion Blustein said of you that when you became a policeman, you became a man of power, a master and a lord. I am sure from the evidence we have heard in this trial, that he was right when he said that.

'You have been convicted of charges properly brought; you have had a fair trial; no jury could have given closer attention to the issues raised by this case than the one that has tried you. You have been convicted of two charges of murder on clear evidence in my judgement. I pass upon you the sentence fixed by law on each count, which is one of life imprisonment.'

Andrusha either still did not hear, or was too stunned to react, and the judge had to repeat the sentence to him before he at last acknowledged that he had heard it. At first, he showed little reaction other than a slight shake of his head, but then he slumped back in the chair and, as the reality of it dawned on him, he put his face in his hands. Having passed his 78th birthday in the course of the trial, he was one of the oldest people ever to have been convicted of murder in England.

Eventually he turned to Steve Law and said, 'What happens now?' and Law later said, 'I had to tell him that he was going to jail and would probably never leave.'

'I don't want to die in jail,' Andrusha said, but that was no longer under his control. Having absorbed that, he asked Law to go to his flat and collect some of his belongings. All he wanted were his photos of his son and his two granddaughters, and the gold watch he had been given after 25 years' service for British Rail.

He 'cut a pathetic figure,' Bill Clegg says, as he was taken down the narrow staircase leading from the dock to the cells, still protesting his innocence.

As his tormentor was led away to begin his life sentence, Ben-Zion, still in attendance as he had been throughout every moment of the trial, turned to his son, Shalom, and in a near-echo of the words the survivor of the Majdanek extermination camp had used to him, said, 'I can die now; I've closed the circle.'

'Ever since I understood who my father was and what he went through,' Shalom says, 'I tried to be worthy of being the son of the partisan Benzi. It was a huge privilege growing up next to him and learning from him almost everything I know.'

Benni Kalina had spoken to Ben-Zion about the need to avenge the dead, but as he later told his grandson, Ben, that had not been his motive in testifying. 'I did not come to seek revenge. Instead, I tried to tell the whole world about those who were murdered and I had to bring their voices for all those who could not speak for themselves: my brother, my mother, my two sisters. I dedicated all my life not to revenge but to the memory of my mother, but the best revenge would be to show the Nazis my big family, living in our own independent country, and say, "We won!"'

Before bringing the proceedings to an end, Mr Justice Potts said those who had investigated the case and prepared it for trial 'deserve the highest praise. I would like those observations to be brought to the attention of the appropriate authorities.' He went on to praise the authorities at Belmarsh Prison for their assistance, though it was unlikely that Andrusha would have echoed those comments.

Potts then turned to the eight men and three women of the jury. 'Last but not least, Ladies and Gentlemen, I want to thank you. I can only say that in my experience, you have been a quite exceptional jury. This has been a difficult case for all of us, in almost every way one could imagine. You have shouldered the burden from Day One when we met in this court, when you went to be injected [with the necessary immunisations] and thereafter when we all went in the middle of February to Belarus. Following that, no one who has observed you could fail to be impressed by the close attention you have given to every issue, and if anybody had any doubts – and I do not think anybody would – they must have been removed by the way in which you have clearly approached the evidence and the issues raised by the case over the last two days or so. All I can do, I am afraid, is to thank you, and I do sincerely, on behalf of the public, for what you have done. If members of the public were not prepared to do what you have done, in the way you have done it, justice could not be done. And justice, I would like to think, has been done in this case.

'I have it in my power to exempt each of you from jury service for the rest of your lives, and I am going to do that. At the conclusion of this case, you will get a certificate stating that you are exempt and you can rely on that should you ever be asked to come for jury service again. However, the option is yours. Provided you keep the bit of paper, you can rely on it. On the other hand, if at a future date you are called for jury service, then you can choose to serve. I make that order and I thank you once again, and I wish you all a pleasant Easter holiday.'

After thanking 'the Bar for their help from the very start — all the Bar, please, Mr Clegg', Potts rose for the last time and Britain's first — and last — successful war crimes trial was at an end.

CHAPTER 37

The media had been constrained in what it could report while the trial was ongoing, and in the immediate aftermath of the verdict, most papers published lengthy features about Sawoniuk and his crimes, and the verdict made headlines around the world.

Charlie Moore, one of the two remaining detectives on the War Crimes Unit, had married his wife Jane, a typist on the Unit's HOLMES database, during the trial and they were on honeymoon in Thailand when the verdict was announced. They only realised its worldwide impact when they picked up the *Bangkok Times* the following morning and saw the headline 'Sawoniuk Found Guilty'.

Only one newspaper had sent a reporter to interview Sawoniuk's former neighbours, and few of them were willing or able to say much about him. The *South London Press* headlined its front-page story 'Butcher of Belarus Jailed for Life', but contented itself with a summary of the case, and only a feature in the *Southwark News* – 'Bermondsey's Evil Nazi Killer: His Life Among Us' – drew on interviews with those neighbours willing to share their opinions.

One rather implausibly complained that Sawoniuk 'should never have been allowed to live here', as if the Bermondsey Housing Department ought to have had the resources to investigate war crimes before allocating its council flats. Another, who surprisingly said that Sawoniuk had claimed to be called 'Mr

Bell', spoke of his rudeness and aggression, but most recalled him only as a taciturn and anti-social figure they had seen walking around the estate but had rarely, if ever, spoken to.

Only one, 77-year-old Bill Cuff, like Andrusha, an original resident of the Rouel Road Estate, who had known him for 24 years, could say much about him. 'I used to talk to him on the road or in passing,' he said. 'He was a powerfully built man although I know he had a lot of health problems and had to go into hospital at least twice. I remember him telling me how much pain he was in after he came out of hospital for a triple bypass opera- tion. He never mentioned the war, nor did he ever say where he was from. I assumed from his strong accent that he was Polish. He did talk about his son but you never saw the two together. He would pass the time of day with me but whenever I was with my wife, he would either cross the road or just walk by without saying anything. Once the story broke, he took a different route and we never spoke again.'

Despite Andrusha having appeared to be 'a pleasant enough man' in their encounters, Cuff said that he 'always had the feeling about him being aggressive. You get a feeling of horror to know that someone like that was living amongst us for so long, a man who ordered women to strip and then machine-gunned them. I hope he spends the rest of his life in jail for what he has done.'

Towards the end of the trial, *Sun* crime reporter Ian Hepburn had been approached by Stewart Payne of the *Evening Standard* to see if he could help him track down Sawoniuk's third wife, who was thought to have returned to her native Holland. Payne knew that Hepburn had excellent contacts in the Netherlands and he was eagerly anticipating a trip over there himself, but instead they found themselves on the doorstep of a bungalow in Whaplode, Lincolnshire, where Christina van Gent, then 76, was living. She reluctantly agreed to talk to them about the 'horrifying' period when she was Sawoniuk's wife.

'She met him,' Hepburn says, 'at a dance in Sussex in 1947,

when she was a 24-year-old maid and he was a forestry worker with the Polish Resettlement Corps. Sawoniuk told her that he was a bachelor – a lie – and they married later that year. She told the two reporters, "My wedding day was the worst day of my life. He was a horrible man – vile and violent. I was with him for two and a half years and in the end I walked out. He used to attack me. He never told me about his past and I didn't dare ask. I was horrified when I heard about his crimes. I shudder to think I have lain in bed next to a man who was such a reviled killer. I can't believe he was a policeman, he was too thick. I've been reading the papers and listening to the news on the radio and TV. All this coming up now is turning me into a nervous wreck. It's a dreadful shock after all these years.'"

As news of the verdict spread, Jewish groups and supporters of the War Crimes Act were quick to praise it. 'Mere passage of time does not make a guilty person less guilty,' Rabbi Jonathan Romain, the chair of the Jewish Information and Media Service, told the *New York Times*. 'It is not pleasant to have to take an elderly man to court, but it is even less pleasant to think of the murders of which he is accused going unpunished.'

Lord Janner of Braunstone, chair of the Holocaust Educational Trust, who had crossed swords with Sawoniuk during the trial was 'very glad that this murderer has received a fair trial and that justice was both done and seen to be done. The Nazis gave neither trial nor justice to their victims. I am sorry that so many other war criminals who sadly found refuge in Britain have so far escaped justice, [but] the trial is a symbolic beacon, relighting memories of the hideous barbarity of the past.'

CHAPTER 38

Under English law, a life sentence for murder must be confirmed by the Home Secretary, taking into account the need for retribution and deterrence of others. He or she then sets the tariff – the minimum amount of time that the convicted person must serve before becoming eligible for parole. In this case, Jack Straw – a former criminal barrister himself – was given sentencing recommendations by the trial judge and the Lord Chief Justice, Lord Bingham. Sir Humphrey Potts argued that Sawoniuk should die in jail, saying that 'given the defendant's age and the nature of the offences, to release him before his death would, in my opinion, defeat the purpose of the War Crimes Act'.

However, Lord Bingham, while admitting that 'The judge's view is a tenable, and perhaps preferable, approach to this unique case, and he has had the experience of living with these harrowing facts for weeks,' still felt that the sentence should allow Sawoniuk some hope of eventual release. 'An alternative approach, to which I myself incline,' he said, 'is that general deterrence has little part in this sentence and retribution must be moderated when delayed for nearly sixty years and visited on a man approaching the age of eighty.' He recommended a tariff of five years but Jack Straw, no doubt well aware of the political ramifications of appearing to be unduly merciful to a Nazi war criminal, rejected Bingham's recommendation and made the decision that life should mean life, ensuring that Sawoniuk would die in prison.

The following year, Bill Clegg appealed the conviction, but three law lords, headed by Lord Bingham, unanimously upheld it and refused leave to appeal to the House of Lords. Clegg then appealed to the European Court of Human Rights, arguing that his client's right to a fair trial had been violated, and that the imposition of a mandatory life sentence upon an elderly and frail defendant was arbitrary and disproportionate.

In May 2001, in a unanimous verdict, seven justices of the European Court of Human Rights rejected the appeal. They stated that the long interval of time between the crime and criminal proceedings did not make the trial unfair, especially as there is no statute of limitations for war crimes under international law. The jury had not been subject to undue influence and had reached its own decision about the validity of the key evidence in the case. No further appeal was possible, condemning Sawoniuk to remain in prison for the rest of his life.

Andrusha Sawoniuk served the first four years of his sentence at HM Prison Kingston in Portsmouth, but in April 2003, a report by Her Majesty's Chief Inspector of Prisons found that conditions in the Elderly Prisoner Unit there were 'unacceptable'. Movement within the unit was severely restricted, and there was a lack of natural light and ventilation.

As a result, the unit was closed and, with other inmates, Sawoniuk was transferred to a unit for elderly life prisoners in Norfolk. However, his health was failing and on the morning of 6 November 2005, aged 84, having been in prison for six and a half years, he died from heart disease, heart failure, chronic renal failure and diabetes. He had refused to go to an outside hospital as his condition deteriorated and instead was cared for in the prison hospital until the end. If his son ever saw the death certificate, he would no doubt have been grateful that the authorities had spared him the ignominy of recording the death-site as a jail. Instead, it merely stated the place of death as 9 Knox Road, Norwich, which only those with local knowledge would have realised was the address of Norwich Prison.

When he heard of Sawoniuk's death, Lord Greville Janner expressed his satisfaction. 'In 1948 our government closed down the Army's war crimes group. We investigators, who were still hunting 10,000 murderers, were furious, but the government was more interested in attacking the Soviets. Well, at least one depraved Nazi escapee has died in prison; his ignominious end should send a message to other war criminals today.'

Benni Kalina died in 2011. Unknown to Ben-Zion Blustein, Benni did finally break his silence and talk to his family about his wartime experiences, but only when he was 80, in the final year of his life. 'And whenever he did so,' his son, Meir, says, 'he would invariably burst into tears.'

Ben-Zion, the man who had saved Benni's life in the forest all those years before, returned to Israel after the trial, but he paid a heavy price for the stress and the traumatic memories it had re-awoken. His family felt that he was never the same man again and he suffered a stroke not long afterwards that permanently affected his health.

In his last days, he told his grandson, Ben, that, 'All his life, every day and every night, the family he had lost came into his dreams, and the day he left the bunker and never saw them again.' Ben-Zion died in 2012, surrounded by his family, having outlived his friend turned enemy, Andrei 'Andrusha' Sawoniuk, by seven years.

Seventy-five years after the end of the war and ten years after his grandfather's death, Ben Blustein tries to live his life by Ben-Zion's example. 'My grandfather told me we should always fight for our country,' Ben says. 'He said the only way to make sure that the Holocaust and Jews being led to the slaughter can never happen again is to have a strong independent state.

'On Memorial Day, we think about Jewish people seventy-five years ago being led to the crematorium, but I can see my grandfather in the forest, hiding from the Nazis, in the depths of winter with no shoes, just strips of sacking wrapped around his feet. Every time I feel things are a little bit difficult for me, I remember my grandfather, almost barefoot in the forest in the middle of winter and I think if he could do that, of course I can do this.'

CHAPTER 39

Sir Humphrey Potts went on to preside over one more very high-profile case before he retired: the Jeffrey Archer perjury trial. An earlier libel trial had ended in Archer being awarded substantial damages against a tabloid newspaper, but that verdict was overturned when he was proved to have perjured himself, and Potts duly sentenced him to four years in jail.

Sir Johnny Nutting and Bill Clegg are both enjoying a contented retirement, Nutting dividing his time between his London residence, his Wiltshire manor house and his Scottish estate, while Clegg has retired to a beautiful town in his native Suffolk.

The junior prosecution counsel at the trial, John Kelsey-Fry, is now one of the leading criminal barristers in the country. Although the junior defence counsel Kaly Kaul's outburst about the revocation of Sawoniuk's bail could have blighted her career, through Bill Clegg she made a fulsome apology to Mr Justice Potts and the incident clearly did her prospects no lasting harm, because in time she became a QC, and later a judge.

Johnny Nutting has never harboured any doubts about the validity of the trial and its verdict. 'The critical factor was the ability to hold a fair trial, and I think that the trial *was* a fair one. Sir Humphrey went out of his way to make sure that every shred of evidence was fair and appropriate, and subject to English law.'

Perhaps understandably, that view was not shared by some members of the defence team who felt the scales had been tipped against their client by the testimony about Nazi policies and massacres in which Sawoniuk had played no part. In particular, Steve Law believes that Ben-Zion Blustein's testimony was crucial. It brought several jury members to the brink of tears and Law believes that this affected their view of the defendant throughout the rest of the trial. After the verdict was announced, he says he saw many jurors looking at Sawoniuk with expressions of undisguised disgust and contempt.

Law still feels that although the first two charges against Sawoniuk were thrown out, the jurors were so shocked by the evidence that they were committed to a guilty verdict from that point on. He remains convinced that the trial should have been restarted with a fresh jury to try the remaining two charges.

'In any trial where the verdict goes against a barrister,' Bill Clegg says, 'there is always a feeling that a lot of time and energy has gone into an argument that isn't accepted,' but even with the benefit of hindsight, he can see no realistic path by which a not guilty verdict could have been achieved.

He has no regrets about not calling any character witnesses. 'Part of the purpose was so that there was no lie being told to the jury that he was a man of hitherto impeccable character. There was no record of any unlawful behaviour from him post-1945, but I don't think the police investigated it particularly, and for obvious reasons, it was of no help to us anyway.' Trying to establish Sawoniuk's good character would also have opened the door to the prosecution calling dozens of other witnesses to testify to his brutality, anti-Semitism and his membership of the Waffen-SS, but Johnny Nutting found ways to draw that to the jury's attention anyway.

If Sawoniuk had not given evidence, Clegg thinks 'it would have been a closer-run thing. We had given him some very strong advice, firstly about whether to give evidence, and secondly, if he insisted on doing so, how to give evidence: listen to the question before you answer it, don't argue with counsel, keep your answers short, don't go on to make a speech – all of which he completely and utterly ignored. He was as bad as we feared, a ludicrously bad witness, saying things that were palpably untrue. So his evidence was disastrous for him, and to be honest, that was all borne of his character in the first place.'

John Kelsey-Fry says that the prosecution did not set out to goad Sawoniuk into giving evidence. The only way to provoke him into taking the stand was by demonstrating the strength of their case, and Kelsey-Fry feels that is what they did. 'The stronger the case – the more it needs to be answered, but it was a happy moment when Sawoniuk took the stand,' he says. 'Johnny and I were slightly surprised but very pleased at this gift, and Sawoniuk didn't disappoint as a witness!'

Clegg had resigned himself to losing from the moment his client took the stand, but he says it was impossible to tell if Sawoniuk realised that. 'I honestly don't know what he thought. It was very difficult to understand what was going on inside his head at any time. He certainly conducted himself in a way that made the chances of a not guilty verdict more difficult, but whether that was just pig-headed belligerence, I don't know. All clients have at least one redeeming characteristic, even if it's only a sense of humour, but Sawoniuk had no redeeming features at all. I had an open mind to begin with, but the more I spoke to him, the more I began to recognise a repugnant, deep-seated anti-Semitism. He blamed the Jews for being on trial and used the words 'Jew boy' in almost every sentence. I remember saying to him that if he ever used that phrase in court, his conviction could be guaranteed.'

Kelsey-Fry adds: 'You could not have written a novel and used Sawoniuk as a character because people would say, "Well, he's such a caricature, a cartoon character," but he really was immensely unlikeable and displayed some very deep-rooted, unpleasant characteristics. The private joke among the prosecution team was that at times he looked like he could only just stop his right arm from going up, like Peter Sellers' Nazi scientist in *Dr Strangelove*.'

The jury did not know about Sawoniuk's ugly clashes with Meir Bronstein, Greville Janner and Jon Silverman, but his fury, lies and wild accusations were obvious. Nutting remained very courteous whatever the provocation, which only made the contrast all the more pointed and, as Clegg ruefully admits, over the course of his cross-examination, Nutting 'reeled him in, slowly, surely, devastatingly'.

When the verdict was announced 'I didn't feel pleased,' Clegg says. 'I didn't feel sorry. It is not for me to be judge and jury, but the evidence in relation to one charge was very weak, hinging on an identification made over fifty years before. The evidence on the other charge was stronger, but as to whether it was a good idea for the trial to go ahead at all, I personally feel that it was too little, too late. You shouldn't be trying people for war crimes after fifty years. The quality of justice was significantly damaged by time and the reliability of witnesses was doubtful.'

Looking back now, Clegg thinks that the eyewitness testimony of Fedor Zan and perhaps even that of Alexandre Baglay was not necessarily the deciding factor. He believes the jury had already decided that 'even if the witness couldn't have recognised Sawoniuk, it was almost certainly him anyway, and if it wasn't, it didn't matter, because he'd killed other people. I think the jury saw him for what he was: not only a compulsive liar but a ghastly anti-Semite.'

Whether Andrusha Sawoniuk also committed the many other murders alleged by those who lived in Domachevo under the Nazis, the weight of testimony surely puts it beyond dispute that he was a brutal killer. Whether that would have been the case if he had not joined the *Schutzmannschaft* and been given, literally, the power of life and death over his fellows, is an unanswerable question, but while his half-brother resigned at once when he realised that murdering Jews was part of the job, Sawoniuk not only remained a member but embraced the role with enthusiasm.

It is undeniable that he had a troubled and poverty-stricken childhood, and was taunted, denigrated and bullied before suddenly finding himself placed in a position of power, but that does not condone nor excuse what followed, any more than the beatings that Adolf Hitler took from his abusive father justify the atrocities of the Third Reich.

CHAPTER 40

If the trial and Sawoniuk's life sentence had given other elderly Nazi war criminals in Britain pause for thought, it soon became clear that there was little prospect of any of them sharing his fate. More than 100 cases were abandoned because the suspects were dead, and 30 others were dropped because the men were either too old or too ill, or because the unit could not gather enough evidence. Martin Dean found some of the constraints imposed on the War Crimes Unit 'frustrating. We found others who had been in units similar to Sawoniuk's but they were really asking us to find an eyewitness to someone shooting someone else and the only one like that was Sawoniuk.'

One of those who got away with it still haunts Maggie Newberry, who ran the WCU's office. A Jewish survivor they traced to New Zealand had been ordered to strip naked and line up beside a pit for a mass execution. Two bullets tore through her and she tumbled into the pit. As the shooting continued more and more bodies fell on top of her. She lay there for over 24 hours before daring to move, fearing that guards would be watching over the corpses, ready to finish off anyone who had somehow survived. After dark the following night, she started to claw her way upwards, pushing bodies out of the way until she was able to crawl out. She escaped into a forest and was eventually found by partisans and treated for her wounds. The killer in that case was a Latvian who, like Sawoniuk, had been recruited by the Nazis as an auxiliary policeman. He was living in the UK and the WCU had his address but, Newberry says, to her eternal regret, 'We could not build a strong enough case to put him on trial.'

While the jury in the Sawoniuk trial was still out considering its verdict, the Crown Prosecution Service released a briefing note declaring that only those who had been in a position of command had been considered for prosecution under the War Crimes Act, adding: 'Responsibility is also an important factor in deciding on . . . culpability.' This startling claim directly contradicted the Nuremberg precedent that 'I was only following orders' was no defence, but may explain why Serafinowicz and Sawoniuk were the only war criminals out of the 97 identified by the Soviets as living in Britain and the hundreds of others who had settled here after the war who were ever charged.

Within a month of the Sawoniuk verdict, the Commissioner of the Metropolitan Police, Sir Paul Condon, announced that the War Crimes Unit was being disbanded 'for operational reasons', having become redundant because there were 'no more leads for the police to investigate'. The reason for that, apart from the age of the crimes and the potential defendants, was the restrictive criteria for potential prosecution.

Although the War Crimes Act 1991 was intended to apply to anyone accused of 'grave violations of the laws and customs of war', following the CPS guidelines, the Met now not only required safe identification and reliable eyewitnesses, but 'proof that the defendant was in a position of command'. As commander of the local *Schutzmannschaft*, Sawoniuk fulfilled that criteria, but ordinary auxiliary policemen, in Domachevo or elsewhere, did not, no matter what crimes they had committed. The decision was seen by many as a shameful abdication of responsibility, taken not on principle, but at least partly on cost grounds.

The War Crimes Unit had been costing upwards of £1.5 million a year, and the Sawoniuk trial had added another £6.5 million to the bill. At its peak, the WCU employed 11 detectives, supported by teams of historians, researchers, linguists and administrative staff. By the time of Sawoniuk's trial, just two detectives, Charlie Moore and Chris Latham, and a single researcher remained, and they had been moved out of Scotland Yard to a small office in the Leman Street police station in Whitechapel.

Having demonstrated once that Britain was willing to prosecute a war criminal, repeating the experience was evidently not a priority. Nonetheless, Moore has no regrets about devoting so many years to a unit that only produced one successful prosecution. 'It meant so much to the survivors,' he says, 'so that's why I'm glad we did it.'

One further obstacle to pursuing war criminals was the wording of the War Crimes Act itself. It laid down a requirement for prosecution for murder but omitted any mention of de-naturalisation and deportation. That had been the preferred practice in the US and, had the Act allowed it, would have been perfectly possible in the Sawoniuk case. He had entered Britain in 1946 under false pretences, having lied on the forms he had completed. Many others had done the same.

Israel and Germany remained willing to put war criminals on trial and the United States showed a continuing readiness to strip them of their citizenship and deport them. To its shame, Britain would henceforth fail to adopt either remedy. The Sawoniuk case would remain unique: the only war crimes trial ever to be held in Britain, with its jury the only one ever to set foot on foreign soil.

ACKNOWLEDGEMENTS

My thanks firstly to Neil Hanson, my co-writer, without whose full commitment and skills this book would never have been written. Likewise to Mark Lucas, our literary agent and The Soho Agency, and to Ian Marshall, Frances Jessop, Kerri Sharp and the rest of the brilliant team at Simon & Schuster for their skill, enthusiasm and whole-hearted commitment to the story. Thanks also to my wonderful parents, Gerald and Rosemary Anderson, my fabulous siblings Bridget, Anthony and Stephen, and my civil partner, Jon Turner, all of whom have encouraged me in never giving up on this project.

In researching and writing this account of the trial of Andrei 'Andrusha' Sawoniuk, we have been helped by numerous individuals and organisations who gave unstintingly of their time and knowledge. My good friends John Kelsey-Fry QC and Russell Jacobs were unfailing sources of support and wise advice, and Russell's sister, Beverley, provided expert translations of Hebrew documents. We're grateful also to Shulem Deen for his translation from Yiddish of the almost illegible recollections of Saul Furleiter. Agnes Grunwald-Spier, a Holocaust historian and a survivor herself, has been an invaluable guide and friend. My history schoolmaster, the late Tony Corten, whom I miss very much, was also an inspiration. Thank you also to Gina Carter, David Burns and David Cummings who helped me to grapple with this endeavour, particularly in the early stages.

Lady Potts and her sons Jacob and George kindly gave us exclusive access to the court transcripts annotated by her late husband, the trial judge, Sir Humphrey Potts. Other leading figures in the trial, including Sir Johnny Nutting QC, Bt, Bill Clegg QC, and defence solicitors Martin Lee and Steve Law, all shared their recollections with us. Thank you also to Sir Adrian Fulford QC and HHJ Mark Lucraft QC, for their very kind assistance and encouragement, and to Chris Watson, Charles Rifkind, Stephen Auld QC, Johnny Levy, Neil Calver QC, Lord David Wolfson and Baroness Scotland, whose enthusiasm has been unstinting. There are many more in the legal community who have provided assistance and support; they know who they are.

We are also grateful for access to the testimonies of Ben-Zion Blustein, Benni Kalina, Saul Furleiter, Miriam Soroka, Michael Omelinski and other survivors of the Holocaust preserved in the Yad Vashem archive in Israel and the Holocaust Museum in Washington DC, and the help of the staff at both institutions is much appreciated.

Among many others, we were also privileged to conduct exclusive interviews with Ben-Zion Blustein's son, Shalom and his wife Hanna, and grandson, Ben; his friend and biographer, Margalit Shlain, author of *One of the Sheep*; Benni Kalina's son Meir; Jack Pomeranc and his son Larry; Sara Omelinsky; and the families of the late Meir Bronstein, Boris Greenstein and Abraham Edelstein, all partisans who fought alongside Ben-Zion in the forests of Belarus.

Professor Chris Browning, who gave expert testimony about Nazi plans and hierarchies at the trial, gave us his insights and reflections, and our thanks to David Hirsh whose chapter about the Sawoniuk trial and support were early motivators. Thanks also to Charlie Moore, a detective with the War Crimes Unit and his wife Jane McCallum Moore who served in the same unit. Charlie shared his insider knowledge of the investigation, and we're also grateful for the input of their colleagues Jill Murray and Maggie Newberry, and other former and current Met policemen, including Eddie Bathgate, Richard Blewett, Mike Charlton, Norman Inniss and Matt Shalders. Dr Martin Dean, the WCU's Senior Historian, gave us invaluable insights into the files that he and his fellow historian Alasdair MacLeod had uncovered in archives across the world.

The comments and research papers of Ian Hepburn, for many years the senior crime reporter on the *Sun* newspaper, have also been invaluable, and we're grateful for the help of photographer Ray Collins, and many other reporters, photographers and broadcasters who covered the trial and the historic jury visit to Domachevo. Mike Hookway and some of Sawoniuk's other former co-workers and neighbours also shared their memories and opinions of him.

The friendly co-operation of all these people and many others is very much appreciated. Any errors are ours alone.

Further details on the story of *The Ticket Collector from Belarus* can be found at www.theticketcollector.com

PICTURE CREDITS

Map p. viii

Plan of Domachevo, produced for the War Crimes Unit: courtesy of the Metropolitan Police Service.

Plate sections

1. Souvenir postcard of Domachevo in the 1920s or 1930s © Stanislaw Kozlowski, www.domachevo.com; refugees following the Nazi destruction of Domachevo: authors' collection.

2. Map © United States Holocaust Memorial Museum, courtesy of National Archives and Records Administration, College Park.

3. Partisans crossing marsh © Sovfoto / Universal Images Group via Getty Images.

4. Members of partisan group © United States Holocaust Memorial Museum, courtesy of Samuel Gruber; group of Jewish resistance fighters © United States Holocaust Memorial Museum, courtesy of the Jack Lennard Archive at The Hull History Centre; Jewish women and children © United States Holocaust Memorial Museum.

5. Sketch map of the Zhukov partisan camp © Blustein family collection; Jewish partisans in Belarus burying comrades © Museum of Jewish Heritage, courtesy of the Jack Lennard Archive at The Hull History Centre.

6. The watch towers and fence at Majdanek concentration camp © United States Holocaust Memorial Museum, courtesy of

Michel Reynders; the crematoria and gas chamber at Majdanek © United States Holocaust Memorial Museum, courtesy of unknown Russian archive; Red Army Soldiers in the ruins of the Reichstag in Berlin 1945 © United States Holocaust Memorial Museum, courtesy of National Archives and Records Administration, College Park.

7. Andrei Sawoniuk in army uniform: source unknown; Sawoniuk photographed in 1948 © PA / Alamy Stock Photo; Ben-Zion and Clara Blustein in 1946 © Blustein family collection; Benni Kalina in Israel in the 1950s © Blustein family collection.

8. Aerial view of Domachevo in the late 1990s: authors' collection.

9. Fedor Zan © Chris Harris, the *Sun* / News Licensing); Fedor Zan pointing to the site from which he witnessed the killing of 15 Jewish women: authors' collection.

10. Alexandre Baglay: authors' collection; Ivan Baglay: authors' collection; Ben-Zion, Clara, Shalom and Tomer Blustein in Domachevo © Blustein family collection.

11. Itinerary of the jury's visit to Domachevo: authors' collection; judge and counsel outside Sawoniuk's home in Domachevo © Reuters / Alamy Stock Photo; the jurors trudging through the snow © Chris Harris, the *Sun* / News Licensing.

12. Local people, inured to the biting cold, watch the British invasion of Domachevo (Chris Harris, the *Sun* / News Licensing; Andrei Sawoniuk's half-brother Nikolai © Ray Collins, the *Sun* / News Licensing.

13. Partisan comrades reunited many years after the war © Blustein family collection; summary of the four indictments: authors' collection; Ben-Zion and Clara Blustein arriving at the Old Bailey © Ray Collins, the *Sun* / News Licensing; Andrei Sawoniuk outside the Old Bailey © PA Images / Alamy Stock Photo.

14. Sawoniuk throwing a stone at a photographer © ITN / Getty Images; some of Sir Humphrey Potts' annotations on his copy of the court transcript: authors' collection.

15. The *Sun*'s verdict on Sawoniuk © the *Sun* / News Licensing; the Blustein family © Blustein family collection.

16. The massacre site in Domachevo: authors' collection.

INDEX